D1433313

SHADOW AND SUN

THE AUTHOR   *Photo by Anne Fischer*

SHADOW AND SUN

by

Neil Campbell

LONDON
GEORGE ALLEN & UNWIN LTD.

PRINTED IN GREAT BRITAIN
BY HENDERSON AND SPALDING
LONDON, W.1

TO MY WIFE
SHIPMATE AND FRIEND
THIS MANY A YEAR

" Shadow and sun, so too our lives are made ;
But think how great the sun, how small the shade."

ACKNOWLEDGMENT

In the following pages an attempt has been made by the author to portray, candidly and faithfully, the scenes of the Passing Show of life.

A small part of the material in this book has been printed before. Thanks for permission to reprint are therefore due, and are hereby gratefully tendered, to the Editors of the following South African publications: *South African Railways and Harbours Magazine*, *The Outspan*, Johannesburg *Sunday Times*, *Cape Times*, *Cape Argus*, *Natal Daily News*, *Salstaff Bulletin*.

CONTENTS

ILLUSTRATIONS

CHAPTER I

DUBLIN DAYS

BROWSING, the other day, amongst the leaves of a magazine, I came across the following statement: "While a number of nonentities have thought themselves important enough to write their memoirs, many men and women who led really important and exciting lives have not left one word describing their experiences."

With the seeds of this book germinating in my brain, that came as rather a subduing slap in the face.

And then, setting out a little later to read that fine autobiography *The Wandering Years,* I saw facing me there the heartening opening words of Weston Martyr: "Men should tell what they know. My father died, aged ninety-two, and he took all he knew with him."

So it is, my brow as yet uncrowned with fame or perhaps even importance, I set about this task—at the risk, no doubt, of offending the caustic literary critic quoted above.

Those of us who have passed the half century of life must surely have something of interest to relate. That must be my excuse for writing this book—if excuse be needed; that and the itch for the grip of the pen which has ever tingled within my fingers.

We have lived through a period unprecedented in the history of the world; we have seen the tempo of human life alter from the *clip clop* of horses' hooves to the strident roar of machinery. On land and sea and in the air this change has taken place, embracing every sphere of our activities.

We have seen sail driven from the seas, after proudly holding sway for centuries; we have seen almost unbelievable speed attained on land and water; in the air mammoth planes, weighing many tons, hurtle across the sky. The last of the 'gentlemen's wars' was fought within our time; chivalry has been replaced by savagery on the battle-field, a savagery undreamed of by the campaigners of old. We have sorrowed through two colossal, world-wide conflicts in which human lives have been sacrificed in millions. What it pleases us to call civilisation has tottered on the brink. . .

Our lives are measured in but a few brief years. Half a century, what is that in the age-old story of the world! Nevertheless, those

9

years furnish us with an ample field for reminiscence and reflection on the remarkable metamorphosis which has taken place in human life. Man's so-called progress in this period has been nothing short of phenomenal. The previous five hundred years brought no such change as we have known. With the present century came inventions the like of which our forefathers would have considered far beyond the realms of possibility.

Looking back, adown the long valley of the years, we wonder— wonder to what end this mad thirst for speed, and yet more speed, is leading. Man's ingenuity continually contrives new means of alleviating the suffering of humanity; at the same time those same immensely fertile brains devise fresh horrors for the destruction of mankind. It makes one wonder if the climax has not been reached; if the time has not already come to call a halt, lest the whole human race be obliterated by that very ingenuity which is not ingenious enough to accomplish some plan whereby the peoples of the world can live in harmony and peace. Some day, perhaps, we will turn again to the simpler things, sated and weary of the immense stride of mechanical progress.

In a world where so much is being destroyed wilfully it is a comforting thought that some of the better things that really matter are indestructible—the wind, the sea, the mountains, the beauty of the dawn and the glory of the sunset . . . all these, and, as my father would have said, the love of God, which is everlasting.

* * *

What are the ideal surroundings and conditions for the writing of a book? A pretty, secluded lakeside chalet in Switzerland? A lovely, peaceful villa on the isle of Capri, overlooking the wide, blue Mediterranean? Yes, undoubtedly, should those charms be within the orbit of your means.

Alas and alack, mine is no such opportunity. In the midst of the resounding drums of war—war again, when that uneasy pause of peace had been so short!—in the alarms and excursions of the conflict, with the sometimes carking care of a family upon my shoulders—I set about the telling of my tale.

It is then, without further prelude or preamble, that I propose to start by stating that my father was a Presbyterian minister who was blessed with, and no doubt ofttimes greatly distressed by, a family of five. Mine was the fourth place in the quiverful of little arrows of that rather delicate but otherwise perfectly fecund man. Nourished in the bosom of the church, I ate of the sanctified bread of religion long before my baby teeth were cut.

That father of mine, a gentle scholar buried perhaps too much in his beloved books, possessed a kindly Christian nature which was frequently imposed upon throughout his life. He was born in Galway, in the extreme west of Ireland, in 1858, his father having left his native Argyllshire to settle there in the early 'forties. My grandfather died eight years before my birth. In his youth he had been a great friend of young Currie, who, later in life as Sir Donald, did so much to bridge the distance between England and South Africa, the latter a land which was to play a big part in the lives of my grandfather's descendants. The two had shared a room as youngsters in the house of Currie's aunt in Greenock.

At the time of his death in Galway my grandfather had become a man of considerable importance and substance in the town. Unfortunately, when the estate was settled up my father did not benefit greatly from the will.

My mother, a pretty, active woman until even late in life, gave up the amenities of an English-city environment to share her lot with my father in small northern Ireland towns before he received the call which brought him to a congregation in Dublin.

This, then, briefly—granite or sandstone—was the rock whence I was hewn.

* * *

Unfortunately for me, by the time the third son had arrived boys were becoming a bit commonplace in the old manse. Long prior to my birth my name had been fixed as 'Isabel,' my parents being firmly convinced that nature would not play them a scurvy trick once more. To their chagrin, the longed-for girl did not appear when my mother's fourth time had come.

Psychologists have touched only on the fringe of the subject of pre-natal influence. I have often wondered what part that influence played in the formation of my character. If my parents had not longed so ardently for a girl would I have had more hair on my chest; would my voice have been stronger and deeper; would I have been more virile and self-assertive? These are questions which as yet, despite the delvings of ponderous minds, no living person is in a position to answer decisively.

On a grey day in February, 1892, my first squall was heard. It was not an event of any concern to the world in general. It was not even an occasion for tumultuous rejoicing in the home circle. There remains to this day an element of doubt as to the exact date. An old lady, a life-long friend of our family still living in Dublin, put down the day as the twelfth. It is likely she is correct, for her birthday falls on that same date. She clearly remembers my father calling from an upstairs window as she passed the house, immediately after the arrival of the persistent stork: "It's another boy!" (That impudent, lop-winged bird made two appearances at our house within one year!)

That old lady goes so far as to say there was a decided note of disappointment in my father's voice.

In due course he called at the registry to record the particulars of my recent advent. When he gave the name which had suddenly replaced the feminine one of the last few months the old registrar, a little hard of hearing, hesitated with pen poised over the column where that insertion was to be made.

"Nil?" he said enquiringly. "Nil? Do you mean to say you're giving the poor child no name?"

Apart from the doubtful, inconclusive effect of pre-natal influence, the choice of my initial was unfortunate, especially for one who was destined to sail the seas. In the International Code of Signals the letters 'NC' have always been one of the most urgent of signals—"In distress—want immediate assistance." Many a time have I been in distress; many a time has the shadow of life almost obliterated the sun before the latter has shone out again.

It was not until some years later, when it became necessary to obtain my birth certificate, that we found the registered date of my launch was 21st February, 1892. For a long time there was confusion when the day drew near for the customary annual rejoicing, some members of the family stoutly maintaining it was the twelfth, others the twenty-first.

* * *

We lived in a big house at the corner of Tritonville Road, Sandymount, a southern suburb of Dublin. It stood in extensive grounds which were enclosed by a rather uninviting wall. In our early days that wall assumed something of the proportions of the ramparts of a prison. A pleasant prison, it is true, and high iron gates gave ready entrance—but to very few children of our own age.

When the fifth—and last—child arrived, a girl, to the great relief, no doubt, of my parents, our circle within that wall was considered complete. Occasionally, but very occasionally, some prim little girl or boy who could be regarded as 'nice' would be permitted to come and play with us. But for the most part we saw little of other youngsters. My parents, good folk though they were, lived under the impression that five children, following closely in age, were all-sufficient to themselves. A favourite remark of theirs was: "There are quite enough of you to play together."

So it was, at a time when we should have been rubbing shoulders with every grubby-nosed kid in the neighbourhood in preparation for the inevitable hurly-burly of life in later years, we were cloistered within the walls of the manse. It is those early impressionable years which I blame for all the inhibitions and idiosyncrasies and introvertive tendencies which have beset me all my days; for my introspective nature, too, and for the difficulty which has ever been mine in adjusting correctly my relationship with other human beings.

The house, a big ungainly place, literally gave my poor father nightmare; that is, when he could sleep at all. His miserable stipend was totally inadequate to keep it going. In the great basement kitchen a huge stove roared, year in, year out, from early morn till late at night, hungrily devouring many tons of coal. Before his death he told me how he used to lie in bed worrying himself into chronic insomnia over the expense of our menage.

While we were small there were always two servants in the house, and also, for some time, a German girl who acted as a sort of governess. Her wages, no doubt, were trifling, for at that time foreign young women, anxious to learn English thoroughly, could be imported readily for next to nothing. I have vivid recollections of that fair fräulein bribing us with a cheap cake, which remained perched enticingly on the corner of a high cupboard until the lessons were over.

Besides these women, employment was also provided for Rumgay, the slow, methodical gardener who loved his plants, and Mrs. Paget, the washerwoman, who usually brought with her on her weekly visits her daughter Maggie. Maggie is best remembered as a rosy-cheeked, fully-ripened girl of seventeen. When first she came to us, on being asked her name she stuck her cheeky nose in the air and chanted saucily: "Butther an' crame, all the ways from Dirty Lane—that's me name."

My father had lived a considerable time in Germany and spoke the language like a native. Up to the time of the first World War, when the Hun bared his teeth and his real baseness became apparent, my father always had the greatest affection for the kindly people he met in the Fatherland, and for their familiar tongue. In this connection my mind recalls very clearly the periodic visits of the touring German bands, which will be remembered by many as a feature of the 'nineties. Our house looked imposing, even if we were not rich, and the Teutonic music often blared out on the front lawn. On such occasions my father carried on long and animated conversations in German with the leader, who never went away empty-handed.

* * *

To this day I can recall the names of practically all that succession of Irish girls who worked for us. Many of their faces appear before me as I write. Some were pert and precocious, others staid and hard-working. One or two disappeared suddenly under a cloud, and their names were breathed no more. In this category was the poor, misguided one who, kicking against the dull monotony of her life, sought diversion with a man in the garden shrubbery one night. She was caught there by my father in circumstances which must have been decidedly compromising. The wrath of the holy man fell upon her unfortunate head. Next morning she hurriedly left our service, bowed with shame. The poor girl could hardly be blamed. Domestic service at that time was the nearest approach to imprisonment one could devise. From dewy morn till dusky eve, aye, and even later, girls worked for £1 per month, sometimes even less, with a few begrudged hours off duty once a fortnight.

No wonder they were called 'slaveys.'

* * *

Many things puzzled my immature mind in those far-off days. I was often bewildered by the cryptic remarks and curious actions of the servants when my mother was away from the house. Foolish women such as those must do incalculable harm, both physical and mental, to sensitive children of tender age. Passing by the physical, on the mental side I could mention many incidents, but two should suffice.

One night one of the girls was shutting the windows of the nursery. "Come and look," she said, "there's the banshee in the garden. She's combin' her long hair. If she throws that comb and it hits you—you're sure to die!"

Tremblingly I left my bed and came to the window. There was, of course, nothing unusual to be seen; but my imaginative eyes saw many things lurking in the shadows of the trees and shrubs. As I ran back to bed to bury my head in the blankets she laughed foolishly, pulled down the blind, and left the room in darkness. But my mind was lit by pictures which took many months to erase.

Fear of that wailing banshee haunted me for weeks. As I lay for hours, listening open-eyed to the peaceful breathing of my sleeping brother and little sister, it was impossible for me to shake free those clutching, frightening thoughts.

Often I would stare in trembling apprehension at the dim outline of the covered windows, expecting any moment to see one of the blinds drawn aside to reveal, peering in, a face distorted with malice. Sometimes I would dive my head beneath the blankets to avoid the impact of that deadly comb.

So great was my anguish, there were nights when I would jump from my bed to flee out into the lighted lobby when I heard my mother coming up the stairs. As her head appeared over the top of them she would see me there. Hurrying the length of the lobby, she picked me up in her arms, soothing my fears with soft, maternal words.

Then came the heavenly security and comfort of the great conjugal double bed, whither I was swiftly borne. Safe at last, secure like some storm-tossed barque which had won its sheltered haven through a stress of wind and wave, I would snuggle down between the warm bodies of my father and mother.

On the wall facing the bed hung the big, illuminated text in its white-enamelled frame. It is nearly a half-century since I last clapped eyes on those imploratory words, yet they are still crystal-clear within my memory:

"Help us, O Lord, our Yoke to wear,
Delighting in Thy Perfect Will;
Each other's Burdens learn to bear,
And thus Thy Law of Love fulfil."

Every night, every time before the light was put out, my eyes rested on that florally-decorated text. It was surely the first piece of adult reading mastered by my childish brain.

As we settled down to sleep my mother would murmur to my father, over my small, curly head: "My poor little Benjamin, why is it he is so much more nervous than the others?"

From some misguided sense of loyalty to the servants, I never told her what had frightened me so woefully.

* * *

Another case of the foolish chatterings of those servants came on the eve of the opening of the present century, when I was nearly eight years of age. Those thoughtless girls had filled the receptive heads of us children with a lot of nonsense, telling us that an earthquake would shake the house at midnight; that a terrible thunderstorm would rage while the New Century was coming in.

That night I lay awake for hours, listening to the ancient grandfather clock in the hall downstairs hammering out the passing of the time. When midnight came with the clamouring twelve strokes of the venerable timepiece nothing unusual occurred. But no sleep came to me, and I remained staring wide-eyed into the lonely darkness of the small hours of the morning of the New Year and New Century.

* * *

My earliest recollection is undoubtedly the loss of the Finnish barque *Palme* and the terrible tragedy involved in that wreck. When I was four years old this ship was blown ashore outside Kingstown in a wild winter gale.

The larger of the two Kingstown lifeboats, *Civil Service No. 7*, put out to the rescue at once. When still nearly half a mile from the wreck the boat, under sail, for there were no mechanically propelled lifeboats in those days, was capsized by the furious seas. She failed to right herself, and the whole fifteen valiant Irishmen of her crew perished.

Undaunted by the horror of this tragedy, the smaller lifeboat *Hannah Pickard* left the harbour, having first called alongside H.M.S. *Melampus* for six volunteers to complete the crew of fifteen. The tug which was to have towed this second lifeboat to the vicinity of the wreck refused to put to sea. Under sail alone, then, the *Hannah Pickard* bravely set out. She, too, was capsized before long, but righted herself without loss of any life.

This plucky crew, however, could not make the wreck, being blown far to leeward, so that they were forced to land on a rocky part of the coast, where the boat was badly damaged. Then the Dublin Poolbeg lifeboat unsuccessfully attempted to reach the stricken *Palme*.

For two days the wretched crew of the barque, facing death at any moment throughout that time, clung to their battered ship. It was a miracle the vessel did not go to pieces on that treacherous sandbank. And then the gallant skipper of the Commissions of Irish Lights' small steamer *Tearaght* took off every soul from the wreck. It was a masterly piece of seamanship, carried out while the gale still blew with unabated force. The captain's wife and baby were aboard the *Palme*. The infant, wrapped mummylike in oilskins, had to be thrown from ship to rescuing boat. I can still remember my father busying himself collecting tiny garments for that baby before the parents left for their own country.

Kingstown and the whole neighbourhood were thrown into mourning by the tragic loss of so many of its brave men. My brothers and I were taken to see the sad sight of their battered lifeboat, lying on the beach exactly as it had been hurled there by the raging sea. Though Kingstown may have changed its name since then, the epic bravery of those valiant Irish lifeboatmen lives on in the minds of many still living. The reward to their poor, widowed womenfolk was paltry enough, but a monument erected by public subscription speaks eloquently though silently of their gallantry for ever.

This occurrence has been dealt with, perhaps, unduly lengthily because it made so deep an impression on my childish mind. It may have been, even in those far-off early days of my life, some bond, visionary yet inexorable, had already claimed me for the sea.

* * *

In 1897, the year of her Diamond Jubilee, the aged Queen Victoria paid a visit to Dublin. Landing at Kingstown, she drove the seven miles to the city in an open carriage. Dublin did its utmost to welcome her. The route was lined by cheering crowds.

The custom on such occasions at that time was for a number of people to hire a brake or dray. This vehicle would be driven in good time to the side of the road of the proposed route. The horses were then unhitched and taken away. The spectators concerned stood on the dray, thus obtaining a better view than the less fortunate ones on the ground.

The cheering reached us long before the Queen had come in sight. Then there was a brave clatter of horses' hooves and a lively jingling of the accoutrements of her bodyguard. Her carriage was drawn by four of Ireland's most magnificent horses. Before us passed a little old lady, plainly dressed in black and wearing a bonnet edged with white. Sunk low in the seat, looking pathetically old and tired and lonely, she feebly acknowledged the plaudits of the crowd.

For many years no British sovereign has dared to pass that way.

The celebrations in Dublin included, of course, the illumination of the city. How feeble that effort would appear compared with modern super-floodlighting. But to us children the spectacle was wonderful indeed, as we were taken through the streets one night in an open carriage behind two spanking horses.

It was a cold night. The lights glittered like fairyland. I can recollect, as if it were but yesterday, my mother's concern over the 'night air'; how carefully we were muffled up to the ears in rugs. Several people we knew had died recently of consumption. Their illness and consequent death were attributed primarily to some malevolent effect the night air had had upon them.

That night air theory must have obsessed my mother. The windows of the nursery were invariably kept closed after dark except in the hottest summer weather. Just before we went to sleep we were told, if it were wintertime, to put our heads underneath the bedclothes. A window was then thrown open for a minute or two before being shut securely for the night.

It was while this was being done by one of the servants that she told us, in a confidential, expansive moment, of the origin of babies. One of my brothers and myself, the only youngsters in the room at the time, were astounded at her news, having been stuffed up with the usual nonsense. When we told the girl we were going to seek official confirmation from my mother she got frightened and swore us to eternal secrecy.

*　　*　　*

People were, it must be admitted, a little backward in those distant days, what with the 'night air' and other ridiculous ideas. Though most publications shouted at us even then, in keeping with the belief that repetition is the soul of salesmanship, that a certain hardy perennial was Worth a Guinea a Box, the power of the printed word had not been so fully realised as now.

Nobody, apparently, had been progressive enough to differentiate between ordinary starvation (suffered by thousands in a land of plenty) and the fashionable "Night Starvation" referred to so repeatedly in the modern newspaper advertisements of a well-known liquid food.

Nobody had been enterprising enough to discover that poor Ann, wilting willowlike at the lively dance, was a silent victim of that pernicious pest, B.O. The present day Ann, so afflicted, is told discreetly by her friend Daphne that she is subject to that dread, hieroglyphic malady. And then, hey presto! with the kindly, salubrious emulsified assistance of a certain brand of soap, all is well. Ann emerges from her bath rose-like, the belle of the ball, sought after by those same young men who heretofore had shunned her—having, of course, been clad in her best dance frock.

In those distant days of which I write, which are yet remembered so well, the traditional Saturday night hot bath was considered sufficient to preserve, except in the clammiest weather, the pristine peachlikeness of a girl.

Then again, there is now that other modern malady about which one sees so much in the newspaper advertisements—Pink Toothbrush. In those days people were not so fussy about the particular colour of their toothbrush as long as it cleaned the teeth. It might be remarked casually, "Dammit, one of my teeth is bleeding." Or perhaps, "I've been rubbing a bit too hard." Now some dire warning is woven into the blushing rosiness of the brush.

How did people manage at all at all (as is said in Ireland) in those dim, dark days when all these pestilential plagues were unknown or unnoticed? They look almost like a series of chemical formulae:—B.O.; N.S.; P.T.—and all the others whose ingenious originators fatten the newspaper proprietors and themselves.

Well, so far as I can remember, we got on fine. In the aggregate there was probably little more actual unhealthiness (even if

Ann *did* occasionally have to be a wallflower) and, as likely as not, a great deal more simple, honest-to-goodness happiness throughout the human race.

*   *   *

The commencement of the Boer War stands out very vividly in my memory. We little thought then that South Africa, which seemed so remote, would ever mean anything to us. My father, a staunch imperialist, took a keen interest in the course of the war. We children played the usual martial games on the nursery floor, smiting hip and thigh the little drab, slouch-hatted bits of lead which represented the Afrikaner warriors.

The initial reverses suffered by the British forces affected my father greatly. It was inconceivable to him that what were regarded as a few thousand ill-equipped farmers should hold at bay for so long the might of the British Empire. I can recall clearly the evening when he opened the paper and read the news of the action at Magersfontein, where the Highland Brigade was ambushed and cut to pieces. Needless to say, the ha'penny local nationalist paper crowed loudly over such reverses. Though my father was Irish-born his forebears were all Scots, and he was intensely proud of his Highland blood. At the news of Magersfontein, he stood in front of the fire with bowed head and would not speak to any of us for some minutes.

Beggar's Bush barracks, at that time, held a considerable number of British soldiers. We watched them marching off to embark for South Africa. That was before khaki had been introduced. The traditional colour for a soldier's coat was red. In their vivid crimson jackets and trappings, the band playing *Soldiers of the Queen, Good-bye, my Bluebell, Dolly Gray,* and other popular and patriotic airs, they made a brave show.

Though even then there were murmurings for all but the deafest to hear, Ireland was different at that time. There must be many living now in that distressed country who, had they the freedom and the courage to speak their minds, would welcome the old regime again.

*   *   *

Those late Victorian days were leisurely and not unhappy. The tempo of life was set to the measure of the beat of horses' hooves. It was as if the world were pausing, breathing deeply and slowly, before abandoning itself to the mad rush of machinery which was to engulf it in the rapid development of the internal combustion engine in the new century.

All the traffic in Dublin was horse-drawn, with the exception of a few steam traction-engines which used to rumble past, snorting fiercely. The little tram we boarded at the end of the road on our occasional expeditions to the city was pulled by two round-flanked, sturdy nags. Sitting beside my mother, I could see their massive sterns bobbing up and down as they trotted along.

When the tram was full and the roads frosty, the horses' shoes would slip and clatter on the glass-like surface until the tram was under way once more. Sometimes it was necessary for the driver to leave his little platform to go to the horses' heads to encourage them with cries of "Gee up ou'er that!," the customary exhortation which was applied to horses and donkeys throughout Ireland. In the winter the driver would be muffled to the ears in his topcoat, his face richly coloured by the keenness of the air and the many pints of 'porther' he had consumed from boyhood. On our visits to the Zoo, a place I remember from a very early age, the gradient made necessary the assistance of another horse. With this help the whole outfit would make its way laboriously up the rise.

Of all the magnificent horses in Dublin (Ireland has always been famous for these animals) probably the finest were those used by the fire brigade. It was a wonderful spectacle of power and speed to see them tearing along with dilated nostrils, a stream of sparks flying from the chimney of the engine behind.

It was about 1902 when the electric trams came to Dublin. I had a ride on one of the first—from Nelson's Pillar to Howth. They were primitive affairs, no provision whatever being made on top for the passengers' protection from the sodden Irish climate. I was alone, sitting on the front seat of the upper deck, the wind rushing past my ears as the noisy contraption tore along at what seemed breakneck speed. I looked in vain for the motive power. Nobody explained to me how the tram was driven.

* * *

At the age of ten I was seeing a little more of the world outside the walls of the manse. I had been given a bicycle, and was permitted to trundle around the quieter roads in the vicinity of the house. That bike was more of a treadmill than anything else. It was, of course, a fixed-wheel machine, with uncomfortable, down-turned handlebars which gave me a permanent crick in the back of my neck. It was, moreover, as heavy as lead and, judged by modern standards, would be considered totally unfit for a child of ten to ride.

I was as proud as a peacock of that primitive gridiron, although it was already old when it came my way. There was only one brake, a rubber pad which pressed on the front tyre. If you got a puncture on a steep hill—well, you were just unlucky, especially if your feet were on the two ugly, saw-toothed footrests on the front fork. To regain those whirling pedals under such conditions was difficult. More than once I have seen a rider thrown over the handlebars when attempting to do so.

It was about this time that my father called the whole family into the garden one day to see the great new invention—the free-wheel. We all stood around wonderingly while he explained the workings of this new-fangled bike. Then he proceeded to mount, with much dignity and ceremony. Placing his left foot on the step attached to the rear axle, he hopped several times and gently raised himself into the saddle. As his feet touched the pedals the latter twirled backwards. The bike lost its slight impetus, fell over and precipitated my father to the ground. He rose, dratting softly (he never permitted himself the use of strong words), and tried again. He had ridden a 'penny-farthing' in his youth in the west of Ireland, but it never gave him so much trouble to master as this new steed of his.

* * *

As I pedalled about the streets around our house, I continually heard the pleasantries which passed between errand boys on their rounds and nursemaids giving the baby an airing. Some of those little verbal passages amused me, but one in particular, which was a favourite witticism with the cheekier type of boy, puzzled me greatly.

The errand boy would call out derisively and mockingly to the girl, usually from a safe distance: "Chase me, Charley, I've got barley—Up the leg of me drawers!"

Now that did set me thinking. The only barley known to me was the delicious sweet on which we often spent our Saturday penny at Miller's shop in Sandymount Road. Yes, that must be it, I concluded. But why did the girl appear to get so annoyed? And why choose such a curious spot in which to stow precious sugar-barley?

Occasionally there would be a clash between the rowdy Protestant and Catholic boys from Ringsend, something in the nature of 'The Twelfth' in miniature form. Blows were rarely exchanged, hostilities usually being confined to the hoarse shouting of vulgar doggerel. The Protestant boys would scream at the rival party:

"Slitter-slatter, howly watter, sprinkle the Papishes, ivery wan; Cut 'em asunder an' make 'em lie under the Protestant boy that carries the drum!"

The Catholics would reply in similar vein, until all grew weary of abusing each other and passed on their way.

* * *

The school attended by my brothers and myself would make a modern educationist burst into ribald laughter. Either that or tear his hair in despair. It would all depend on whether or not he had a sense of humour.

The entire school was housed in one hall, with the exception of one privileged class which occupied the outer vestry of the church. This, as can well be imagined, was hardly conducive to the easy and rapid absorption of knowledge.

The class presided over by the headmaster was stationed on the platform at the end of the hall—the post of honour. Below that, in the body of the building, three or four other classes were spread out, if that word can be used when they were almost rubbing shoulders with one another.

When all the teachers were in full cry the pandemonium was almost indescribable. From one part of the hall the intricacies of the *pons asinorum* would be in process of explanation in strident tones; another class would be listening, as attentively as the circumstances permitted, to the pugnacious adventures of the Romans; a third would be having hurled at it the dates of the Glorious Deeds that Won the Empire.

It was, of course, almost impossible to concentrate on the one subject, to fix one's attention rigidly on the particular teacher at the head of the class. Occasionally, when the masters became a little too enthusiastic in their efforts to howl one another down, the principal would advance to the edge of the platform to gaze sternly and rebukingly through his imposing pince-nez at his noisy satellites below.

We were all glad when we found ourselves in that quiet back-eddy, the outer vestry. But even there the sound of the warring masters in the big hall came through the heavy door like the muffled roar of angry surf on a rockbound coast.

In spite of all this, miraculously, almost unbelievably, results were obtained, and we appeared to be as far advanced as other boys of our own age.

*   *   *

The headmaster, and sole proprietor, of this establishment was commonly known as 'Wag,' his initials forming that snappy little sobriquet. His bald head and long, flowing gown created a considerable amount of awe in the hearts of the boys. This was heightened by his firmly established faith in the use of the cane. It was always at hand, ready for use. Sometimes my poor palms were almost crippled by its vigorous cuts.

At times some older boy, more courageous than his fellows, would carefully and surreptitiously split the cane, so skilfully that no defect was noticed until the instrument of torture was grasped for use. That foolish, defiant act availed nothing, for there was always a plentiful supply of fresh canes in the locked cupboard. On such occasions the wrath of Wag was terrible to behold, the distended veins standing out like cords on his bald pate.

The title of this emporium of learning was most euphonious. The proprietor had somewhat pompously named it Sandymount Academical Institute, Dublin. That looked well in the prospectus, and must have been the source of great satisfaction to the founder of this somewhat weird and wonderful seat of learning.

We wore dark blue caps with bright concentric yellow stripes. In front a confused mass of yellow thread was worked into what faintly resembled a burning bush. Underneath, in small letters, appeared the motto, 'Ardens sed Virens.' Around the lot were spread four large letters—S.A.I.D. The whole thing was most impressive—to those who had not taken the trouble to peer beneath the surface. Those four letters were the subject of much rude jocularity on the part of impudent boys from other schools. Standing in front of us, gazing intently at our brightly-embroidered caps, they would enunciate slowly: "S.A.I.D.—Said. Said WHAT? Tee-hee-hee!"

There was a subsidiary title represented by the letters P.C.D. (Presbyterian College, Dublin). This must have had some bearing on the reason for the attendance of my brothers and myself at the school. The Academical Institute supported my father's church. Every Sunday the boarders tramped noisily into the back seats, rattling heavily at collection time their meagre pennies and ha'-pennies into the plate. *Ergo,* it was but befitting that my father, with his four boys, should support the school, no doubt on a sort of 'You scratch my back—I'll scratch yours' basis.

There were, of course, much better schools in Dublin, but none so conveniently near. Wag's was literally on our threshold, for the hall abutted the church, which stood in close proximity to the manse. The orthodox route to the school led around the front of the church and into the playground. There was also a small door at the lower end of our back garden which gave immediate access to the playground.

The official summons to the scholars at play was given by Wag striking on the lock of the lower door with its heavy key. On the hollow lock it sounded like, but was far more insistent than, the *cluck-cluck-clucking* of a fussy hen gathering together her wandering brood. Many a time when we had lain too long a-bed, or had dwelt too lengthily on our breakfast, we would take the short-cut down the back garden. If the door was locked—a necessity in summer when our trees were laden with apples—a convenient, partially-hidden hole in the high hedge gave precipitous entry to the school grounds.

Wag's *cluck-cluck-clucking* would rise to a crescendo just before he prepared to shut the door. That was the time for an extra spurt. Hot and flushed, we often dashed past him on the last *cluck*—to receive a disapproving look from his cold, pince-nezed eyes.

There was one occasion, and one only, on which the imperious summons was ignored. That was the morning of the accident.

One of Boland's heavily laden bread vans, just emerging from the lane at the end of our playground, collided with a young man cycling to town. The man was knocked down; one of the van's wheels passed over his body.

The news of the tragedy spread like wildfire amongst us, just as Wag started clattering his key on the lock. In spite of this, a mad rush was made for the end wall, which was soon festooned with jostling boys gaping wide-eyed down on what they saw below.

The unfortunate man was lying on the pavement, where he had been lifted by the vanman and several passers-by. The great horse stood patiently close by, turning its head occasionally to give that poor battered body a compassionate, wondering look. Meanwhile Wag was hammering a wild tattoo and shouting angrily at us. Presently he left the door, came down to the wall, and attempted to pull off it one or two of the boys. Then, peering over, he too was overcome by morbid curiosity.

The injured man's face had turned a ghastly greenish-grey; he seemed beyond all aid. Shortly before he died he disgorged, before our horror-stricken eyes, the entire contents of his stomach. The heterogeneous mass of his recently eaten breakfast oozed slowly down the pavement to the gutter, a hideous flood. . . . .

*   *   *

The boarders of the school were housed in a building somewhat pretentiously called Sandymount Castle. Often in the most inclement weather they walked the full length of Sandymount Road to reach the school hall. No regular conveyance was supplied for their use.

So much for Wag and his strange so-called Academical Institute. Where are all those boys who felt the weight of his tingling cane? How many, if any, achieved greatness? how many died in the gutter? Not one of them all has ever crossed my path since those far-off Dublin days.

CHAPTER II

ERIN, FAREWELL TO THEE!

My father ministered to the spiritual, yes, and often the bodily needs of that Dublin congregation for many years—to be exact, from 1890 to 1903. It would be difficult to estimate what measure of success crowned those ministrations. The task of a parson is, at best, a thankless one, and it is almost impossible to assess statistically the ardour of church goers, or the benefit they derive from their attendance there. The little band of real enthusiasts, as every minister knows only too well, is far outnumbered by the others of his flock, the goats amongst the sheep, whose devotion is not so strong.

Throughout those years my father toiled for his church, never sparing himself, thinking only of others. His salary all that time was little more than the wages claimed by the present-day dustman or humblest mechanic. If you had asked him to tell you his favourite prayer he would have answered simply, without any attempt at rhetoric: "O Lord, make us faithful in the *little* things." That was characteristic of the man. It was, indeed, the lode-star which guided him through life. Duty to him was everything; to my way of thinking, his sense of duty was so high that it put him prematurely in his grave.

As was but befitting, once we had passed babyhood days we were expected to attend regularly the church services. My father used to say to us: "How can I encourage people to come to church if the manse pew is empty?"

Hundreds of times I have watched him as he stood in the high pulpit. Arched over his head on the wall behind glittered the illuminated text which I remember so clearly from early childhood:

"O Worship the Lord in the Beauty of Holiness."

To my childish eyes its gaudy lettering formed a gigantic halo over my father's head. Never a robust man, he looked lonely and almost ethereal in that setting.

Though our pew was fairly well filled, room was found for an elderly woman who was unable to pay pew-rent. A maiden lady, she lived in a tiny house in rather straitened circumstances.

Poor Miss Drimmie, unconsciously she caused us youngsters much vulgar amusement which also embarrassed us greatly. As she sat with hands folded devoutly on her lap while she raptly absorbed the tit-bits of my father's sermon, there would be a little trilling deep within her tightly-laced, black-clad body. It commenced like elfin music, rose to a chirping, tremulous note which sounded clearly along our pew, and then subsided—to be repeated several minutes later.

There would be a suppressed titter from one of my older brothers. That would start us all off. Often I leant forward in agony, nearly choking myself by stuffing my handkerchief half-way down my throat. Horrified glances from my mother only made things worse. The children of a large family in front of us would gape over their shoulders with disapproval in their cold, staring eyes.

I grew to dread Miss Drimmie's presence in our pew. I used to pray that she would not be there; that something would prevent her from attending church—anything. She did eventually become ill, poor woman, not as an answer to my prayers, but through attempting (so rumour had it) to make a somewhat fly-blown joint last throughout the week.

* * *

Church services at that time were intensely dreary. So strict were the doctrines of Presbyterianism that no instrumental music whatever was allowed inside the place of worship. As a small child I had long puzzled over the little *ping* of the choir leader's tuning fork, which rang out clearly before the commencement of the singing of each psalm or hymn.

And then, after a long and heated discussion, the conclusion was arrived at that instruments could hardly be classed as profane. A harmonium was installed in our church. The sharp *ping* rang out no more, its place being taken by the flip-flap of the organist's feet on the pedals.

My father always realized the dreariness for children of the long services through which they sat so patiently. Soon after coming to Dublin he introduced children's sermons—just a few words or a short story for the sole benefit of the youngsters. This was an innovation which met with immediate success, enjoyed quite as much by the adults as by the children. My father must have been one of the pioneers of this movement.

He wrote and preached hundreds of sermons during the years he occupied that pulpit. His study was a *sanctum sanctorum* which few were permitted to enter while he wrote. I can see it all so clearly; the long wall with its shelves covered by many hundreds of volumes; the old desk at which my father always sat.

There were evenings when I was privileged to be with him while he worked, on condition, of course, that I kept as quiet as a mouse. Curled up in the huge armchair before the fire, I would study one of the big tomes from the bookshelves. Even at an early age the *Encyclopaedia Britannica* (especially the volume dealing with ships) was a great favourite of mine.

There would be perfect peace within that sanctuary. The only sounds the busy little scratching of my father's pen; the hundred and one companionable prattlings of a well-lit coal fire; the gentle ticking of a marble clock on the mantelpiece; the continuous, soothing hiss of the mantled gas-jet overhead.

Dublin was lit by gas in those days, not only the houses but also the streets. Every single street lamp in our district had to be lit and extinguished by hand. As dusk fell the hurrying feet of the lamplighter would be heard on the pavement. With his little charcoal brazier on its staff he lit each lamp in turn. First a sharp click as the lever of the gas-jet was pulled down; then a soft *pop* as the escaping gas ignited.

Next morning the same feet hurried on their rounds again, as the lights were put out for the day.

Downstairs our house was quite brilliantly illuminated, all the burners being fitted with incandescent mantles. Upstairs, most of the rooms were lit by old-fashioned fish-tail jets—a dim light which did not encourage a great deal of reading after dark. Those mantles must have been a continual source of expense. So frail were they that often the romping of us children overhead was sufficient to shatter them to a white powder on the carpet.

My father, tenderest of men, had yet a fixed belief in the use of the rod of correction. But corporal punishment was not a thing to be treated lightly. The High Place of the study was always the scene of its painful application. No careless cuts must be applied in any lesser place in the house, however strong the provocation.

I have a very vivid recollection of one of my brothers clinging, limpet-like, to a leg of the heavy dining room table while my father struggled to drag him off to his lair for punishment. Later, when that had been administered, another brother boldly scrawled with chalk on the study door: "An ogre lives in here"—a defiant act which brought upon his head, and body too, the wrath of the good man.

* * *

My father, with his broad, loving outlook on humanity, rich or poor, was in truth no ogre. His keen wit and deep sense of humour must often have carried him through the difficult times he had to face so frequently. He had a ready store of anecdotes and little stories of a mild and blameless nature. His repertoire held no place for smut, nor for the bawdy taproom yarn.

One little story which he sometimes told to the many people who visited us concerned a boy, son of a colleague, who had been sent to boarding school. The boy's frequent requests for more pocket money became so insistent and disturbing that his father finally demanded, and eventually received, a detailed account of the boy's expenditure.

After perusing this carefully, the minister turned to his wife. Tapping the letter with his pince-nez, he remarked contentedly and reassuredly to the good woman: "There you are, my dear. That's a son after my heart. You see these repeated items: 'S.P.G. 2/6; S.P.G. 3/-; S.P.G. 1/9.' There can't be much wrong with a boy who denies himself so often to send his pocket money to the Society for the Propagation of the Gospel."

At the end of the term the boy returned for his holidays. On the very first day, another divine happened to be dining with the family. As they all settled down to dinner, the father, turning to his guest, said proudly: "This is the lad who devotes so much of his pocket money to the splendid work of the Society for the Propagation of the Gospel."

Choking over his food, flushed to the roots of his hair, the poor boy stammered out: "I'm sorry, Father, if you were misled by those S.P.G.s. They really meant: 'Sundries, Probably Grub!'"

* * *

Though, as has been said before, few children came to our house, there was no shortage of adult visitors; for my father presided over frequent clerical gatherings, and other meetings which took place in the manse.

Sometimes we crept from our beds to watch the arrival of the black-clad divines from the vantage point of the bannisters, high overhead. We soon grew to recognize the different voices. That of one minister in particular boomed out repeatedly, and his loud, rumbling laugh vibrated through the house.

My father repeatedly left home at week-ends to exchange pulpits with some other minister, usually 'up North,' that stronghold of Presbyterianism. It was a beneficial practice which 'freshened the nip' (as we sailormen say) for both minister and congregation.

Some of those visiting parsons, who always stayed at our house, must have been a severe trial to my mother. There was one big, pallid-faced man who occasionally came to us, a Northerner with that objectionable, adenoidal twang which is disliked so much by the Southerner in Ireland. He filled us youngsters with a strong distaste from the first.

Cornering me in the hall, immediately after his arrival, he patted my curly head while he clasped my small paw with his other cold, flabby hand. "Well, my little man," he enquired fervently, "and do you *really* love your Redeemer?" The little man only scowled at him. For his touch sent a shudder through my childish body; it reminded me of a slug which my brothers had dared me to pick up from the garden path.

Talking of a curly head reminds me that my mother, loath apparently to cast aside for ever the knowledge that I was not a girl, kept me in a sort of hermaphroditic state for five and a half years. Until that age was reached, long curls dangled about my shoulders. Recently the old lady mentioned before sent out from Dublin one of those curls which my mother had cut off and given her in 1897. Though that friend had labelled it 'a great treasure' my children showed no interest whatever in that pale, almost straw-coloured lump of hair. My own reaction was wonderment that my grizzling thatch could once have been so fair and finely spun.

* * *

In connection with the interchange of pulpits which took my father away from us so often at week-ends, an amusing incident which happened some time later in South Africa comes to mind.

It was long before household refrigerators were thought of. The weather was intensely hot that week-end, when a visiting preacher came to stay with us. My mother, having heard that this particular man of God was reputed to be an excellent trencherman, had ordered a specially large sirloin of beef.

After the butchers' shops had closed that Saturday evening my mother made the horrible discovery that the enormous joint was 'off.' It was, indeed, worse than 'off,' for it was humming more loudly and insistently than any humming bird.

There was no hope of getting any other meat that night. Taking the protesting joint from the meat safe, she carefully washed it and anointed it with liberal doses of vinegar and salt. Unfortunately, she had to go out that evening. On her return that darned old trek-ox was shouting out so loudly that my mother was nearly demented. Within the narrow limits of her restricted, ladylike vocabulary, she called the butcher all the low down things she could think of.

And then she decided on the only possible action—to cook the meat immediately, before it had decomposed entirely. That decision did not mean the mere switching-on of an electric stove, as would be the case nowadays. All our cooking was done with wood, and it takes a long time for a wood-fired oven to get heated properly.

When the poor woman went to her uneasy couch after midnight the joint reposed once more in the meat safe, partly cooked but still telling the world that though it was dead it wouldn't lie down. And my mother lay trying to glean some comfort from the thought that if pheasants were eaten "high" there was no reason why the same practice should not be applied to trek-oxen.

Already in my mind the vow had been registered that it would be a meatless Sunday, although we were all particularly fond of roast beef.

*   *   *

Our visitor apparently considered his morning service had been quite a hit. He was obviously intensely pleased with himself as we all sat down to dinner. His black-clad paunch rested comfortably against the table-end, waiting to be filled, while he smiled blandly upon us and passed the usual fatuous remarks peculiar to such occasions.

My mother, looking anxious and worried, was at the other end of the table, ready to carve in the absence of my father. When

THE BEAUTIFUL FIGUREHEAD OF THE BARQUE " FAVELL "   *Photo by the author*
REPRESENTING MISS FAVELL HILL, DAUGHTER OF THE BUILDER

FINNISH BARQUE " POMMERN " LEAVING TABLE BAY IN 1931   *Photo by F. Rogers*

she had helped the reverend gentleman, my eldest brother's voice rang out:

"No meat for me, thanks, Mother."

"I don't want any meat either, thanks," came from my second brother. Then the third piped up in the same strain.

When it came to the turn of my sister and myself an appealing glance from my mother kept us silent while she put some slices on our plates. These we carefully pushed on one side, for old Klaas, or Blesbok, or whatever the trek-ox's name had been in life, had defied the charring of a hot oven, and still sniffed strongly and cheerfully.

Our guest was so full of his own unctuous importance that he apparently noticed nothing wrong in our behaviour, or in that of the sirloin. His dinner finished, he retired to the study for an afternoon nap. Several of us hung anxiously round the closed door, thinking of poor Miss Drimmie, and expecting to hear any minute the groans and cries which we assumed would accompany the symptoms of ptomaine poisoning, or whatever toxin was found in the carcasses of decomposing trek-oxen.

* * *

Though never really a heavy smoker, my father liked his pipe. He never touched cigarettes, and in later years begged us, if we must smoke, to stick to the pipe. It was but one of the many wise counsels he gave his sons. Strong drink of any sort never passed his lips. Over and over again he told us how much he had seen of "the curse of drink" in the west of Ireland and other places. Never would he entertain the thought of spending one penny on it.

There were times when he temporarily came to regard even smoking as a weakness. Then he would throw his pipes out of the study window, denouncing the foolish habit and vowing he would smoke no more. A few hours later he would be seen probing the bushes for his beloved pipes.

One rabid non-smoker (he must have been a pest to my mother) who exchanged pulpits occasionally with my father was a gnome-like little man from the North. The frugality of his Scots ancestry must have been deeply embedded in his bones. The first time he had dinner with us we were surprised to see him carefully scrape back into the salt-cellar the unused salt on his plate.

Next time he came to visit us we youngsters nudged one another under the table, waiting expectantly to see this performance repeated. Laying down his knife and fork, he peered short-sightedly around for the salt-cellar, drew it close to the edge of his plate, and scraped into it every grain of salt he had not used.

* * *

As has been said, my father was born in the extreme west of Ireland. But his forebears had sprung from the soil of Scotland. He was intensely proud of his Highland blood. For generations either the army or the church had claimed the majority of the male members of our particular branch of the clan. On the walls of the big dining room in the old manse hung the life-size oil portraits of those red-coated warriors who had led their men in the campaigns of the eighteenth and early nineteenth centuries.

If I were left alone in the room at night as a small child an uncanny feeling invariably crept over me, as if those long-dead men were intently watching my every movement. No matter where I went in the room their eyes never left me, and it seemed to me they were about to speak.

We children all wore kilts of the Campbell tartan in our younger days. Dressed up in them, with the square silver buttons shining, the buckled shoes and swinging sporran, I thought myself no end of a fine fellow, in spite of my spindly legs, which were quite unsuited to that garb.

From kilts we graduated to Eton suits for Sunday wear. How I loathed those Eton suits! As there were four of us each suit, on being outgrown, was passed down from one to the other. By the time it reached me that fourth-hand outfit was showing decided signs of wear. The coat would be frowzy and shabby at elbows and cuffs, the trousers baggy at the knees. Dry cleaning had not become the fine art it now is; those defects just had to be put up with.

To this day the Eton suit appears to me to be the acme of sartorial smugness. When I was forced to wear one, rude boys used to enquire with mock tenderness, especially in chilly weather, if my backside was not cold.

* * *

The summer of 1901 was one of the best Dublin had enjoyed for years. Donn Byrne, that young Irish writer who died so tragically before his zenith had been reached, must have been thinking of such a summer when he wrote the opening words of his book *Hangman's House*: "Once more had come now the miracle of the Irish June; red of clover; purple of the Dublin mountains. Everywhere the white of the hawthorn. And wherever a clump of trees was, there grew great crops of bluebells. And the primroses lingered, who should have gone three weeks and more . . . And from the mountains there blew a little breeze, cool as water. All the population of the trees was busy. The cheery blackbird sang, and the thrush whistled. There arose the little piping of the finches . . . "

Week after week we had many of our meals out of doors, the table set beneath the sycamore trees—surely a procedure of uncertainty in that treacherous Irish clime. The big apple trees in our back garden were laden with delicious fruit, tempting venturesome boys to make repeated raids over the stone wall. Those apples were a continual source of trouble during the fruit season. Hundreds of them must have been stolen while our backs were turned.

The tired old Queen had passed on to her long and well earned rest. The coronation of Edward, her son, had been postponed on account of his illness. It was, indeed, his famous operation for appendicitis which started a new fashion throughout the world. It must have been hailed as a God-send by surgeons everywhere. Hundreds of society folk, wishing to be in the regal fashion and having money to burn, insisted on having their appendices carved out.

* * *

During the summer of 1902 I took part, though so small and not particularly strong, in the activities of the local cycling club. On Saturday afternoons often thirty or forty members would meet, the men in natty knickerbockers, the ladies in leg-o'-mutton sleeved blouses, inconveniently long skirts, and the most unsuitable headgear.

Some destination in the country had already been chosen where tea and cakes were procurable. Off we set, the ladies having demurely adjusted lengths of elastic from the front hem of their skirts to their feet, lest any indecorous and disturbing glimpse of their legs might be shown to the male riders or to passers by.

That will surely amuse the modern girl, used to exposing without a blush her lower limbs from keelson to truck.

The country roads were delightful in those days, though, of course, the surface was not what one is used to now. There was little or no traffic; we could with safety spread ourselves out over the road. A hay wagon might be met; an elderly lady taking the air in her smart brougham; perhaps a doctor hurrying behind his spanking horses to some urgent case.

During that year the South African war came to an end. There was great rejoicing in Dublin, though there were many people in Ireland who sympathised openly with the Afrikaner cause, and admired the brave fight which had been put up against the overwhelming might of Britain. We had no inkling then that we should soon be living in the country on which so many people's attention had been fixed for two and a half years.

Shortly after the close of the war somebody who had just returned from South Africa came to dine with us. He told us many interesting stories about that beautiful country, but what impressed us most was his description of the delicious fruit. We found difficulty in believing him when he said, quite casually: "The finest grapes can be bought for a penny or twopence a pound."

It was in that same year, 1902, that we youngsters experienced real tragedy for the first time.

Up to this no mention has been made of Major, a most important member of our family. He was a magnificent collie dog with a beautiful black-and-tan coat. He was not of the sharp-nosed, narrow-headed breed of collies one sees to-day. His great skull was broad, the muzzle heavy. His intelligent eyes were the most beautiful one could wish to see in man, woman or dog.

He was given to my father about the time of the birth of my eldest brother in the north of Ireland. As each child made its appearance Major welcomed the new arrival and took it under his canine wing. Nobody ever had more faithful or dearer friend than Major. He was always with us, watching over and guarding us from any harm. With us all he was as gentle as a kitten, though we often pulled him about and rode roughly on his back. But woe betide anybody who tried to interfere with any of us when we were out for walks. Many a time when we grew tired he supported our weary footsteps as we held on to his long dark coat.

Dear, faithful old Major. He was with us throughout his whole life from 1888 to 1902. In all those years he gave so much—freely, lovingly, ungrudgingly.

Major had grown old with us. In those days dogs had a chance of running fully their normal lives. No motor-cars rushed madly about the roads, dealing death and destruction not only to dogs but also to human beings, as is now the case.

He was no longer so active as before. His teeth had worn down to the gums. In spite of this, though his muzzle had turned white, he still kept in wonderful condition. One or two people advised my father to have him destroyed. None of us would hear of this.

And then the morning came when we heard queer little choking sounds from the shrubbery. We found Major lying in the bushes, practically *in extremis*. A bone, thoughtlessly given him by one of the girls, had lodged in his throat; slowly it was choking him.

My father clapped his flat parson's hat on his head and hurried off for the vet. There were few telephones in Dublin at that time, though, of course, some of the more progressive business houses had installed them.

We stood around the poor dog, utterly helpless to do anything for him. Every time we spoke to him he wagged his tail feebly and tried to come to us. When the man arrived it was soon over. Forcing open Major's jaws, he placed a little poison on the dog's tongue.

The dear old fellow looked up at us, bewildered. Then his head fell back and his beautiful eyes glazed for ever.

But was it for ever? Is there not surely some happy spot where such good doggies go—where their joyous barks ring out again; where there is an inexhaustible supply of juicy bones? Who is vile man, much vaunted lord of creation, that he should monopolize for himself the belief of an everlasting soul? Any day, any hour of the day, that good dog could have taught the average human being many lessons in love, and faithfulness, and honesty, and devotion.

* * *

We buried him at the foot of the garden, down beyond the gnarled trunks of the old apple trees. We boys all helped to dig the grave. We dug it deep, so that his earthy bed should be secure.

There was not a dry eye in the whole family as we laid our dear friend to rest. For fourteen years he had lived with us, giving everyone so much—yet asking so little in return.

One of my brothers laboriously carved his name and the date on the heavy slab of wood which served him as a headstone.

* * *

I never got to know what decided my father to tear himself and his family away from Ireland. He loved his native soil; his roots were imbedded deeply in that emerald land. The wrench required to pull them out must indeed have been a hard one. It may have been that he considered there would be more scope abroad for his growing family than was offered by the narrow, restricted horizon of Dublin; it may have been that he thought the health of all would benefit by the change; it may even have been that he had grown a little weary of the grey weeping skies, the sadly-falling tears which seem symbolic of the soul of Ireland.

Whatever the cause, he did not lightly make the decision to plunge into the unknown. It took courage and much forethought to even contemplate the transfer of a big family and a great deal of our furniture so far across the sea . . .

It would be early in 1903 when whisperings went around the house that we might be leaving Ireland for ever. We youngsters did not take much notice of these rumours. The people around us had been born, lived their lives, and died in Dublin. Why, then, should we be different?

And then my father called us together to tell us he had received a cable from South Africa—a call from a church not long established there which was seeking a permanent minister.

He did not accept immediately. He spent many hours worrying how it could be done, whether it was the right thing to do. And then at last the cable of acceptance was sent back—the die was cast. It had been arranged that we young folk should go to our grandfather in Liverpool, while our parents remained behind to supervise the packing of the furniture and the sale of that part of our possessions which had been decided not to take with us.

* * *

I paid a last visit to Howth, that old-world fishing harbour which had known me so well since a little toddler. Standing on the East Pier I looked over the strip of water which separated Howth from Ireland's Eye, romantically named, uninhabited island which had been the scene of many of our picnics, bringing to us on such occasions the additional spice of the boat trip across the water.

Walking the road which fringed the harbour, I came to the West Pier, where the brown-sailed fishing smacks were discharging their finny freight. The whole place was redolent of the sweet sadness of the sea. The crying of the gulls a-wing, or fighting for the offal on the quayside; the incense of the tarry cordage and netting; the ripple and flap of unstowed canvas—these sounds and smells stirred me strangely. It must have been in Howth that the seed of unrest was sown which sent me off one day to earn a livelihood on the broad bosom of the ocean . . .

Looking out over the little harbour I saw many yachts at their moorings; I watched the comings and goings of the sturdy sailing smacks. And in all that fleet of little ships there was not one which had not to rely on the wind in its sails, or the stout arms of its crew, to find its power of movement.

Later, we stood at Nelson's Pillar for the last time. Here was the heart of Dublin city. All around were the familiar cries which had greeted our ears every time we went to town. The newsboys, raucously shouting their rival papers; the flower and fruit sellers, shawl-clad girls and women, monotonously calling their wares: "Panny each thim nice juicy oringes an' limuns . . . panny each thim nice juicy oringes an' limuns . . . "

Entering the Pillar, several of us clambered up the cold stone steps to the top. The whole place, like so many old buildings in the British Isles, smelt strongly and sourly of stale urine. But the view from the top was fine. For the last time we gazed out over the old grey city where we had been born, and which we were to leave so soon.

In spite of the excitement of the coming voyage, a sort of numbing nostalgia crept over me. I wanted to return to the home where we had lived all our lives. South Africa was so distant—an unknown quantity—while here were the people and things with which we were so familiar.

* * *

Looking back on our time in Dublin, the amazing thing to me

is how my father, poorly paid, and burdened, and harassed, managed to take us all away from Sandymount every summer for a holiday.

We spent a number of happy months on Dublin and Wicklow farms. It was amongst the purple hills of Wicklow in the river Dargle that we all learned to swim as very small children. My father had no time for any of the new-fangled strokes. Breaststroke was good enough for him. Captain Webb had swum the Channel some years before, using only breaststroke. So it was we all became good swimmers in the cool, slightly peaty water of the Dargle.

On a number of occasions we "crossed the water" for our annual holiday—to Colwyn Bay and Ayr, even as far as Elie, on the Firth of Forth. It was while we were aboard the steamer bound for Scotland that one of my brothers made the remark which caused my parents so much amusement, and with which he was twitted long afterwards.

Two ladies were talking to the boy (he was about seven at the time), and in the course of their conversation one of them asked him: "Is your mother an Englishwoman?" My brother stuck his snobbish little nose in the air, and then replied haughtily and freezingly: "My mother's not a woman—she's a lady!"

During a stay on a farm at Rathfarnham, outside Dublin, I obtained my first real insight into the Great Facts of Life. The farm was run by an old woman and her sharp-nosed, sharp-tongued daughter.

Early one morning the young farm boy (he was not a great deal older than myself) came down a leafy lane, driving before him a restless-looking cow which twitched its tail continually and lowed mournfully at frequent intervals.

"Where are you going, Tom?" I asked him.

"I'm takin' Daisy to the bull," he answered simply.

When I told him I would come with him for the walk he looked around to see that nobody was about before consenting. We set off along the country lanes to a neighbouring farm. It was a lovely morning . . . "Once more had come now the miracle of the Irish June; red of clover; purple of the Dublin mountains . . ."

The birds were singing blithely in tree and hedgerow. And Daisy was singing too, her plaintive, mooing song of love as she stalked restlessly ahead.

Though I was so young the farmer apparently saw no wrong in my presence there with Tom to see what polite people call the "mating" of Daisy. Two magnificent bulls were penned in adjacent paddocks. Daisy's appearance set them afire, each pawing the ground and snorting fiercely, vying with his neighbour for her favours.

We made our way back along the same leafy lanes, Tom whistling shrilly and cheerfully, while I pondered silently and wonderingly over the Great Facts of Life. Noticing at last my preoccupation, he came out with a little bit of his boyish philosophy. "That's nothin'," he said, "we take all our cows there. They like it."

Tom must have been right, for I noticed Daisy mooed less now as she plodded contentedly along. The daughter of the house met us on our return. Her eyes blazed angrily at Tom and me as her sharp tongue scourged him for permitting "the child" to accompany him on such an errand.

* * *

We joined the Aberdeen-White-Star liner *Nineveh* in the Royal Albert Dock on 9th June, 1903. If we could see her now she would look small indeed, and strangely obsolete. For she was barquentine-rigged and, like so many steamers then, still clung stoutly and tenaciously to her sails.

To us, however, she was the finest thing afloat, with her beautifully-moulded green hull and graceful clipper-bow. Looking up an ancient Lloyd's Register, I find she was not a great deal bigger than the sailing ship in which I first went to sea some years later.

We sailed the same afternoon, hauling out into the river while a few of our friends and relations stood at the quayside and wept copiously. It took many years for Africa to live down its Dark Continent reputation. Though our ship was not large, she carried about 90 first class and several hundred third class passengers, practically all bound for Australia.

The *Nineveh* rolled south, setting sail when the wind was fair, furling it when the south east trades headed the vessel. Only one call was made, at Teneriffe, whose towering peak had been in sight for many hours. First seen nearly ninety miles away, its snow-clad cone peeped coquettishly over the horizon. And then the bulk of the island grew, proving to us the rotundity of the world far more conclusively than any of Wag's teaching.

CHAPTER III.

SUNNY SOUTH AFRICA

The *Nineveh* dropped anchor under the huge, unmistakable bulk of Table Mountain on 2nd July, 1903. We were taken ashore in a tender, landing at the little quay where the pilot boats now lie. The present big red building which houses the port captain's offices was not then in existence, the site being occupied by a humble galvanised-iron shed.

Several of the elders of my father's new church were there to meet him. While we gaped around with interest at the unusual sights which surrounded us, I noticed my father had become strangely preoccupied, having had a long and deep conversation with the men who had met us. I did not know until long afterwards that, for him at least, our arrival in the promised land had been darkened by bitter disappointment.

He had been told there was no manse ready for us. It is true, a plot had been purchased, but so far not one brick of our new home had been laid. We were faced with the prospect of being scattered to the care of new-found friends who were prepared to accept one or two members of the family. The position, too, of his newly formed flock had been made known to my father. The Dutch Reformed Church apparently more or less dominated the religious character of Stellenbosch. The Presbyterian element was relatively small, and the stipend miserably inadequate for the needs of a minister with a large family.

* * *

When we emerged from the station at Stellenbosch a full moon bathed the scene in its silvery light. Lifting our eyes, we saw the amphitheatre of great, aloof mountains which almost surrounded our new home. Though it was mid-winter the afternoon in Cape Town had been intensely hot. The air was now surprisingly cold and penetrating.

It was some weeks before an empty farmhouse was rented for us, and we came together once more under the one roof. My mother, brave soul that she was, found herself faced with in-

42

numerable difficulties in this strange land to which we had come. To make matters worse, my father contracted enteric and required weeks of careful nursing.

We young folk were not slow to appreciate the joyous sunshine and freedom which had been brought into our lives. Around us, almost at our front door, reared majestic mountains, sublimely aloof yet so near at hand, silently calling us to scale their heights. Compared with them, the green hills of Dublin and Wicklow were but molehills.

But there were many things we missed. We missed the sweet song of the birds in Ireland, the lovely scent of the primroses, the mayblossom, the bluebells, and all the other flowers which grew so profusely, each in its season, in the dells and glades of the Irish countryside. It did not take long to find out that the unusual birds and flowers around us had little or no song or smell.

* * *

As can be imagined, there was some difficulty in adjusting our position at school. Wag's Academical Institute had apparently not conformed to any recognized standard of education, so that it took some weeks of patient experiment for the headmaster to find our correct niche.

We had reached South Africa shortly after the conclusion of the Boer war. That unhappy shedding of blood was over, but the aftermath of bitterness and sorrow remained. Alas, it remains to this day, darkening the relationship of some sections of the people of this much-blessed country. Though that war was a mere picnic compared with the hideous slaughter of modern, mechanised combat, many Afrikaners are determined not to forget it. This, too, in spite of the fact that Britain has shown in the past years much goodwill and complacency towards her one-time foe.

While on this subject of warfare it is of interest to note what wonderful strides have been made in the evolution of man. He surely has much to be proud of! Forty years ago it was considered a heinous crime to make use of dum-dum bullets. I believe the Boers blamed the British, and the British blamed the Boers, for the use of this type of ammunition. That was the last gasp of brutality—forty years ago. Now, thanks to our wonderful progress throughout nearly twenty centuries of Christianity, dum-dum bullets are about as trivial as babies' rattles.

We were amazed to find in that school huge young men with flourishing moustaches. These, we learned, were youthful warriors who had taken part in the stand of the South African Republics against the British Empire. Strangely enough, these fine fellows seemed to bear no grudge or malice. That spirit came mostly from other boys who had been born, and lived their lives, under the Union Jack, and who had taken no active part in the war.

Frequent opprobrious epithets were thrown at my brothers and myself. Often we were referred to derogatorily as "rooineks" or "rooibaaitjes," and on some occasions were not even allowed to look on at the books of the more embittered.

My rich Dublin brogue caused intense amusement to the boys in my class. I grew to dread the days when we had to stand and read aloud extracts from our books. One occasion I remember particularly well. It came to my turn to read out a passage relating to a train which had caught fire, and was in immediate peril of complete destruction owing to part of its load being blasting powder.

It was all very dramatic, but the whole class rocked and roared with merriment, and I felt foolishly confused, when I read out the bit about the "blastin' pow-wowder."

* * *

My father toiled faithfully and self-sacrificingly for years, endeavouring to create a better spirit amongst the warring elements in Stellenbosch. Many a time he was disheartened and dispirited but carried bravely on. He must often have longed for his native soil and for the familiar Irish countryside he had always loved so well.

And while he toiled and worried we youngsters revelled in our new-found freedom, the bright sunshine, and the wondrous change which had been wrought in our lives. It became our habit, nearly every week-end throughout the summer, to set out for some spot up the beautiful Jonkershoek Valley. With a rolled-up blanket, several days' provisions, and a billy-can, we would be off when Friday's school was done.

As daylight faded from the sky our blankets were unrolled, and coffee was boiled on a glowing wood fire before we lay down to sleep on the ground. Above us stretched the huge canopy of the starlit sky—our only covering—bejewelled with constellations we had never seen in Ireland. Around us often the cries of baboons, jackals and leopards would ring out. These, strange and unnerving at first, soon grew familiar in our ears, and no longer disturbed our sleep.

And then, when the cool, fresh dawning came, there was the first invigorating plunge in the prattling river, which had been talking merrily to us all night. As the sun topped the giant peaks of the near-by mountains we dried our naked bodies in its warming rays.

* * *

My first love affair—I must introduce a love interest into this book somehow—came at the age of about fourteen. It was the usual foolish boy-and-girl temporary infatuation through which we all must pass before reaching the sterner associations with the opposite sex. It led me, however, unwittingly into a most unpleasant situation.

The object of my affection was a boarder at one of the several local girls' schools. Our first meeting took place at a Sunday school picnic organised by my father. Shortly afterwards the young lady spent her school holidays at Gordon's Bay, where we also had been taken for our annual change of air.

On the girl's return to boarding school it became my habit to cycle up and down the road which bordered the school grounds. Occasionally I was rewarded by a glimpse of HER, when the girls came out just before dark to spend a few minutes walking about the grounds.

One happy evening she saw me and came over to the iron railings. Greatly daring, emboldened, no doubt, by the deepening dusk, I kissed her awkwardly as she pressed her face between the cold, hard bars.

And then the crash came, suddenly and without any trace of warning. The headmaster of my school called me to his study one morning. Fingering a letter, he gazed curiously at me while he informed me that the principal of the girls' school wished to see me at 8 o'clock that evening.

Punctually, with trembling knees, I presented myself at the grim, frowning door. It was opened immediately, and I found myself in the presence of the Ogress. The stage was well and truly set for my discomfiture.

A solitary oil standard-lamp (we had no electricity in Stellenbosch) lit the room, or rather, lit the chair underneath in which I was commanded to be seated. The principal moved away into the outer gloom of the big room. Full on my face the light shone, and I knew she was watching me intently. It was, of course, a mild form of Third Degree, and it disconcerted me more than a little to find she was not prepared to encounter me on equal terms.

From the outer darkness came the voice of the Ogress, cutting and as cold as ice: "It has come to my knowledge that you have been trifling with the affections of one of my girls." (There was something decidedly Victorian in that touch.) "These girls are entrusted to me for the pursuit of their studies, not to attract the attention of foolish boys such as you. Your notes have been found in her work-basket." (Silly ass of a girl, thought I.) "This is a serious matter which I feel strongly inclined to report to your father. No doubt this girl's school work has suffered by your thoughtless action. You have, moreover, just sent her a gift. That, as you must be aware, is strictly forbidden. I am returning that gift to you now."

The Ogress rose from her seat to open a drawer. Coming over to me, she placed a thin, flat parcel in my hand. I knew that parcel only too well, for I had saved up every penny for months to buy the contents.

Returning to the kindly semi-darkness, the Ogress continued her discourse. (She wasn't really an Ogress, for she never told my father.)

At last I found myself out under the quiet, aloof, disinterested yet friendly stars. A little cool wind fanned, with kindly gesture, my burning cheeks. It stirred the dry autumn leaves with crisp rustlings; it spoke small, soothing, almost inaudible words of comfort to me as it played upon my red-hot face. Never before had the fresh night air been so sweet to me.

On my return home I made a clean breast of the whole affair to my mother. My motive in doing so was, it must be admitted, not only mercenary but also one of dire necessity. The flat parcel contained a dozen fairly expensive initialled handkerchiefs, representative of my pocket money over a considerable period. Unfortunately, the initial was not that of my mother, but the good woman consented to buy the handkerchiefs from me. I never quite forgave her, however, for refunding me only half their cost. That, no doubt, was her idea of punishment.

* * *

All through our childhood and years of adolescence my father was a stickler for his family worship. Every morning we had prayers before breakfast. (In the Dublin days they were sometimes the cause of that mad rush past old Wag on his last *cluck*.) I firmly believe that little ceremony meant more to my father than the food he ate.

On Sunday evenings, with more leisure on our hands, family worship became a much more important ritual than the somewhat hurried morning prayer of the ordinary day of the week. We all sat around the dining-room table. My father would choose a passage and we each would read one verse aloud from the Bibles in front of us, working clockwise around the table.

Surreptitiously, without incurring the notice of my father, we would each calculate which verse would be ours. Then, concentrating on those particular lines, we would read and re-read mentally, until we imagined we were word-perfect.

My father, thoroughly conversant with the Bible from beginning to end, carefully avoided what might without irreverence be termed the twiddly bits. But there were times when some unfortunate one of us was forced to read out, blushing with embarrassment, and stumbling slightly on the ugly words, the names of such vulgar people as the Gurgashites and the Shittimites.

* * *

I have often been asked what decided me to go to sea. It is a question which is a little difficult to answer. So far as I can remember no actual decision was ever made, the idea having been there, deep in my mind from my earliest years, growing apace as time went on.

Prying into our family history, I find that heredity played but a vague part in my choice of a career at sea. Our genealogical tree is almost entirely devoid of seaweedy branches. There was, in the manse in Dublin, a musty old book on the fly-leaf of which were inscribed the words: "Peter Campbell, Master *Stormy Petrel*." That, and a date of the early part of last century. Unfortunately I am unable to discover whether the bold Peter, who, I understand, was my great grandfather, and his aptly-named ship ever achieved greatness.

Then, of course (I nearly forgot them), there were those two uncles on my mother's side. I grew weary of their sad story, which was told me so often when the suspicion took hold of my parents' minds that my heart was set upon the sea.

Those two young men had set out for a life on the ocean wave, their father having paid fat premiums and equipped them with expensive outfits. They soon found the sea life less attractive than they had anticipated. They found it so unattractive, indeed, that they deserted their ships abroad, never to return to sea again, their father naturally losing the premiums of both.

Those two avuncular backsliders, apart from the aforementioned Peter, are the only relatives of mine whom I can locate as having sallied forth to sail on the rolling deep.

* * *

For my part, I have always loved the sea. Born within its sound, I have lived at its fringe, or upon it, practically all my life.

I love to hear it in its milder moods, caressing the land where it is met on pebbly beach or bastion rock. And when a winter gale lashes it to fury, hurling the maddened water against the coast in boisterous strife—it leaves me undismayed. For, to me, the sea is the one true friend of whom one never grows weary . . .

The Sea. One of God's greatest gifts to man. Perhaps the one decent clean thing left which the human race, with its petty squabblings and so-called progress, can neither defile nor desecrate. The Sea, that great purifier of the world which man has never really conquered—nor ever will.

Let me quote from a far abler pen than mine will ever be ; from the heart of a practised writer who, too, has always loved the sea. List to this, ye landsmen!

"The sea is the consolation of this our day, as it has been the consolation of the centuries. It is the companion and the receiver of men. It has moods for them to fill the store-house of the mind, perils for trial, or even for an ending, and calms for the good emblem of death. The sea has taken me to itself whenever I sought it and has given me relief from men. It has rendered remote the cares and the wastes of the land; for of all creatures that move and breathe upon the earth we of mankind are the fullest of sorrow. But the sea shall comfort us, and perpetually show us new things and assure us. It is the common sacrament of this world. May it be to others what it has been to me . . . "

Good old Hilaire Belloc! And up to recently I have always regarded you as a rather pompous individual whose writings were far above the level of the common herd.

Probably the seed of my unrest was sown in those happy days I spent as a child at Howth. That little old-world village was then the home of a flourishing fishing industry. All day the circling gulls surrounded the brown-sailed smacks. Somehow their sad, wailing cries have always breathed for me the very spirit of the sea. And when those brown sails were hoisted no more, and the death-knell of those little wind-driven ships had been sounded, that small port, too, seemed to wilt and die.

Perhaps the seed was sown even before that, when the nurse-maid used to take me for a walk along the causeway which led to the South Wall. From there we had a full view of the river and all its activities. There were many sailing vessels visiting Dublin in those far-off days. Sometimes we were lucky, watching there, for a ship or two would pass close by, towing majestically to sea behind one of the old "Flying" paddle tugs. And I would long to be aboard, setting out upon the great broad highway which was theirs.

The last two years at school were purgatory for me. I found myself unsettled and incapable of studying with any degree of concentration. There were times when the fever within me became so insistent that, like Masefield, I felt I must go down to the sea again. And the only way an impecunious boy could go down to the sea was by bicycle. Setting out for Cape Town on Saturday mornings, tip-toeing out of the sleeping house, I would be a-wheel long before the sun had topped the peaks of Jonkershoek.

In those days no macadamised road stretched smoothly along the seemingly endless miles. The going was heavy over the sandy track; but the reward was ample when I finally sat eating my sandwiches aboard some ship in the docks. All around were other ships in whose lofty masts and rigging the wind whispered and murmured to me.

Often I would board one of Andrew Weir's four-masted barques at the Collier Jetty, where they discharged nitrate from Chili. That was better than the West Quay, for there one felt the ship rolling slightly and moving restlessly at her moorings.

D

Recently I have passed many times along the smooth, hard road to Stellenbosch with no greater effort than the pressing of a motor-car's accelerator. Every time, every mile of the way, I see a thin-legged boy on a heavy bicycle. Head down against the buffeting of the south-easter, he plugs his way home along the sandy track —the sea-fever within him appeased if not abated . . .

Sometimes I wonder if the modern boy would cheerfully face a sixty-mile push-bike ride just to feel the tang of salt water again. At the risk of being called an "old has-been" or a foolish sentimentalist—I doubt it.

*　　*　　*

It was solely due to the encouragement of my father's promise of one pound reward that I succeeded in obtaining a pass in the Cape Matriculation examination of 1908. It was a base thing to expect and accept such a bribe, and to work so grudgingly, when my father had so few pounds to spend on anything.

After leaving school it seemed impossible to make any progress in my wish to get to sea. I was headed off in every way, the joys and advantages of some alternative career always being graphically put before me. My father repeatedly referred to the sea as "a dog's life." He may have been right, though many self-respecting dogs would have turned up their canine noses at the coarse fare on which we were forced to subsist in windjammers.

For some months I worked on a fruit farm, the idea being that, miraculously, I might suddenly decide to till the soil instead of ploughing the ocean for a living. Then, when that phase was over, I was persuaded to consider the prospect of becoming an analytical chemist. In cap and gown I trod the learned precincts of the old Victoria College, attending the necessary classes with little enthusiasm or interest. It was, indeed, a shameful waste of my poor father's money.

Then, in a weak and wavering moment, I consented to fill in an application form for a junior clerkship in a Cape Town bank. That was surely the last straw. How could anyone hope to be happy sitting on a high stool when one's dearest wish was to be swinging on the footrope of a topsail yard?

At first I lived with a sea captain's widow and her large family in the Gardens. The widowed lady's two sons were fine, athletic young men with whom my skinny figure compared most unfavourably. When I told her of my intention to get to sea some-how—anyhow— she shook her head sadly, and said: "You will never be strong enough for the life in a sailing ship. I know, because I sailed with my husband for years, and realise the hard-ships only too well."

In that house it soon became apparent to me that "the lodger" was considered entitled to extra tit-bits unshared by the others. This embarrassed me so much that I left and took up residence —candidly, not from any religious tendencies—at the Y.M.C.A. The food was reputed to be very good there and the building was conveniently near the bank. The never-ending prayer and holiness meetings were a little tedious at first, but these, of course, could be avoided provided one had the courage not to shrink from the consequent disapproval of the management.

Those months in the bank held for me no joy and little pleasure. It is true the life had its lighter moments, but, looking back, I regard that period as one of unalloyed monotony. Running around the city delivering bills, drafts, etc., gave me a very clear insight into the money-grubbing nature of the many customers of the bank.

One of the members of the staff, a single, middle-aged man of rather eccentric habits, took in me what seemed an almost fatherly interest. Sometimes he would come and stand beside me as I attended to my work. Occasionally, if nobody were near, he would peer intently at me through his bulging glasses, pinch my cheek playfully, and remark: "You've got nice roses in your cheeks, Campbell." I have often wondered since what thoughts were passing through his mind behind those spectacled, quizzing eyes with their unblinking gaze.

Every minute of my spare time was spent at the docks. There was relief in the habit of wandering amongst the ships I loved so well, the smell of bilge water and tar incense in my hungry nostrils. One hand invariably clutched an old quarter-plate box camera loaded with twelve glass plates in sheaths. There were many sailing ships visiting Cape Town in those days, and I snapped the most of them.

* * *

That bank had become for me a prison house. My life had grown so irksome that I decided, if my father would not permit me to go to sea with his consent, I would go away without it.

The barque *Gulf Stream* was sailing for Australia in the morning. I hung around the quay close to her after dark, watching for any sign of life aboard. A dim light burned in the galley; beyond that, the ship lay in darkness. Creeping quietly up the gangway I reached the deck, and was making my way forward when a voice called out and a man came towards me. "What are you after, sonny?" he asked me.

I told him I wanted a warm-up at his fire. We sat in the galley, talking and smoking, friendlylike, in front of the cheery blaze. Outside, the rain lashed the deck, and the wind boomed and roared aloft. For it was a particularly filthy night. A nor'-west gale, sweeping in from the sea, drove before it sheets of rain.

He was the only one aboard, a member of the crew who had hurt his arm, and had consequently been given the night watchman's job. All the others were up town for their last spree ashore before sailing. He seemed so friendly that I was misled into telling him of my wish to get away in the ship, foolishly going so far as to ask him to show me some snug spot in which to stow away.

Unlike W. W. Jacobs' night watchman who cried cheerily "What ho!" as he blew the froth from his beer, this man nearly spat blood, cursing me foully when he realised what I was after. He even threatened to call a policeman from the nearby dock police station. Eventually I pacified him somewhat by saying I would wait to see the skipper on his return aboard.

Hour after hour passed. The crew came up the gangway, full of hops and good cheer. When the apprentices returned they heard of my plan to get away in the ship. "We've got all our crew," they told me, "but why not see the old man when he comes aboard?"

Though I waited until the wee small hours the captain did not show up. Had he done so, what I was going to tell him I do not know to this day. Down the gangway I went at last, the baleful eye of the night watchman fixed steadily on me lest some attempt should be made to return. I reached my room in the Y.M.C.A., disheartened, dispirited—and soaked to the skin.

The *Gulf Stream* sailed next day. Some months later that unfortunate ship, on a westerly passage round the Horn, just disappeared from mortal ken. No trace of her was ever found; it was assumed she met her end, like so many other fine sailing ships,

from collision with an iceberg. Ice was particularly prevalent off
the Horn that year. In those square-rigged vessels there was no
handy engine-room telegraph to jam down "Full Astern" when
the dread cry: "Ice right ahead!" rang out in the darkness of
a blustering night.

* * *

Life was becoming almost intolerable in the bank, and the
holiness meetings were getting a little of my nerves when my
deliverance came about.

On my comings and goings to the Y.M.C.A. I had often noticed
and nodded to the old caretaker of the Michaelis House in Green-
market Square. One night, as I passed disconsolately by the door,
he called me in for a chat. Learning that I was interested in ships,
he produced an ancient dog-eared Lloyd's Register, in which the
blue-edged "Sailing Ship" section was as fat as that of the steamers.
This book absorbed me for an hour, and then the caretaker handed
me the latest Lloyd's Shipping List, a little green book giving
details of the movements of thousands of vessels.

In it, poring over the tiny print, I found the short notice which
was to lead to my happy emancipation from the bondage of the
bank.

"Br. bq *Elginshire* passed Tatoosh Island, for Table Bay." That,
with a date, was all. But it was enough for me. I had never heard
of Tatoosh Island. Reference to the big atlas at the Public Library,
whither I hurried before closing time, soon proved it to be in
British Columbia.

Sitting down that night in the loneliness of my little room, I
penned a long letter to my father, telling him of the *Elginshire*
and appealing to him to write immediately to the owners in
Glasgow.

Two days later he walked into the bank. Good man that he
was, he had seen at last the light of reason—and I knew that I
had won. He urged me to think wisely once more before the
die was cast. He said again his little piece about the two avuncular
backsliders; he dwelt lengthily on the "dog's life" which I was
contemplating.

"All right," I answered angrily and impatiently, "if it's a dog's
life—then I'm content to be a dog."

Then ensued a period of some weeks of painful suspense. Would
the *Elginshire's* half-deck be full up, leaving no room for me?

Would the owners say I was beyond the customary age for starting apprenticeship?

In due course a letter from T. Law & Co. arrived. My father sent it on to me immediately. It stated that though my age was above that of their first voyagers they were prepared to permit me to sign indentures with them. The master would be instructed to transact the necessary business connected therewith.

The ship would probably reach Cape Town in several months. I respectfully approached the manager to inform him that it would be necessary for me to terminate my association with the bank. He peered at me incredulously through his spectacles.

"Are you bereft of your senses, boy?" he asked. "Is it really your intention to give up a brilliant career in the bank for a life such as that?"

Perhaps my eyes were dimmed by the eager thought of my early emancipation, for I failed to see the brilliancy. It may have been, of course, that he anticipated my eventual transfer from the tiring message running and salival stamp licking to some more important branch of the service.

I left those gloomy portals without one regret. For months the front door key had been in my keeping overnight, it being one of my many duties to open the door and straighten up things before the others arrived in the morning.

Often, as I stood alone in the office, changing pen nibs with which the customers had obviously been playing darts, altering the wall calendars, opening the window grilles, the thought would come to me: What would you do if some ruffian came slinking in, revolver bulging sinisterly from his pocket? Would you hurl yourself against the safe, defying the marauder to open it only over your dead body? Or would you welcome him in, close the door obligingly, and assist him in every way—providing he slipped you a fiver?

Probably this latter action would have been mine, for my salary was a paltry fifty pounds per annum.

That key was a source of continual anxiety to me. My mind was filled with the ridiculous idea that every rogue in Cape Town knew it was in my possession. As I made my lonely way about the city after office hours, I frequently pressed the most secret pocket of my clothing to reassure myself the key was there. And when I went to bed it always lay under my pillow. Even within the pious walls of the Y.M.C.A. I did not consider it safe. For the first few weeks I woke occasionally to slip my hand underneath the pillow.

* * *

And then the *Elginshire*—MY SHIP, at last—came in from the open sea. She had made a long passage round the Horn, hampered by the burden of timber which had been piled high on her deck.

One of my brothers in Cape Town at the time wrote to me at Stellenbosch next day: "I have been down to the ship at the West Quay. She is very rusty and there are planks stacked high on her deck. Her masts look very lofty, and I can't imagine you climbing to their tops."

Several days later my father took me to interview the captain, future arbiter of my fate. Before reaching the station I was thrilled, looking over towards the docks, to see the ship's four masts towering aloft.

So the dog's life was to be mine after all! For me no more the fetters of the stuffy bank with its 'brilliant' career. Instead, the freedom of the great, broad highway of the sea, stretching across a windblown immensity to distant, fascinating, foreign lands.

We were shown into the saloon under the poop, where the master received us. It would be more correct to say received my father, for the captain took little or no notice of me, giving me something of a wormlike complex from the start.

One of the apprentices came in to report to the captain. He was a rosy-cheeked, sturdy boy, barefooted and clad in soiled dungarees. I watched him carefully, noting every detail, my own outfit not as yet having been purchased. A formidable sheath-knife which stuck jauntily from his right haunch was one of the items not overlooked by me.

Having made our obeisance to the captain we returned home, It had been arranged that I should sign indentures and join the ship shortly before she sailed for Australia.

* * *

And then came the last night, momentous occasion, in the old home. My father called me to his study when all the others had gone to bed. Seating himself at his desk, he opened the Bible.

In the silence of the hall outside the study door, the ancient grandfather clock ticked unusually solemnly and ponderously. I had rather dreaded this final interview, yet in reality there was nothing to fear.

My father read some passages, but my thoughts were far away, and no impression was made on my wayward mind until he turned to Corinthians. And then his slow words suddenly grasped my wandering attention. . . . "Watch ye, stand fast in the faith, quit you like men, be strong. . . ."

It seemed to me those words were written specially for a weedy boy setting out to sail beyond a far horizon. Many a time, in the months and years to come, I was to think of them; many a time when the ship was hard pressed; when she was in distress, and mere boys had to play the part of men for her, and their own, safety.

Closing the Bible, my father rose from the desk and spoke some words of kindly counsel. He was, I knew, a little sad at heart over my determination to go to sea. He had repeatedly said to my brothers and myself, regretfully: "Though I have four sons not one of them is following in my footsteps by going in for the ministry."

I sensed he wished to warn me against the wiles of women and the woes of wine, and wondered how he would approach the subject. Sex was a matter which had not been discussed between us, for it was considered taboo.

He stood with his kindly eyes fixed on me for a minute or two, and then said quietly: "Always treat women with the same respect you would show your own mother." Shaking hands, he wished me good luck and fair winds while he handed me a brand new Bible. To my immortal shame—that book remained with me for years with practically uncut leaves.

Quit you like men, be strong. Fine, heartening words for a boy who was not strong and yet was setting out to face the endless trials and tribulations of sail; fine, heartening words too, for that matter, for anybody met with the crises of life. I hear again my father slowly repeating them, and the deep, solemn ticking of the ancient grandfather clock.

*   *   *

Next morning we had a rendezvous with the captain at the

Shipping Office on the West Quay. That humble little building still stands unchanged to this day.

We were a bit early, and were standing there contemplating a smashed-in window when the captain arrived. He was a shortish, thick-set man with a very red face. The weather was unusually warm. He looked hot and uncomfortable in his tight-fitting go-ashore serge suit, high collar and pot hat.

Having noticed the direction of our gaze, the captain pointed a stubby finger at the bashed-in window. "One of my men did that when he was drunk yesterday," he remarked. "Wait till I get him to sea—I'll fix him." There was something sinister in those words, "I'll fix him." He looked at me as he spoke, so that I wondered whether I too were going to be included in the fixing process.

After we had entered the building the shipping master babbled a stream of words which were so garbled that I grasped little of their meaning. The Apprentice's Indenture, which lies before me as I write, was placed in front of us, and our signatures appended in diminishing order of importance—first the captain's, then my father's, and finally mine in a boyish hand.

I find now, though I took no heed at the time, being prepared to sign anything to get to sea, that the clauses of the indenture were rather exacting. The solemn words which follow appear therein : ". . . . the said Apprentice covenants that he will not frequent taverns and alehouses. . . . ." That tickles me, as it must have tickled many a bygone generation of sea apprentices. The worthy owners must have lost sight completely of the fact that the briny fare supplied by them produced a thirst that would not be denied.

It was only right that the owners, having virtually claimed my soul for four years, should on their part have made some suitable provision for my welfare during that period. Oh yes, they did. It is all down there, clearly stated with meticulous care and many flowery words.

They agreed to furnish me with Meat, Drink, Lodging, and to pay me the munificent sum of £5 per annum. That was surely a poor reward for the toil and hardship of a whole twelvemonth.

The signing of the indenture complete, my father handed to the captain the premium, a sum of money which must have meant a heavy sacrifice to him. If was, if I remember correctly, forty pounds.

Leaving the shipping master and the captain to transact some other business, the two of us stepped out of the dingy office. My father had become very quiet and preoccupied, as though he were wondering whether we had done the right thing. And I? In my heart there was a great elation, tempered, perhaps, by the thought that I was leaving a comfortable home which had not, strictly speaking, fitted me in any way for the hardships of the sea. Silently, deep within me, I hoped and prayed that I might have the guts to see it through.

Close by, at the southern end of the West Quay, lay the ship. She stood high in the water, her discharge almost complete. Her immense masts towered loftily towards the sky, the great yards standing out from them horizontally like the sturdy branches of an oak tree.

High above the quay the graceful stem traced its delicately curved line, topped by the newly-painted, glistening figurehead which nestled under the long spike boom. The rust of which my brother had complained had disappeared under a coat of paint which freshly covered the hull from waterline to t'gallant rail. She looked very smart with her grey hull and black topsides, the band of white between the two showing up boldly the oblong black-painted ports favoured by some owners. T. Law's "Shire" fleet of square-riggers were always painted so, a colour scheme which was most effective.

Aloft, the crew were bending sail, swinging on the footropes of the fore lower topsail yard with a nonchalance which I hoped would soon be mine. To us came the sound of the sou'easter singing its age-old song, tearing at the unruly canvas. The hands were stretching the head of the sail along the jackstay, the time of their pull being given by long-drawn, musical cries. Perched precariously on the yard-arms sat two men who were passing the head-earrings.

The *Elginshire* was a steel vessel of 2,229 gross tons, rigged as a four-masted barque. When I joined her she was about to celebrate her coming-of-age, if ships do that, and was still in fine condition, having been well looked after throughout her life. She was steel from truck to keelson, there being no wood aloft except the jigger-topmast, the spanker gaff, the plugs in the yardarms, and the various blocks for the running rigging. It was a slight disappointment to me to find she carried only single t'gallant yards. Those single t'gans'ls always gave me a slight inferiority complex with regard to my ship.

Occasionally, trying to do a bit of swank in some port while speaking to another sailing ship boy, I would swell my puny pigeon-chest and remark: "My ship is a fourmasted barque." Then would come the devastating answer: "Yes, I know that. But your ship has only single t'gans'ls. We carry double t'gallant yards —*and* a main skysail!"

But as she lay at the West Quay that morning all those years ago, much admired by my father and myself, I found much satisfaction when we noticed that she literally towered over the other windjammers in port.

* * *

When I made my way aboard with my sea-chest the half-deck, the official residence of the apprentices, housed only four boys, though there were bunks for twelve. Two, I soon learned, had come to a sticky end, one having fallen from the main t'gallant yard to be pulped on deck. The other had suffered so much from chronic and apparently incurable seasickness that he had to be sent home from British Columbia. Several others had completed their time, thus being able to leave the ship to sit for their B.O.T. examination for second mate.

The half-deck was just a cheerless steel box built on the after deck, where it carried the skids for the lifeboats. The deck-house was divided into four, the largest section being our sleeping quarters. It contained twelve metal-lath bunks, four on each side and four across the fore-end. Abaft this, on each side, were respectively a very small so-called wash-house to starboard, and a tiny two-berth 'hospital' to port. Between the wash-house and hospital a narrow opening led to the messroom, where all our meals were eaten. This was furnished with a deal table scrubbed (more or less) white, two benches, a water-tank to hold our precious issue, and twelve lockless 'lockers', in which our simple eating utensils were kept.

A door in the after-end of the half-deck faced the break of the poop; thus we were always under the eagle eye of the austere authority which ever paced the poop in the shape of the officer of the watch at sea. As we ate in port, or in fine weather at sea when the door could be kept open, constantly before us was the big brass plate which the builders had proudly screwed to the foot of the jigger mast when the ship had left their yard. That plate was polished many times by me in the two years I spent in the ship. Its wording was as follows: ELGINSHIRE—BIRRELL, STENHOUSE & CO., IRON AND STEEL SHIPBUILDERS, DUMBARTON, 1889.

* * *

I formally took possession of one of the 'thwartship top bunks, the top fore-and-afters being occupied by my lords and masters, the four apprentices who had been many months aboard the ship and had already rounded the Horn twice. It did not take long to realise the disadvantages of a 'thwartship bunk once the ship had got to sea. When the vessel was rolling badly one's feet were up in the air one minute; the next, one was looking down at them as from the top of a hill. It also meant continual shifting of one's pillow as the ship went about, otherwise one woke to find the barque sailing 'on her ear' and one's head away down to leeward. This did not often happen, for the heavy gear usually required all hands to put the vessel about.

It was strange the following morning to be roused at 5.30 a.m. by the A.B. who was acting as night-watchman. He came roaring into the half-deck: "Come on, me hearties. Rise and shine, you sleepers. Show a leg, me lads, and come and get yer coffee!"

Sound sleep had not come to me throughout the night. The strangeness of my surroundings had kept me awake, staring wide-eyed at the deckhead so close above my face. The ship, too, had been restless, stirring with queer little hollow noises against the fenders. Somewhere below me, in the darkness of the empty hold, the thin piping cry of a rat in pain had rung out clearly once or twice. Up aloft the wind had been talking to the masts and yards all night; some slack running rigging had been *tap-tap-tapping* continuously against the spars.

While the crew completed the bending of sail, I worked down the great, gloomy hold, shovelling the ballast which had been dumped anyhow into the ship. It was the heaviest task faced in my life as yet; I was glad when the mate called me on deck to assist him tend the gear as the hands cried out from aloft. He was a fine fellow to whom I took a liking from the first.

We had hoped to sail without any further addition to our number in the half-deck. Our hopes were dashed the next day. Five youngsters marched aboard, newly come from London in a steamer. Our ranks had now swollen to ten, a decided crush, particularly at meal times.

Three of the newcomers were from one of the training ships which cater solely for the 'Sons of Gentlemen.' Though they turned out good sailors and not bad shipmates, they always gave me the impression that it was a great condescension on their part to spend their lives with a motley crowd like the rest of us. I have nothing against these lordly training ships which confine their superior activities to the sons of gentlemen—provided they do not foster an uppish spirit which is alien to the sea. Those three never went ashore with any of the other boys. Secretly they were dubbed by me The Training Ship Trio.

The day before we towed into the bay two of my school contemporaries, whom I had not seen for some time, passed along the quayside. My sole clothing a particularly grimy shirt and filthy dungaree trousers, it is little wonder they had difficulty in recognising me. We were washing decks at the time. Barefooted and dirty, I stood bending my back at a portable hand-pump, while opposite me a villainous-looking Scandinavian, even dirtier than myself, toiled at the same work.

The two boys gazed at me and my shaggy vis-a-vis. Surveying the ship and myself in a deprecatory manner, one of them asked, in all seriousness: "Are you doing that for a joke?" "No," I answered, "but I'm going to sea, and this is just part of the job."

Shaking their heads sadly, they passed on their way. It was obvious they did not understand, for in those days South African boys had little or no soul for the sea. Many people who knew me, indeed, seemed to imagine I was suffering from some obscure mental aberration.

CHAPTER IV

I GO TO SEA AT LAST

THE ship hauled out into the bay next day. She lay to a long scope of chain while the south-easter boomed and roared aloft.

The following morning I turned out to see my last sunrise over Table Bay. Standing on the fo'c'sle head, I watched the greyness growing in the east. The mountains I knew so well stood out clear-cut, like the jet-black silhouettes of our great-grand parents before the discovery of photography.

A tug came nosing out of the docks, heading our way. The great hearty voice of the mate called along the deck: "Man the windlass!"—and I knew that we were soon to sail.

As we marched around the windlass, bending over the bars, there was ample time to take stock of my future shipmates. They were truly an oddly assorted lot. But amongst them it was easy to pick out a number of real shellbacks. At the bar in front of me a grey-headed Norwegian with a heavy white moustache was putting all his strength into the work. He wore only a thin cotton singlet and a pair of cleverly-patched dungaree trousers, his bare feet thrust into the coloured plush slippers so beloved of the Scandinavian sailormen.

The mate, leaning over for'ard, watching the chain make its slow entry into the hawse-pipe, called out: "Give us a song, one of you men." One of the older hands piped up, and we all joined in. The clanking of the windlass pawls and the cry of the wheeling gulls was a fitting accompaniment to the rough song.

The tug *Manila* had been lying off, watching the scene which she had witnessed so many times before. She was to take us to an offing, the morning being entirely windless. When the chain was almost up-and-down the mate roared to the skipper on the poop: "Hove short, Sir!"

With the tug fast, we manned the windlass again. The anchor was loath to leave the ground. We sweated at the capstan bars, the mate encouraging us with shouts of: "Heave and bust her! Heave and break her out!" And then the big barque swung slowly round as the tug took up the tow. We were really off—and I realised that I was bidding good-bye to Table Bay for four years at least.

Some of the hands ran aloft to loosen sail as the ship swept past Sea Point, nodding her trucks and tilting her long yardarms as she met the deep-sea swell. But the morning remained windless, and the sails were left hanging in their gear until we were fifteen miles out to sea. Then the south-easter came ruffling the water. The fore-and-afters went rattling up their stays; the topsails were sheeted home and the foresail set. With the tug let go, sail was crowded on the ship as she bore away close-hauled to the south-west.

It seemed the *Manila* did not want to leave that ever-interesting spectacle—a square-rigger making sail for a long ocean passage. At last the tug's whistle blew three long blasts of farewell as she turned back for Cape Town.

The wind was freshening. Soon the ship, with everything set, was leaning steeply to the breeze. For the first time I experienced the easy, joyous motion of a big sailing vessel under way. To the eastward lay the long windswept trail which would lead us to Australia.

* * *

Before joining the *Elginshire* I had greedily devoured every book of the sea within my reach, and had been aboard many windjammers in dock. Foolishly I had imagined that the work of the ship would come easily to me. It did not take long to realise that I was hopelessly lost, running around the decks endeavouring to be of some assistance.

There was a temporary ban on the new boys going aloft, one of the apprentices having been killed by a fall from aloft when the ship was off the Horn. Had that tragedy not occurred so recently, so much solicitude would not have been shown for our welfare.

When all sail had been set and the confusion of running rigging coiled up, there was time to look around. Being in ballast, the ship was lying well over, doing about six knots. The familiar rugged mountains of the Cape Peninsula were already assuming the bluish hue of distance. Later, when the sun was setting, the land was but a shadow to the northward. As darkness crept over the water that distant shadow was shut out from view.

Then, it must be admitted, a sort of reaction set in, and the first touch of melancholy swept over me. Would I, too, be like that wretched pair of gutless uncles; would I, like them, admit defeat? Behind me lay the soft upbringing of a good home; before me lay the unknown but undoubted hardships of life in a ship where the food would be of the coarsest; where there was no comfort or let-up from the endless watching of ship and warring with the elements. My father's slowly-enunciated words came back to me then. The thought cheered me that an attempt could at least be made to quit myself like a man, even if I was not particularly strong.

As night enveloped the sea, shutting out the last sight of the now distant land, I swore a mighty oath in the name of old Peter who had sailed the *Stormy Petrel* a century before. Fair weather or foul, come weal come woe, I would never return until the proud possessor of, at least, a square-rigged second mate's certificate.

Throughout the night the ship made over six knots towards the south-west. I had been picked by the mate for his watch, a great stroke of luck. At four bells, 2 a.m., the wind freshened, necessitating the furling of the royals and the fore and mizen t'gans'ls. Up aloft in the darkness the sails threshed and pounded, until the watch on deck had run up the rigging to muzzle them with the gaskets. The outer jib was hauled down too. As we pulled lustily on the down-haul it carried away. The husky third mate, holding the parted end of the rope in his hands, roared out above the slatting of the sails: "Jesus wept and bust his waistcoat!"

In my innocence it seemed to me, unused to the blasphemy and roughness of the sea, an odd and foolish remark. Standing there on the fo'c'sle head in the middle of the night, I waited for the wrath of Heaven to descend upon him. As truly as I write these words, I expected some fiery symbol of the Lord's displeasure to strike upon his curly pate. He remained very much alive, however, and a line was soon taken aloft, and a bowline passed around the t'gallant stay by means of which the struggling sail was hauled down and stowed.

The memory of that first little blow remains very vividly with me. The booming of the wind aloft and the thunder of the unstowed sails; the steep incline of the deck; the eerie cries of the men as we hauled the canvas to the yards; the pitch darkness in

which men found the correct ropes and then made their way
aloft to lay out on those huge swaying yards. The most vivid
recollection of all is that of the Herculean third mate, looking up
and crying out blasphemy and obscenity at the dark, lowering sky
which overwhelmed us.

That first night brought me face to face with the stark reality
of the Great Adventure on which I had embarked. Here was no
pleasant romance such as one found in the reading of a fireside
sea story. There was, nevertheless, a strange elation about it all
—and I was glad that I had come.

* * *

For a week the barque made no progress whatever towards Australia. Her course was persistently to the south-west, her limita-
tions as a square-rigged vessel in ballast preventing her from
heading higher than that in the stubborn south-east winds we
experienced. She was actually being carried further from Port
Adelaide, whither we were bound.

But the captain remained unperturbed and the mate, in an expansive moment, explained to me that the most important matter
was to make *southing*. Soon the brave west wind would come to
drive us on our way. Then the ship would square away for
Australia, sailing on the arc of a Great Circle, biting deeply into
the "Roaring Forties" to retain the strong favourable winds of that
region.

For the most part that first week was spent by the crew in
cleaning up the great lower hold, empty but for the three piles of
stone ballast. From the for'ad collision bulkhead the ship stretched
aft like an enormous warehouse, pierced by the boles of the four
massive masts. We worked down there in the semi-darkness,
sweeping and clearing up in preparation for the cargo of grain we
hoped would be ours when we reached Australia.

Often the weatherbeaten face of the mate would appear over
the hatch-coaming as he summoned us hurriedly on deck to stand
by the halliards or to trim the yards.

The sea had been empty of all ships until the second day out,
when a sail was sighted. She was a very small vessel, from the
mast of which two little wisps of bunting were flying. The captain,
thumbing the signal book, made out their import—"YR: Want
water immediately."

"Back the main yard!" he sang out to the mate. A boat was dropped from the little vessel, and soon the two men in it had clambered on to our deck. They told us they were from the cutter *Elizabeth,* of Cape Town, bound from Great Fish River to their home port. There were three men aboard, one having remained to tend the hove-to vessel.

I knew this little ship well, having often been aboard her and her sister *Stella* in the docks. She was one of that fleet of hardy cutters which plied regularly up and down the South African coast before marine motors had come to mean anything at sea. Frequently they made long passages, sometimes being blown many miles off the land, as on this occasion.

A cask of water was lowered into the boat, and a hefty lump of salt beef. Then the main yards were filled again, and the barque gathered way to the southward. Soon the *Elizabeth* was only a little speck on the waste of water.

It took the ship a week to find the west wind. In the middle of the night it came roaring on its way around the world. With a great *cluttering* of brace-blocks and wild, yodelling song from the leading chantyman, the barque squared away before it to start her long run to the eastward. The wind soon brought its fellow, the long high swell in which the ship rolled and staggered, her jib-boom soaring and falling like some gaunt finger pointing the way.

At last we were really on the road to Australia, romantic, one-time bushranger-ridden land of my dreams.

*　　*　　*

At midnight a heavy pall of black, lowering cloud hung overhead, almost touching the wildly swaying mastheads. In a rising gale the mainsail was hauled up and furled by all hands. In the inky darkness, I jumped into the rigging and made my way aloft with the crew.

It was my first serious attempt at taking a man's part in the handling of sail. I had, of course, been aloft a number of times before, but only in the fine weather we had experienced since leaving Cape Town. Now the ship was storming through the darkest of nights. There was no glimmer of light to guide us as we clambered out on the footropes of the main yard. The huge sail, its struggles to be free only halfheartedly curbed by the clew-garnets, buntlines and leechlines by which we had hauled it up, was threshing and pounding madly in the high wind.

My neighbour on the footrope was a huge lout, one of the senior apprentices. When he realised who was next to him, he cursed me roundly for coming there at all.

Old Wilson, one of our stout-hearted real sailors, cried out eerily in at the bunt, where the best men go. Wailingly his cry gave us the time of the pull. Clawing painfully with my nails at the cold, iron-hard canvas, I hauled to the best of my poor ability, the mate's injunction ringing in my ears: "One hand for yourself and one for the ship," an important piece of advice which was rarely heeded. For most of the work aloft required both hands for the ship.

The footrope swung back to the time of the united pull. I found myself lying horizontally on top of the yard. The jackstay gouged painfully into my vitals, and it seemed to me I was faced with the immediate prospect of being hurled headforemost over the yard. Fifty feet below, the main deck showed up blackly in the darkness, framed in the leaping white crests of the big seas alongside.

And then the strain of the pull relaxed—in preparation for the next concerted effort, the time of our drag being perfectly punctuated by Wilson's long-drawn, minor-cadence cry.

Finally the big sail was muzzled and rolled on top of the yard. Clinging there precariously, 'twixt sea and sky, the thunder of the mighty wind in the topsails above, the phosphorescent crests of the breaking seas far below, I heard the voice of the bully alongside shouting at me. He wanted me to kneel down on the footrope to pass the gasket to him up the foreside of the yard.

This was a physical impossibility for me to do. (The work aloft became so familiar later that there was no difficulty about it.) The ship, hard pressed, was rolling and plunging heavily. As if that were not enough to imperil my position there, the great lout started belabouring me about the head and shoulders with his enormous fist.

What with the wild swaying of the yard, the storminess of the night, and the unpleasant attentions of my next-door neighbour, it is amazing I did not lose my insecure hold and fall—to be mangled on the deck below, or to drop overboard, where I should not have lasted long clad in oilskins and heavy seaboots.

And then old Nelsen, the Viking who had bent over the capstan bar in front of me in Table Bay, came to my assistance, threatening to throw my assailant off the yard.

* * *

The days which had intervened since sailing had given me an opportunity of settling down in my somewhat strange environment. What, then, were my feelings throughout that week?

First, most unpleasant of all, was the entire lack of privacy in the half-deck. In that narrow steel box ten of us ate, slept, and had our being. To my sensitive nature this was something entirely new, for I had never been at boarding school For some days and nights I foolishly pulled my clothes off, and dressed again at the end of the watch, in my bunk.

This unprecedented modesty was, of course, noticed by my shipmates from the start. After much twitting while I protested violently, they dragged me from my bunk, pulled every shred of clothing from me, and left me entirely naked and much ashamed.

One of the greatest hardships which we had to suffer was the terrible loss of continuous sleep, which followed me all my days in sail. It was impossible under the four-hour watch system to obtain more than three to three and a half hours' sleep at a time. During the four hours of one's watch below, meals had to be eaten in the daytime, and at night it was difficult to get to sleep much before the half hour after going below.

The call to turn out again came all too soon. At one bell, a quarter of an hour before eight bells, one of the watch on deck came roaring into the half-deck: "One bell, you sleepers! Show a leg, rise and shine!" Then often followed: "And you'll need your oilskins, for it's a lousy night." Setting a match to the dim light, he left us to crawl protestingly from our warm bunks.

It was an unforgivable and severely punished offence not to appear on deck immediately eight bells had been struck. The watch which had just completed four hours on deck was not permitted to go below until the entire relief had mustered aft.

As eight strokes rang out from the small poop bell—to be answered by the big one for'ad—we stepped out on to the windswept and often seaswept deck, to be joined by the fo'c'sle hands as they made their way aft. Then took place the relief of the watch, a ritualistic procedure which was carried out three times every night throughout a long voyage. It was, in its way, equally important as the famous Changing of the Guard at St. James' Palace.

We stood huddled together in the darkness while the second mate carefully checked us and then reported: "The watch is aft, Sir!" From the Holy of Holies of the poop the mate, leaning over the teak rail overhead, shouted: "Relieve the wheel and lookout!" The new helmsman would climb the lee poop ladder, carefully avoiding the weather side where, in sail, the smooth planking was always regarded as having been impregnated with some mystic holiness, which transferred itself to the other side immediately the ship went on the other tack. The rigid ceremonial of the change of the watch at night was made necessary by the exactions of a sailing ship, where everybody had to be ready at all times for instant action.

* * *

It did not take long to realise that life at sea was going to be no bed of roses. Little or no consideration was given to the comfort of any of us. In sail one was expected to be tough, and to stand uncomplainingly unlimited hardship and discomfort. Perhaps that is why the sailing vessel played so well its part in the training of men for the sea.

The food was coarse, not too plentiful, and unlike anything I had been used to at home. A day or two after sailing the supply of fresh meat gave out, its place being taken by alternate salt pork and beef, which were soaked for a few hours in *salt* water to remove the brine. This daily issue shrunk considerably in the boiling, and the hungry boys in each watch usually sat down to a greasy kind of unappetising, often evil-smelling, meat of unknown age and origin.

To counteract the salinity of this briny fare, and to act as an 'anti-scorbutic' (hideous word, that), lime-juice was issued daily at noon from the tenth day onwards until the end of the passage. It was from this practice that all British windjammers came to be known as 'lime-juicers' or, more shortly, 'limies,' a slightly opprobrious term which originated in the United States. This item did not appear on the ration scale of American vessels, being considered unnecessary, a fact which bears witness to the superiority and greater variety of the fare aboard ships of that country.

Some theorists maintained that this rough, unrefined lime-juice had a subduing effect on whatever glands govern the amorous activities of sailormen, which could not, of course, be fulfilled at sea. In this light I remember well one day on which the steward was ill, just before we made the chops of the Channel after a long passage.

The master and mate were sitting at dinner while I, deputising for the steward, stood by watching them munch their salt beef. Lifting his tot of 'anti-scorbutic,' the master remarked facetiously to the mate: "It's time we were cutting this stuff out, mister. We're getting near home now."

All hands were called aft at noon to partake of the communal cup. The steward appeared from the pantry, bucket in hand. As the men lay aft, half-masticated chews of tobacco would be hiked from their jaws. Each quaffed his allowance scornfully, wishing, no doubt, it was a drop of 'Nelson's blood.'

One or two of the more fastidious boys brought their own pannikins, but most of us, having regard to the brotherhood of the sea, used the common mug, the A.B.s drinking first. And when all had had their 'daily dose' the remainder was given graciously by the steward to the half-deck. Strained through a none-too-clean handkerchief to remove the inevitable tit-bits of tobacco-chew, it usually gave us an extra tot apiece.

* * *

Had I come aboard with any exalted ideas about my status in that ship, those would soon have been dispelled. The apprentices, whose parents had paid heavy premiums for the privilege of having their sons berthed apart from the crew, received no preferential treatment of any sort. It was, indeed, the exact reverse. Our food was identically that of the fo'c'sle, but while the A.B.s had a recognised name and some sort of official position, we were usually referred to as 'them bloody boys.'

Most of the dirty work came our way. We did this more or less uncomplainingly, considering it part of our job. We kept the same watches as the men, with the additional task thrown in of time-keeping, i.e. striking the half-hourly bells on the poop at night, and acting as general run-abouts for the officers and men.

Many little annoying jobs were found for us, particularly in the second dog watches (6 to 8 p.m.), the traditional period of relaxation, should the weather permit, from the stern discipline of the ship. That was the time for a noisy sing-song, a bit of playful wrestling or boxing. But often the officer of the watch would imagine we were enjoying ourselves too much. Spitefully he would roar from the poop, the High Seat of authority: "Three of you boys—up aloft and overhaul the buntlines from the royals down!"

Buntline overhauling, the bane of our lives, was an important part of the work of a sailing ship, and requires some explanation. Buntlines are those ropes which run aloft from the deck to each and every square sail. Their purpose is to enable the sail to be hauled up close to its yard before the hands go aloft to make it fast. Those buntlines, hanging down on the foreside of each sail, caused considerable friction on the canvas, which would soon chafe through if continual attention were not paid to them. A boy would go up each mast with a few lengths of sail twine, haul up sufficient slack on the rope concerned, and then put a small 'stop,' or lashing, of twine around the buntline or leechline. By this means the chafe was minimised. If a change of weather necessitated the furling of the sail, a jerk on the rope was sufficient to break the 'stop' from the deck.

Sometimes the officers would go down on to the main deck and wilfully and deliberately jerk the buntlines until the stops were all broken and the lines bearing heavily on the sails. Then the voice of authority roared out, and we made a toilsome journey aloft to do the job all over again. In the end we often got so exasperated that we stopped the gear with *rope-yarns*—a foolish and dangerous action which usually meant a hurried trip aloft to cut the rope-yarns if a sudden squall struck the ship.

* * *

To revert to the matter of food, a most important subject at sea, and one which has probably contributed more than any other to the many murders and mutinies on the high seas.

Rations were issued once a week, on Thursday, which consequently came to be known as 'whack day.' Each one received from the steward his Board of Trade allowance—and no more. This rather niggardly handling of stores was observed throughout the time I was in sail. The responsibility of making the ration last its allotted week rested entirely with the individual. If certain articles were used up in a day or two, which often happened, no more was available until the next issue.

Tinned milk was our greatest difficulty. One third of a tin per head was doled out weekly. This amount was totally inadequate for the prescribed period. My mother, on expansive occasions when she had been particularly pleased with me, had often given me a whole tin to eat at my leisure with a spoon.

One third of a tin did not go far in rendering more or less palatable the burgoo (porridge) which was our solitary breakfast dish on three or four mornings of the week. Sweetened milk, moreover, was far to attractive a food to keep in our cockroach infested lockers.　After several attempts to make the milk trickle out its span, I for one gave up the problem and fell into the habit of devouring my 'whack' immediately after its issue on Thursdays.

The steward, noticing this, came furtively to me, whispering that a tin was available—at a price. Weakly I handed over to him a brand-new, unworn pair of dungaree trousers which must have cost my poor father at least five shillings. It was a shocking case of 'sea price', the tin having cost no more than fourpence wholesale.

The whack of sugar, too, was not over generous. Tea and burgoo were rather unpalatable at first without milk or sugar, but it is surprising how soon one gets used to their absence. Provided one's stomach does not shrink from a bit of sediment at the bottom of the pannikin, jam or marmalade or mollasses can be used for sweetening the tea.

The only item on our food list which was unrationed was the biscuits, great square, flintlike slabs in the overeating of which it was unlikely anybody would ever indulge. These appeared to be sound when I joined the ship, but later on became decidedly weevily. The high-sounding 'calavances' which appeared conspicuously on the B.O.T. list turned out to be ordinary beans—musical fruit as they were called by the vulgar wits of the ship. These, too, harboured their own particular type of animal life after a brief sojourn aboard the barque.

Of the whole, decidedly restricted, menu available to us, Sunday morning's feed of curried tinned-mutton and rice was the most enjoyable. Sometimes, when we were in the good books of the cook, it was possible to beg the remains when all had been served. Judged by the standard of culinary art ashore, it would, no doubt, have seemed a sorry mess, the rice soggy and the meat stringy and badly curried. To me, at least, it was the all-sufficing blow-out of the week.

There was another item, a tit-bit, though perhaps a little indigestible, which appeared with monotonous regularity at meal times in both fo'c'sle and half-deck. Though no women were aboard, they were with us every time we sat down to eat. We had them fricasseed for breakfast, minced for dinner, and devilled for supper. The youngsters in the *Elginshire's* half-deck were not particularly dissipated or vicious. It may, perhaps, have been a compliment to the weaker sex that reference to, and remarks about, them filled so much of our conversation.

But it was a little disconcerting until familiarity had wrought its usual work and brought a measure of contempt or indifference. In the atmosphere of my home women had been enthroned, to a great extent, on a pedestal. It takes a long time for that pedestal to crumble, and for the feet of clay to make their tardy appearance.

Before the hardening process has become complete, it gives one a little shudder, having been nurtured in the somewhat narrow surroundings of the manse, to hear one's shipmates continually referred to obscenely and illogically as a particularly low type of woman, and to find them constantly likened, opprobriously and indecently, to parts of the male and female anatomy.

CHAPTER V

THE ROARING FORTIES, AND THEN—
AUSTRALIA

Up from the south, up from the region of eternal storm and cold, a huge albatross came sailing majestically. The word sailing has been used advisedly, for there is none other to describe adequately the flight of these birds.

With no visible movement other than the flickering of the delicate feather tips on wings and tail, it soared proudly over the poop. Its eyes, black and beady, scanned the ship's wake for scraps of food.

I stood deep in admiration of the splendid bird. It seemed to me the fitting companion for our barque—both wind-borne gipsies, both essentially of the sea.

There was a quick tread behind me, and the sound of laboured breathing. It was the mate, a hardy veteran of the sea, who had spent his life roaming the ocean in windjammers.

"That's a splendid bird, sir," I ventured. Tearing his gaze from the albatross he faced me, his eyes ablaze with a malignant light "Splendid bird!" he snarled at me. "No, that's no splendid bird! It's just a dirty, low-down piece of murderous carrion. You wait until after eight bells and I'll show you what I'll do with your 'splendid bird'."

The four double strokes rang out; the second mate came on to the poop to take charge. While the mate passed the usual desultory remarks about the wind, course and work in hand his eyes never left the albatross. Over the poop it hovered, riding the wind as easily as a piece of thistledown.

The mate clattered down the poop-ladder to his room. Though my watch was over, I lingered there. For I sensed some strange vendetta between the man and bird. He soon returned to the lee side of the poop, carrying a coil of stout fishing line and a piece of pork. With the latter he carefully baited the hook, to which was attached a cork float.

The baited hook was cast over the taffrail, the line being paid out at the same speed as the ship was moving. Hovering a moment, the bird settled its huge bulk near the tasty morsel. Paddling close to the floating pork, it made several darts at the bait. The mate, watching keenly, struck in the manner of a fisherman; the hook bit home. Hand over hand we hauled the floundering bird aboard. It reached the poop-deck snapping fiercely, complaining gutturally of its harsh treatment and unfamiliar surroundings.

The mate straddled it and made a swift pass up its neck with one horny hand. A few quick turns of spunyarn, and the cruel beak was lashed securely. "Fetch Chips' tenon saw—quick," he ordered me.

With the saw he carefully severed the upper beak, cutting off the tip an inch from the end. The cruelty of this act filled me with helpless rage. Then the beak lashing was cut and the poor bird hurled over the rail, the scattered blood crimsoning its beautiful snow-white breast.

The mate swung his gaze around the empty horizon. "No more of the swine!" he said. "But they'll come, damn them, they'll come—and then I'll get them before the wind freshens too much." He laughed harshly, took up his line and left the poop, taking with him the severed beak. As he passed the ladder he remarked callously: "That bird will surely die, either by slow starvation or killed by its own dirty breed."

* * *

It was in the middle watch early the following morning. After six bells had been struck I heard the mate calling to me from the weather side of the poop. Weary of the monotony of the lengthy watch, he wished to pass some of the long-drawn time in conversation.

"You must have thought that a pretty brutal piece of work when I maimed that bird," he commenced. "Anyway, you looked a bit squeamish about it. In case you should misjudge me, I'm going to tell you a little story.

"It happened many years ago when I was master of a smart little ship. I had with me a fine young fellow about your age. He did not float around in port in a brass-bound uniform like you youngsters, for he was only an Ordinary Seaman. His father believed the fo'c'sle was the proper place to learn sailorising, so he put him there. And he was already a fine sailor, fearless aloft and equal to any two of the average A.B.s. I saw in him the makings of a first-rate officer, and eventually he would command a ship himself.

"We were outward bound, in just about the same position as we now are. It was in the afternoon, and the lad was aloft busy on some job on the mizen lower topsail yard-arm. What happened I don't know, but I saw him suddenly pitch headlong into the sea. The wind was not very strong, and there was only a moderate sea running, but I had a poor crew, and it took a long time to bring the ship to the wind, and still longer to get the boat out.

"The masthead lookout reported the boy some distance off by then. But it took no lookout to tell me where he was, for half a dozen albatrosses wheeled low in the vicinity. We got the port lifeboat out at last. . . ."

The mate stopped speaking. Aloft in the darkness a sheave whined softly. He left me to cross the deck to peer into the yellow glare that was the compass. Then he threw up his head to sniff the wind.

Around us lay the mystery and the vastness and the majesty of the dark, lonely sea. A greyness, almost imperceptible as yet, heralded another day. Towards it the barque rolled on her way.

The mate returned to my side. He stood so long staring out across the water that I thought he had forgotten his story. "Did you find him?" I asked at last. He turned fiercely on me.

"Did we find him? You ask did we find him! My God, you could have heard the poor boy crying out miles away! Yes, we found him—what was left of him. For those dirty, lousy birds had pecked the eyes out of him, and almost scalped the lad before we got him into the boat. He died before we got him back to the ship. The mate said it was more drowning than anything else, but I knew better. . . ."

He stopped again and stiffened as he looked out across the water. Up from the south, sailing majestically, came an enormous, solitary albatross. As it passed close over the poop, even in the half-light we saw the gaunt greyness of the old bird.

"That's the grandfather of all the albatrosses in the southern seas," said the mate. "Perhaps that's one of the swine that destroyed him. Wait till daylight. I'll have him. An eye for an eye, a tooth for a tooth, and a life for a life. No, not a life for a life, but many lives for one life. That's my law—and a good one too!"

* * *

These were the vanguard of that great host of wandering albatrosses which people the limitless wastes of the immense Southern Ocean. For days they followed the ship, ever a-wing, sweeping at great speed far ahead of the barque, and then, 'bracing sharp up', they returned, sailing with the greatest ease into the eye of the wind.

I spent many hours watching those grand winged nomads of the south. They never seemed to sleep or weary on the wing. I saw them many times later, when the weather was so bad for weeks that to alight on the water would have been impossible. A little has been learned of their habits, but much will never be known. They nest and rear their young in the wildest and most inaccessible of places, far from the haunts of men.

The true Wandering Albatross is not found north of the Line. I believe attempts have been made, without success, to transport them to northern latitudes. The huge birds for some reason thrive only in their own domain—the illimitable and almost landless vastness of the 'Forties' and further south. Capt. Dixon, in his fine book, *A Million Miles in Sail*, estimates the number of albatrosses in these regions at one and a half million birds, surely a noble host of God's beautiful creatures.

The very word which names them conjures up for me the picture of a square-rigged ship storming through the 'Roaring Forties', her shortened canvas straining at sheet and shackle as the vessel flies, with a bone in her teeth, to the eastward.

There is a general belief ashore that these big birds are greatly respected by sailormen, and that a superstitious opinion exists amongst them that the destruction of an albatross brings dire calamity or, at least, head winds. I saw no evidence of this belief amongst the men with whom I sailed, with the exception of one or two of the oldest, who sadly shook their heads and muttered solemnly when they saw the birds being hauled aboard.

It was, to my mind, little short of a crime to catch and destroy these beautiful creatures, especially as their capture, as described, was so simple a matter. Under the right conditions, with the ship travelling slowly, I have seen many albatrosses caught from the poop. In other than light airs they usually arrived aboard half-drowned, and almost immediately disgorged the contents of their stomachs.

Though so graceful in the air, where they float with the fairy lightness of thistle-down, these birds are actually extremely heavy, weighing often as much as twenty-five pounds. Their wing-spread is enormous, sometimes as great as fourteen feet, the wings being very long and narrow. One specimen of almost these dimensions was caught on this passage to Australia. Albatrosses are utterly incapable of rising from a ship's deck, their great weight necessitating a long run such as is required by a heavy plane.

It caused me sorrow to witness the capture of so many of these magnificent birds. It was senseless, wanton destruction of one of God's most lovely creations, a living thing which is the embodiment of grace and of the great, free spirit of the sea, and a fitting companion for man's most beautiful fabrication—the sailing ship.

It was considered 'the thing' to make tobacco pouches out of the big webbed feet; to use the long, hollow flintlike bones for pipe stems, and to preserve the snow-white breast for ladies' muffs. These were poor excuses for committing murder. The art of the taxidermist being almost unknown aboard, little success followed such efforts.

I, for one, was always glad when the wind, after its temporary rest, came roaring at us again, driving the ship at a speed which prevented any further capture of the birds.

* * *

Sailing on the arc of a Great Circle, the ship bit deeply into the 'Roaring Forties.' We lived in a world of grey sky and still greyer sea which depressed me a little at first, fresh from the bright sunniness of South Africa. There was a general, unavoidable dampness which permeated the ship, our clothing and our bedding. The half-deck, that Lodging so conspicuously mentioned in my indenture, sweated continuously and insufferably, its steel plates dribbling wetness on our bunks. In the end we gave up undressing, merely pulling off our oilskins, seaboots and outer clothing before turning in.

Little or no consideration was shown on deck by the officers for the comfort of the crew. Sailors were not expected to look for comfort—especially away down south with the ship 'running her easting down.' We were set, watch after watch, day after day, to the dismal task of sand-and-canvassing the paint-work of the deck houses and bulwarks.

For four hours at a time we would stand or crouch at this work in pouring rain, with an ever-ready eye to the needs of the ship herself. It was intensely dreary, particularly when the upper parts of the deck houses had to be done. As one scoured the paint with upraised arm, rivulets of rain trickled down the sleeves, and none but the finest and newest of oilskins could stand the continuous soaking. In spite of all this I had no regrets, tackling unpleasant tasks with the feeling that the life would make or break me. And somehow, I had no intention of being broken.

The flight of the ship to the eastward as she shouldered the grey, foaming seas; the song of the great west wind aloft; the goodly company of those grand white birds; the endless dangerous work on the wildly swinging yards—these things filled me with a strange elation.

Climbing out to the tip of the jib-boom one dog watch, I took my place with legs jammed inside the backropes, one hand upon the royal stay. Behind me the big shark's tail, nailed, as was the custom, to the spar-end, touched my back as I faced aft. Frank Bullen had gone many times to this vantage point in the ships in which he served—and now I found myself there too.

The sight before me was truly magnificent. It was as if I were on a moving stage outside the ship, watching her striving to run me down, yet never doing so. The barque was storming along under fores'l and six topsails, the wind slightly quartering, so that every sail was bladder-hard and pulling its full weight.

An enormous following sea was sweeping up from the westward, and the ship rolled and pitched heavily in her stride. One minute I soared swiftly upwards on the cold steel tip of that finger-spar; the next found me plunged seaward so steeply that it seemed the maddened water beneath was about to engulf me.

The thunder of the bow-wave was almost deafening as she lifted aft and hurled her stem into the boiling water till it surged, clutching upwards, to the figurehead. And then her bows went flying skywards again till the dripping forefoot showed many feet below. At such times the roar of the broken water decreased and another sound was heard—the deep boom of the gale as it threw itself exultingly against the rain-darkened topsails and great, bellying foresail. . . .

One of the men was standing at the heel of the bowsprit

beckoning to me, his lips moving while no words reached me. I made my way back to the foc's'le head. "Go aft," he said, "the Old Man wants to see you."

The skipper was waiting for me in one of his severest moods. "Do you know you were in the most dangerous part of the ship in bad weather?" he remarked, his keen blue eyes boring into me from under the thatch of his sou'wester. "How long would you have lasted if you had gone overboard? Not five seconds! If you must go out there for pleasure—go in fine weather!"

He turned from me to continue the watching of his ship as she drove along. For hours in such weather he would stand like that, hardly speaking to the officer of the watch unless it were to give some curt order for the safety of the barque. He was a fine sailor, his life having been spent in square-rigged ships and no others. If we thought him hard at times, he was hard for our own good.

* * *

One member of the ship's company had been giving considerable trouble to the officers. Things came to a head one day when we had run about half the distance to Australia. He was put down the fore-peak as punishment, in darkness, with the hatch secured.

Several hours had passed when a frantic pounding was heard on the underside of the hatch. When this was lifted, smoke bellied out from the opening. The culprit was quickly hauled on deck.

"I've set fire to the bloody ship," he announced, in a tone which denoted he considered he had done something remarkably clever.

There was no time to lose. Down below there were barrels of tar and the whole supply of coal for the galley. The wooden deck was saturated with inflammable substances and was already well alight. The wash-deck tub was hastily rigged and filled, and a chain of buckets passed by all hands under the foc's'cle head to the hatch.

The fire was eventually put out, but it took many weary hours of toil to clear the fore-peak of the water we had poured down there. The young man who had so wilfully set the ship on fire worked no more amongst us after that. With cancelled indentures, he was sent home from Sydney, the master having no further use for his services.

"ELGINSHIRE" UNDER SHORTENED CANVAS

Photo from a Painting

Curving northwards as we drew east, we passed several hundred miles south of Cape Lleuwen, western limit of the Great Australian Bight. As we worked towards Cape Borda, on Kangaroo Island, the weather became warmer and less stormy. The usual preparations for making port were now in evidence. The cables were hauled up and shackled on to the anchors; the fish-tackle was aloft, ready to lift the two anchors from where they had lain lashed on deck.

*   *   *

During a passage in ballast such as ours the rats aboard frequently had a very thin time, and often became exceptionally daring in their search for food. This was especially the case if the stores in the lazarette were well protected against their inroads.

One night I was sitting on the grating at the foot of the jigger mast. It may have been that I was dozing—the lack of continuous sleep was an agony at times—for I suddenly realised there was something pulling at the pocket of my monkey-jacket. Putting my hand down in the darkness, it came in contact with the furry coat of a huge rat half buried in the pocket.

The brute sprang away without biting me, and then I remembered the slice of bread and butter which the third mate had given me earlier in the watch. The officers had bread (known in sail as 'soft tack') every day, but to us boys even a plain, homely slice of bread and butter represented a luxury. The rat ran off with the bulk of mine that night.

When Kangaroo Island was but a few miles away the wind headed the ship. For some days we beat about outside Investigator Strait, waiting for a slant. It is almost impossible to work to windward in a big square-rigger flying light in ballast.

A number of other ships were also held up by the head wind. Then, when at last it freed, we all started romping up the Strait for Adelaide. It was a wonderful sight to see those big ships standing into port. Those playtime sailors at Cowes have never seen a nobler sight, nor yachting on such a titanic scale.

The first glimpse of Australia was disappointing. As we passed close to Cape Borda to make our numbers, the land looked intensely parched and barren in the glare of the bright sunlight. The breeze which bore us along carried with it half a dozen other windjammers, all running in for the crowded anchorage. The

F

masts of the great fleet of sailing ships were now visible as they lay off the Semaphore.

It was no light task to bring a vessel to anchor under such circumstances without the aid of a tug. But our skipper was a real sailor, and he took his vessel through those other ships and then rounded her head to wind. As she lost headway the anchor was let go, the ship settled gently astern on the chain—and my first passage under sail was ended.

At that time Adelaide was a favourite rendezvous for sailing vessels, being a convenient port at which to lie while negotiations were carried out for their chartering in dusty offices thousands of miles away. So it was that 'Adelaide for Orders' came to have a significance second only to that of Falmouth and Queenstown, those handy homing ports for the gipsies of the Horn.

Our work of 'harbour stowing' the sails complete, we had time to look around for old friends amongst the surrounding ships. Two little barques were getting under way in our vicinity, apparently having loaded grain at Port Adelaide. One was the dainty *Phyllis,* a ship which had discharged several times at Cape Town, on which occasions I had often been aboard.

The *clank-clank-clank* of her windlass pawls came clearly to us as she hove short. And then she was under way, her topsails filling as she paid off. The haunting cries of her crew rang out across the water as they piled the canvas on her. She passed very close, her numbers and the handsome ensign of Norway streaming from her gaff-end. Feeling the urge of her growing canvas, she headed down the Strait, the long, broad highway before her. We cheered her lustily, for the time had not yet left the world when an ocean passage was still a great adventure.

Close to us lay the British full-rigged ship *Cumberland.* The four-masted barque *Dowan Hill* of Glasgow came in and anchored on the other side of us. And then a big, black-painted German ship came flying through the shipping—arrogantly, defiantly, at great speed. As she rounded to the wind and clewed up everything with Prussian precision, she reminded me of some great sea-bird folding its wings and coming to rest upon the water.

* * *

Our barque had made no clipper run from Cape Town, the passage (46 days) having been spoilt by the loss of a number of days' head wind at either end.

Standing on deck, smoking the strong, nutty 'Fair Maid' plug of the slop-chest (my supply of South African tobacco had long since been exhausted), I reviewed that month and a half which had passed. Contrary to my father's gloomy forebodings, the life was not entirely doglike. While it offered little comfort or security, it had its brighter moments. We had pitted our strength against the elements—and won. And there was surely something of the spirit of the Vikings in setting out to cover vast distances equipped with nothing more than one's courage and God's good wind to take one safely to the far-off destination.

Forty-six days is not a lengthy period, but it was one in which I had learned a great deal. I had, moreover, been well and truly initiated into the brotherhood of the sea. I had lived close to it and had seen its majesty and greatness. The everlasting elemental forces of Nature had been my companions, and it seemed to me some little portion of their strength had become mine.

Never again, fair weather or foul, would I sit effetely on the padded comfort of that high stool in the bank. The footropes of those yards, swinging so far above 'twixt sea and sky, were good enough for me. . . .

* * *

It was not my lot to be chosen for that post of honour—the captain's gig. One of the senior apprentices and the Training-ship Trio filled that role. Clad in well-washed shirts and spotless dungarees, they were the gentlemen of the half-deck, rowing the skipper ashore every day.

So it was I did not have the chance to set foot in Port Adelaide. But there was much to see and much to occupy my time. As I worked in the chart-room by myself, cleaning and painting it out, I had full access to the binoculars and long glass. While the mate was busy on the main deck, I scanned that grand fleet of sail lying in the roads.

We had been at anchor over a week when the captain came off with our orders. There was jubilation aboard for we were to proceed to Sydney to load wheat, calling thereafter at Queenstown for orders. That was a great stroke of luck, when so many ships were loading coal at Newcastle, N.S.W., for the West Coast of South America.

Unfortunately the wind was a dead muzzler for us to beat out to the s'uthard. For several days it remained the same, and then, having freed slightly, the Old Man decided to sail. Three other ships were also heaving up: *Lados, Komet,* and the five-masted schooner *D. K. Hall.* We had heard a great deal about the windward qualities of these big American fore-and-afters, and welcomed the opportunity of comparing the relative sailing ability to windward of the square-rigger and one of the larger of those schooners.

The wind decided to haul dead ahead again, giving us a tedious beat down to Backstairs Passage, the narrow exit from Spencer Gulf at the eastern end of Kangaroo Island. The *D. K. Hall* was lying much higher than us but, being in ballast like ourselves, made a great deal of leeway. As we both zigzagged down the Gulf, tacking ship every watch, neither vessel made much progress, though undoubtedly the big schooner had an undeniable advantage over us.

It was dreary work, the wind holding persistently ahead. Two days after leaving our anchorage the masts of the shipping lying off Adelaide were still visible. At last the wind freed, the *Elginshire* slipped through the narrows of Backstairs—and we squared away for Sydney.

* * *

Throughout the day the ship had been sailing fast, running before a strong following wind and carrying perhaps a little more canvas than was prudent.

The weather had become surprisingly vile, frequent hard rain squalls beating down on the ship, necessitating constant standing by the halliards and other attention to the sails. Visibility, too, was poor, and the captain, usually most imperturbable of men, showed all the customary signs of anxiety.

He paced restlessly between the wheel and the chart-room, where, from my post of lookout on the lee side of the poop, I could see him measuring off distances on the chart. Though I did not know it then, the ship was being driven hard because her master was running a race against time.

With a strong wind we were tearing through Bass Strait, graveyard of many a fine sailing ship in thick weather. Only a few months before, the British full-rigger *Carnarvon Bay* had been lost on one of the numerous islands of the strait.

So it was our skipper urged his barque to the utmost to clear that particularly dangerous region off Wilson Promontory before the night set in. As is often the case at sea, when clear weather is of vital importance to the ship, the master found himself forced to put up with the exact reverse.

As late afternoon wore on it was obvious the Old Man was feeling the tension a bit. For the day was already drawing to a close, while some doubt existed as to the vessel's true position. The log was hove more frequently than usual; one or two extra lookouts were placed about the ship.

And then the rain squalls lifted, and the heavy cloak of lowering cloud to the nor'ard, showing us the desolate-looking headland of the Promontory in the grey, failing light. The weather conditions made it an intensely dreary sight, and one which filled my boyish mind with dread. Against the grim point the enormous swell was bursting, climbing high the gloomy cliffs.

But there were other dangers to grasp our attention. The whole vicinity was literally sown with the dragon's teeth of rocks, reefs, and small islands. We passed very close to Rodondo Island, a steep-to, uninhabited rock which reminded me of Ailsa Craig in miniature. The tides here are reported to run as much as five knots; the impact of tide and wind-maddened sea caused a disturbance which seemed about to demolish the island. The angry turmoil of their meeting sounded close in our ears like the savage snarling of some vast sea monster.

No wonder the captain had wished to pass this hell-gate in daylight. To essay such a passage at night in heavy weather, any shore lights obscured by blinding rain or driving squalls would indeed have been to court disaster, a fate which has overcome many a fine windjammer in Bass Strait.

Later, when the barque had run out clear into the open sea, a great truth entered my mind for the first time—a truth which has governed the lives of those who have set out from the earliest days to cover the oceans of the world.

It is not the *sea* which the sailor fears—it's the *land*.

CHAPTER VI

SYDNEY—QUEEN OF THE SOUTH

THE powerful South Head light was blinking at us, only six or seven miles away, when we backed the main yard to await a tug. Over the land a great glow from the city was illuminating the dark night sky. We had reached our destination, for Sydney lay before us.

A number of bluelights were burnt from the poop to attract the attention of the watchers ashore. In those days sailing ships were not provided with powerful signalling lamps carrying their beam for many miles. As the flares burst into spluttering flame they showed up clearly every detail of the ship's decks and rigging; the great motionless sails aloft; the eager faces of the crew, lining the rail on the shoreward side.

We lay hove-to for several hours, and then, in the middle watch, the tug *Heroic* came out to us. There was none of the sordid haggling so prevalent between sail and steam when dividends were shrinking and every pound a consideration. The tug passed her rope to us. Before long we were slipping between the famous Heads of Sydney.

We knew before we entered the harbour that we should be in the goodly company of many other well known sailing ships. For that reason we took pride in putting on the sails an extra special harbour stow. The graceful pilot boat *John Cook,* which must have been admired by many thousands of seafarers, put our pilot aboard. He left us when we had dropped anchor in pretty Double Bay.

Dawn was creeping over the water as we brought up to our chain. I lingered aloft alone while the others sought the comfort of their bunks (we had been up all night). Swinging there high up on a footrope, I watched the new-born day bring to life the activity of the great harbour.

Never had my eyes gazed on fairer scene. As far as could be seen stretched that glorious sheet of water. Already the numerous ferries fussed about their business, for that was, of course, long before the bridge was thought of. Green-clad islands dotted the almost land-locked harbour; numerous bungalows nestled on the slopes of the headlands and in the little bays, some with their shady verandahs almost lapped by the smiling water.

Sydney, Queen of the South! Queen, indeed, of the world! Swinging aloft there as the sun arose, gazing enchanted far over the wide and lovely bay, I felt that here, in truth, was Paradise....

* * *

The original name of Sydney was Port Jackson, it having been so called by Captain Cook on 6th May, 1770. The brave captain must have been a most phlegmatic man, for his journal states baldly: "Abreast of a bay or harbour wherein appears to be good anchorage which I called Port Jackson." Brief words, surely, with which to dismiss so enchanting a subject. But then, Cook did not enter the Heads to explore fully the great inlet.

Rio de Janeiro and Sydney are universally regarded as the two finest natural harbours in the world. Rio is unknown to me, never having had the luck to call in there. It must indeed be beautiful to compete for pride of place with Sydney.

This great Australian port is almost ideal, being practically land-locked—its entrance is only about three quarters of a mile wide—and affords fine anchorage for ships, and also a magnificent cruising ground for the many keen yachtsmen who indulge in the sport of sailing. And there are few keener than those amphibious Sydney-siders who sail their boats so daringly.

Double Bay offered us a splendid vantage point from which to feel the pulse of the great harbour and to watch the passing show. We lay a few days there, unbending sail, discharging ballast, and sweeping out the hold in readiness for its load of golden grain.

The big liners steamed close by, arriving and sailing; square-riggers towed in to their loading berths, while others towed out to face the long broad highway of the open sea which led to home.

At the week-ends it was sheer delight to watch the swift yachts scudding about the bay. It was an unforgettable sight to see the 18-footers sweep past, packed with human ballast, their little hulls dwarfed by what seemed a ridiculous overload of men and canvas.

On our first Sunday in Double Bay the Seamen's Institute held a service aboard, permission having been granted graciously by our captain. The boys from some of the other sailing ships in the vicinity rowed over in their boats. The poop looked gay with the brightly flag-covered benches from half-deck and fo'c'sle.

The service was conducted by a lay preacher from the Mission. His squeaky voice was imitated long after in the half-deck. He brought with him a portable harmonium and a young lady to play it. We were naturally far more interested in the girl than in either the preacher or the wheezy instrument. As she flip-flopped the pedals with her dainty little feet she showed a very pretty pair of legs.

"And now, dear boys," squeaked the missioner, "I am going to teach you a little hymn to sing while you are going about your work. You must be sure to sing it when you are aloft. Yes, dear boys, it is particularly applicable to your dangerous work up there on those great masts and yards. This is how it goes."

He nodded to the young goddess at the harmonium. Her nicely curved calves rippled as she struck up the music:

> *"He will hold me fast, He will hold me fast;*
> *For my Saviour loves me so, He will hold me fast."*

It sounded fine as we sang it in our croaking voices, but we were a little sceptical. And when somebody asked profanely how it fitted in with the time-honoured custom 'one hand for yourself and one for the ship' he received in answer from the missioner nothing but a stony stare, and from the girl's lovely eyes a decidedly disapproving glance.

* * *

Close to us lay the British barque *Almora,* a notorious slowcoach with some very long passages to her discredit. She was bending sail, deep loaded, almost ready for the homeward trail. Devitt and Moore's fine old warrior, the four-masted barque *Port Jackson* came to anchor nearby, and lay there several days before sailing for London. We were greatly interested in her. Her heavy lanyard-rigging smacked of olden days, set up as it was to channels outside the hull. This grand old training-ship, in which hundreds of boys learned their sailorising, fell victim to a prowling Hun U-Boat in the first World War. An enormous black-painted German barque passed in tow, her sails already loosed before she had gone through the Heads. Those German sailing ships were regarded by us with a certain amount of awe. They certainly were fast sailers with many splendid passages to their credit.

* * *

Several days after our arrival we boys were treated to an illuminating example of what my father used to describe so dramatically as 'the curse of drink.'

The boat had returned to the ship after putting the captain ashore. It would be our duty later to pull to the beach to bring him aboard for the night. In the meantime the gig lay astern on her painter.

The mate had been wandering aimlessly about the poop for some time. Suddenly he roared out: "Four of you boys—man the boat!" As I made my way aft to bring the boat to the gangway I clearly heard him remark to himself: "Hell, I'm going to get a drink somehow!"

We rowed him in to the landing place. "Wait here," he said, without further explanation. We did wait; we waited until it was getting dark. There was now every sign of a change in the weather. A s'utherly buster was brewing—one of those sudden fierce squalls which periodically sweep over the harbour. Lowering black clouds were flying overhead, and soon the wind struck at us like a wild beast.

Out at anchor the big barque, with little ballast in her, was yawing wildly, lying over dangerously, as she swung from one tack to the other.

The mate came running down the path. Jumping in, he roared to us to shove off—and there was fear in his voice. We all gave way, the water boiling around the boat and covering us with spray. As we pulled frantically, the mate leaned forward to put his powerful hand on the stroke oar.

The buster was soon over, but the mate had lost all the benefit of his drink, his unofficial absence having undoubtedly 'put the wind up' him properly.

After dry-docking, the ship hauled into a loading berth at Pyrmont. There were several other sailing vessels in the neighbouring berths—the *Verbena* and the *Ballachulish*.

A steady stream of bags of golden grain poured down a chute into the hold. Great husky Australians shouldered their 200-lb. weight with ease, carrying them out to the wings, stowing them closely. We of the crew meanwhile prepared our ship for her long mid-winter passage of the Horn. Careful attention was paid to everything aloft; new gaskets were placed on the yards, footropes examined, running rigging renewed where signs of wear were evident.

Though we went ashore practically every evening we did not, in the usual manner of sailors, see a great deal of the place other than the centre of the city. Saturday was always red-letter day, for everybody was then issued with a few shillings. Into the apprentices' meagre £5 per annum slop-chest accounts made a big inroad; the remainder had to be doled out with discretion by the master so that none fell into debt to the ship. The customary practice was to permit each boy to draw five shillings if a short stay in port were anticipated. Should the vessel be delayed unduly, the amount shrank to a measly half-crown.

One cannot have a very hilarious time on half-a-crown, or even five shillings, a week. Mine was spent not on wine, women and song but principally on food. Never shall I forget those delicious meals of ham and eggs (sailors' favourite blow-out) on George Street. Our appetites were so abnormal and the lure of grub so insistent that usually our financial resources were almost exhausted when we returned to the ship on Saturday night.

That was where the Mission to Seamen came in. No money was necessary to give one entrance there. The real old salts scorned the home of the 'Flying Angel,' considering it decidedly 'sissy' to be seen in there. But those good folk who ran the place did splendid work in those far-off days. They still do, though their work is not perhaps (in peacetime, that is) so important with the coming of short voyages and all the comforts and amenities of modern sea life. In all the Australian ports sailing ship boys were particularly welcome, a free feed being supplied on Sunday evening, the only stipulation being that those who fed should worship.

To our shame, we sometimes dodged the services. Why, I do not know, for they were always short and undenominational. When we did attend, it was an unforgettable experience to hear thirty or forty sailormen singing with all their hearts that grand hymn, "Eternal Father . . . ."

Several happenings, trivial perhaps in themselves, came my way in Sydney to broaden—I almost said enrich—my outlook on life. It is not entirely correct for me to say that *none* of my money was spent on wine, women and song, for I entered the first pub of my life. Yes, and in defiance of that solemn clause in my indenture. How does it read? ". . . . the said apprentice covenants that he will not frequent alehouses or taverns."

The suggestion came from a thirsty soul who walked from ship to town with me. Up till then, though I did not tell my companion this, I had been what might technically be termed a pub-virgin. Feeling a little uncomfortable as we came out, my hymenean pub-virginity gone for ever, there was some solace in the thought that by no stretch of imagination could the process of drinking timidly *one* beer be described as 'frequenting' alehouses or taverns.

Later that same day, strolling alone through a quiet part of the beautiful Domain, enjoying the cool of the dusk, I almost stumbled over a couple on the grass. It was obvious they were "in the very lists of love," as dear old Bill Shakespeare so aptly puts it. I stood there for a moment, pondering foolishly on the ethical side of the situation. Before I could quietly fade away the ardent swain looked up and saw me there. Jumping up, he menaced me hugely, with upraised fists and foul words.

Though there was actually nothing of the Peeping Tom in my presence there and no guilt was mine, nevertheless a feeling of guilt came over me. Never a boy of great courage, I turned and ran, hotly pursued by the long-legged cornstalk, who lent wings to my feet by the horrid threats he shouted at me.

Later, having by a miracle evaded that swift pursuit, I sat on a bench to regain my breath. Somehow my thoughts turned to the far-off leafy lanes of County Dublin . . . . and to Tom . . . . and Daisy.

* * *

Squatting low in the water, her load complete, the ship towed to Double Bay again, to prepare for her long passage home. There was still much to be done—sail to be bent, chafing gear placed aloft, and everything made shipshape for the stormy run which lay ahead.

We spent several days in Double Bay, viewing again the panorama of the beautiful harbour which I was so loath to leave. Three or four of our men had 'skinned out,' leaving their wages behind, but taking with them their few belongings. Did I, too, toy with the idea of deserting my ship? Perhaps I did, though I knew it would be a low-down trick.

It was not that I had grown weary so soon of the sea; it was not that I did not feel man enough to see the job through. It was just that Sydney had placed upon me her wondrous spell. . . .

But it was foolish even to toy with the idea of remaining in Sydney. What about that poor tired man bent over a desk a few thousand miles away, industriously scribbling sermons for a living? What about those two faint-hearted uncles who had botched things up by deserting their ships so many years ago?

On the last evening in port I stood swinging on the footrope of the fore royal yard, alone, for the others had hurried down from aloft for their evening meal. Already the harsh clamour of their greedy quarrelling over the rough food reached me faintly. Otherwise there was peace up there, on the fore royal, where one felt so near the sky and so aloof from the petty, over-exaggerated affairs of the ship. In the still warm glow of the sunset the beautiful bay was spread far around me. But it was useless to give it any further thought. . . .

The barque towed to sea next day, bound for Queenstown for orders.

*   *   *

Outside the Heads the sweetly-lined *John Cook* lay off to receive our pilot. The tug took us a few miles off-shore before letting us go. Blowing three long blasts of farewell, she severed our last link with Australia. There were other windjammers awaiting her, many other well-known ships which would soon be following on the long, wet trail. *Howth, Oweenee, Killarney, Kildalton, Verbena,* several *Invers,* and some other British sailing ships, for the age of sail was not entirely dead.

It did not take long for us to realise the difference between a ballast passage and one in a deeply-loaded ship. As the *Elginshire* rolled in the long swell outside the Heads the sea already surged through the scuppers, flowing freely over the main deck as if to give us a foretaste of what was soon to come. And when we stuck our noses over the rail the water, lapping hungrily the deepseated sides of the ship, seemed far too close for safety on that midwinter passage of the Horn.

The wind being unfavourable for the southward passing of New Zealand, the captain decided to go north about. It took eleven days to clear the north end of the islands—a disappointing start of our long journey.

Reading through the discoloured diary kept so religiously by me, often under the greatest discomfort, during my time in sail, I find myself occupying a most unsailorlike and unsavoury job for those first few days.

The new steward, a Dutchman named Tromp, was an anaemic, humpbacked, emaciated individual who bore no semblance whatever to his doughty namesake who swept the seas of old. The poor wretch cut his hand badly just after leaving Sydney. The mate allotted me the task of helping him. When I complained he said curtly: "You're a colonial. The captain reckons you're the most suitable one to help the steward."

So it was I stood in the little pantry off the mess-room, attending to the officers' needs while they ate. First came the master and mate, munching their food in stolid silence, for there was no great bond of friendship between them. Then came the second and third mates, the steward and myself following them, taking the leavings. But those leavings were for me Paradise enow. For there was on the table a more or less clean white table-cloth, and the food was epicurean compared with the coarse fare of fo'c'sle and half-deck.

That little pantry upset my stomach completely. The lazy steward had let the place become so filthy that it stank perniciously. That foul little pantry disordered my stomach as never the sea had done. On the second day out, with the ship rolling heavily, my tummy rebelled. My diary records the matter as follows:

"To-day, standing in that vile little hole, my whole inside turned up. The captain and mate had just gone up on deck, the second and third mates had not as yet come down, when the pangs of sickness assailed me. The steward had gone along to the galley. There was no time to go on deck; besides, it was naturally my wish that no one should be witness to my apparent sickness. . . . There was, conveniently in the corner of the foul, smelly place, a dump-bucket. Into this I retched, wholeheartedly, and with the utmost abandon. . . . As the officers came in, I just had time to straighten up and compose myself sufficiently for them to notice nothing particularly amiss. . . ."

There were, however, some compensations during the week of that odious job—once the pantry had been well scrubbed out and disinfected. Another entry in my diary reads: "It is fine to sit down again to a table-cloth. The steward and I clean up what is left by the officers. There is usually plenty, and should there be any left over, my shipmates in the half-deck are not forgotten...."

*   *   *

We were off the northern end of New Zealand when the first gale of the passage came down on us, shrieking, under a wicked sky, from the nor'east—the very worst direction from which it could have blown. For it pinned us down on a lee shore too close for comfort. All day the weather had been growing worse as we stripped the ship to foresail and topsails. Head-reaching, lying with scuppers awash, huge seas striding the weather rail, it was obvious the ship could not carry even that small amount of canvas through the night.

I was standing in the pantry, struggling to wash the supper things, when the call came. In the wild rolling of the ship two dishes had evaded my soapy hands—to crash to splinters on the deck. I cared nothing for their loss, scenting in such mishaps deliverance from that filthy job. Out on the after deck the mate was bawling: "All hands on deck! All hands t' th' fores'l!"

That, undoubtedly, included me. Dropping the greasy swab, I ran out into the gathering dusk. There was no time to prepare in any way for the ordeal which lay ahead. Barefooted, clad only in thin shirt and trousers, I made my way for'ad through the seething water which flooded the main deck. Already the wailing cries of the watch on deck could be heard as they took up the slack of the leechlines and buntlines.

Slowly we dragged that snorting monster to the yard, fighting for every inch we gained on the gear. In that oilskin-clad, sea-booted gathering, continually swept by leaping seas and driving spray, my figure, its thin clothing plastered to my body by wind and water, must have looked oddly naked.

"Up aloft and make it fast!" The mate roared out the few trite words which sent us up to that colossal task. Once on the yard, the wind hammered at us like a wall, blowing clean through me till my teeth were chattering. . . .

We were still descending the rigging when the mate bellowed from the deck: "Lower away fore and mizen upper topsails!"

So we fought the iron-hard sails in the night, until finally the barque lay under the little strip of her main lower topsail, of the stoutest canvas, the small triangle of the fore topmast staysail, and the storm spanker.

Though the gale had reached an unbelievable ferocity, the ship lay a little easier now. But she was drifting bodily down to looard under such small canvas. And down there, somewhere in the black night, lay the snarling lee shore of the north coast of New Zealand.

On the poop, in the scanty shelter of the jigger weather-cloth, which he often scorned, stood the master . . . . anxiously watching his ship. In his ears, in booming topsail and twanging rigging, thundered the voice of the gale—a titan voice to which he had been listening since his boyhood days.

* * *

My term of office as a scullion came to an end next day, to my joy. Those two smashed dishes had done the trick! Crockery was by no means plentiful aboard. The steward, no doubt fearing further casualties amongst his dishes, decided to carry on by himself—and I was released from my odoriferous duties. My treatment throughout that period had been most unfair, for besides spending all day working in the cabin I had been forced to keep my usual watches on deck at night.

For several days the gale blew with unabated force, the ship lying hove-to under that little rain- and spray-soaked rag of her main lower topsail, her lee scuppers awash, huge seas leaping the weather rail. The main deck was usually a maelstrom of deep, surging water. On the second day an immense sea climbed aboard, tearing from their firm hold hatch-wedges and battens, lifting from the main hatch its threefold covering of tarpaulins, gravely menacing ship and cargo of grain below.

All hands were called once more. In the growing darkness we worked, often waist-deep in swirling water, until those tarpaulins were secured again.

Next day the storm-wrack cleared; in the morning the sun shone wanly on us, the wind falling away so that sail was set once more. With a freeing wind, the barque squared away, the land showing up close aboard. Sail after sail was spread to the favouring breeze, and the vessel swung away on the long, long trail. The land faded out of sight, the last we were to see for many weeks.

* * *

We had shaken off the fetters of the land. If the weather were fine and clear—a great uncertainty in those high latitudes—we might be privileged to sight that grim sentinel, that lonely outpost of the sea 'twixt southern west and east—Cape Horn itself. If heavy, leaden skies and continual gales accompanied us on our way we would pass far to the s'uthard, to the s'uthard, too, of the treacherous Diego Ramirez Rocks, sixty miles sou'west of the Horn.

No shipmaster, running for many days on dead reckoning, would risk meeting the land in such a dread vicinity. . . .

"ARCTIC STREAM" IN THE TROPICS

Photo by Capt. C. C. Dixon

CHAPTER VII

MIDWINTER PASSAGE OF THE HORN

IT is, it must be admitted, with a certain amount of trepidation, that this chapter is approached by the author. So much has been written about Cape Horn that it has become something of a fearsome bogeyman in the world of nautical literature. Some of this verbiage may be an exaggeration; a great deal is undoubtedly the plain, unvarnished truth.

With pen in hand I pause before plunging into the subject. . . .

* * *

If I were asked to name the writer who popularised the rounding of Cape Horn in the comfort of an easy chair, before a cosy fire, I would assuredly say that man was Basil Lubbock. He little thought, when he signed on in the four-masted barque *Ross-shire* in 1899, that he was to write a book which would bring him a measure of fame and fortune.

Round the Horn before the Mast captured the imagination of the British public from the first, when it was published in 1902. It has passed through a number of editions since then. The theme was new, though, it is true, R. H. Dana had done the task before.

But it was left to Lubbock, the ex-public-school boy, replete and complete with the old school tie, to tell how he graced the fo'c'sle of a windjammer, amongst those rough, tarry salts where ties of any sort were rarely seen. Writing with an intimate simplicity, Lubbock produced a fine book which has become almost a classic of the sea. He did more—for that single passage from San Francisco to Liverpool so fired his enthusiasm that eventually he became an authority on the last phase of sail. From his able pen has come that splendid series of volumes dealing so vividly with the subject. They are all grand books. One cannot help being impressed by the enormous amount of time and energy he must have expended delving into musty log-books of ships long dead, his thirst for correct information covering the smallest detail.

* * *

It may well be asked how Cape Horn came to be so dreaded? How came it to bear so evil a name? Its latitude is but 56 degrees

south—about that of the northerly position of Glasgow or Edin-
burgh—yet the weather experienced off this stormy outpost of the
world has always been regarded as the worst that can assail a ship.

A glance at a map of the world will explain more vividly than
words part, at least, of the reason why 'the Horn' acquired its foul
reputation.

The southern tip of South America, stretching gauntly like a
grasping finger far down towards the Antarctic, stands isolated in
an immensity of thousands of miles of stormy sea. This great
southern ocean is the home of the prevailing westerly gales which
sweep around the world. Unhampered, unhindered by any bastion
continent, they raise the sea to tremendous height and violence,
setting up too an easterly drift against which an ill-found, west-
bound ship was often powerless.

The westerly passage was the worse. Many ships spent weeks off
the pitch of the Horn, zigzagging drearily north and south with
exhausted crews, striving to make westing against those raging
gales.

Some of the older salts regarded the eastward passage as almost
a picnic. But it, too, had its dangers, and was often full of peril.
Many ships have been lost while homeward bound on what was
considered the easier rounding of the Horn.

Running before a gale on a dark night there was always the
menace of broaching-to; once a vessel fell beam on, the great seas
literally engulfed her. Many a man—even a whole watch—has been
washed overboard while at the braces in such circumstances.
Hatches have been battered in like egg-shells; fine ships have disappeared suddenly, leaving no trace of their passing.

When summer came, bringing some relief in the shape of shorter
nights, there was always the terror of ice, enormous bergs
frequently being encountered at this time. Sailing fast in the darkness, it was often impossible to avoid an iceberg. The 'ice blink'
came too late, if come it did at all; no warning fall in temperature
would work to windward in a gale.

No proper record has ever been compiled of the loss of windjammers through colliding with icebergs—because there were rarely
any survivors to tell the tale.

*   *   *

Though it is one of the most dangerous, isolated and desolate spots in the world, no lighthouse has ever existed on Cape Horn. A lighthouse is an inestimable comfort to a shipmaster, provided, of course, he is not on a dangerous lee shore, or in too close proximity to it for safety.

No such light has ever shone out over the lonely, storm-tossed waters which surround this cape. Yet a great cavalcade of ships has passed this way since Schouten discovered in 1616 that South America did not stretch right down to the south pole.

The brave little wooden ships such as Dana's brig *Pilgrim*, and the small copper-ore vessels of Swansea, all of which traded regularly to the west coast of the Americas long before the Panama Canal was thought of; the swift passenger sailing ships who did so much towards the colonising of the Antipodes, winging their homeward way; the beautiful clippers—wood, composite, iron, steel, each in its progressive succession—carrying the valuable wool-clip, striding hot-foot to the east.

And then came the huge steel vessels of the last days of sail, their great hulls loaded almost scupper-deep with grain. They were the last of the windjammers to pass this way, many of them old and tired and insufficiently manned by a handful of plucky boys.

All these have known this lonely, wind-torn trail. But they will pass no more. And now that grim, scarred cape looks out on the empty seas again—empty almost as on that day in 1616 when Schouten crawled past in his lubberly craft. . . .

* * *

Cape Horn is not on the mainland, as most people imagine, being situated on Horn Island, the southernmost of the Hermite group. To the south-west nearly sixty miles away, lie the treacherous Diego Ramirez rocks, a deadly menace to the unwary navigator in thick weather. They are but an outcrop of jagged fangs, on which many a ship must have been lost with all hands, leaving no soul to tell of her unhappy end.

The whole of this region has seen more of the blood and the sweat, and the toil and the tears of the seafarer than any other part of the world. West-bound ships sometimes spent weeks in this vicinity, fighting gale after gale under such shortened canvas that it was impossible to make westing.

Some of the old school maintained it was unnecessary to spend all that time off the pitch of the Horn. The more timid shipmaster was too prone, they contended, to strip his ship down to lower topsails, waiting patiently and hopefully for a slant. The courageous master, on the other hand, kept his vessel under a press of sail sufficient to drive her to windward. This theory, it would seem, is borne out by the remarkably consistent passages—east and west, summer and winter—of the nitrate carriers regularly using this route. Rarely were they long delayed off the Horn.

* * *

Take a chart of the world, or, failing that, an ordinary school atlas, and you will see at a glance what our ship was facing; that great, lonely stretch of ocean where no land exists, where ships are rarely seen—the wet, windblown, watery road from New Zealand to the Horn. But though we would see no human beings, we would see some life there. For our companions would be the hardy albatrosses, so closely akin to the sailing ships they followed for weeks. Sailing, like them, sometimes with squared yards, fleeing to looard; then, bracing 'sharp up,' working back to wind'ard with an ease which has never been attained, nor ever will, by any square- or fore-and-aft rigged vessel.

As we worked to the south and east the smiling, sunlit skies were left behind. A great melancholy seemed to overwhelm both sea and sky, turning our universe into a drear immensity of greyness in which sea was as grey as sky. Already the high swell cradled restlessly the heavy ship on long crest and in deep valley. When the west wind took us in its titan grip the rain and driving spray came with it, beating down remorselessly on us till our clothing was all soaked and no means wherewith to dry it.

In the half-deck, whose occupants had paid heavily for the privilege of being berthed apart from the crew, conditions were particularly miserable. Being situated on the main deck, their quarters were continually swept and battered by huge seas which squirted in through the doors so that the deck inside was always more or less awash. The A.B.s, on the other hand, housed in comparative comfort under the fo'c'sle head, the highest part of the ship, rarely had any water invading their home.

As the weather worsened, the customary social life of the dog-watch was practically abandoned. Now and then, in a temporary lull, a half-hearted attempt would be made to cheer ourselves with a little music from the gramophone. Perched precariously on one of the sea-chests, a lashing securing the instrument to a bunk stanchion, it would blare out the sugary notes of *Valse Septembre* or some other favourite.

One of the younger boys tended the old-fashioned horn, steadying it in the rolling of the ship as the disc gurgled round. That tune will, so long as breath is in my body, however long I live, bring back vividly the scene at such times. . . .

The steel box in which we live is dimly lit by the smoky little lamp. The whole place reeks with the stench of wet clothes, and is blue from the smoke of our pipes. The watch below, with the exception of the youngster at the gramophone, are lying in their hard, damp bunks—still clad in seaboots and oilskin pants. For our leisure is brief, and the call of 'All Hands!' may come at any moment.

The steel walls of the house dribble moisture continuously; it trickles down in little rivulets, running into the already damp bedding. Several of the boys have pasted up their favourite actresses on the clammy sides of their bunks. Pretty Lily Elsie smiles out at us, her damp face glistening as though she were shedding tears at our discomfort. In another bunk the well-known face of Gladys Cooper gazes soulfully upon us. The all-pervading soddenness has sadly affected her too, for the adhesive which held her secure in sunnier climes has almost dissolved away, leaving her clinging precariously to the cold bulkhead.

Outside, the turmoil of the long, black night which is facing us beats upon the ship. We know she is carrying too much sail; we know that soon we shall be waist-deep in icy, swirling water as we drag that iron-hard canvas to the yards before going aloft to furl it . . . . to furl it! Have you ever tried to bend a piece of sheet iron with your bare hands?

The noise of the wind in the cavities of the straining topsails comes to us clearly, like the booming of some colossal drum, sounding above the shrilling of the gramophone. Every now and then the ship falters in her stride, there is a deeper rumbling—and we know, before the water comes squirting into our domain, that the main deck had been filled up again.

The gramophone gives a squeak and fades out, for the needle cannot retain its groove. "Put the damn thing away," growls one of the older boys from his bunk.

Then, except for the slightly muffled voice of the gale outside and the periodic pounding of the main deck by seas, there is peace of sorts within the steel walls of that cheerless hole of ours. The pipes glow and fade, glow and fade as the silent smokers draw quietly in their bunks. Occasionally a pipe gurgles faintly, and Farmer, his back festered with boils, stirs restlessly and curses softly with the pain. . . .

There is the clatter of heavily shod feet coming down the poop ladder, the shrilling of a whistle, and the hoarse cry out on deck: "All hands on deck! All hands shorten sail!"

Somebody curses foully as he crawls from his bunk. "Christ! What the hell ever made us come to sea—to this!" He scowls around at us as we pull on our oilskin coats and secure the body and soul lashings of spunyarn with which we try in vain to thwart the rude invasion of the heavy water out on deck.

The wind is increasing rapidly. After the comparative quiet of the deck-house it seems to us the elements have gone mad. The night is intensely dark; it takes some minutes for the eyes to become used to the inky blackness. And then we realise that though the sky is heavily overcast there is *some* light, even on the darkest night. For the tops of the great, leaping seas, swiftly overrunning the ship as they boil alongside, illuminate her faintly with their foaming crests.

At the mizen rigging we gather, for the mizen upper topsail is about to be lowered. Heavy water repeatedly thunders over both weather and lee rail, sweeping us from our feet as we clutch at downhauls and spilling lines. But we return again and again, and at last the sail is snugged up as much as possible. And then aloft to make fast that snorting, pounding chunk of canvas. We spread ourselves along the footropes of the yard, feeling our way carefully, for the dim light of broken crest and surging water does not reach us here.

The sail is bladder full between the half-hearted curbing of the gear. With the wind almost aft there is no hope of any further spilling of the sail. It rears over the yard, threatening to hurl to destruction the unwary. As we snatch and tear at the heavy canvas, the wind batters madly at our upturned backsides, sleet rattles noisily on our oilskins. . . . Far down below, the long, slim hull shows up dimly, outlined by the leaping white seas which surround it—following, oppressing, never leaving for one moment the fleeing vessel. Now and then the main deck disappears under a solid load of invading water. At such times we feel the weight of that onslaught in the tremble of the mast and wildly swaying yard as the ship rolls and plunges, striving to rid herself of that deadening weight. . . .

* * *

The barque had been made ready for the real stormy weather to the south. Life-lines, six-inch ropes, had been stretched along the main deck from fo'c'sle head to poop, set up taut with the powerful capstan. Every single roband on the jackstays had been doublebanked, stuffing to their fullest capacity the eyelets on the heads of the sails. Particular attention was paid to foresail and lower topsails, that heavy-weather canvas which is always forced to bear the brunt of the stormy high latitudes.

When there was little else that could be done, we were set to sand and canvas the poop. In pouring rain and bitter cold, watch after watch, we got down on our knees and rubbed those holy, yet soulless, planks. That was the most dismal, most monotonous, of tasks, but the crew must be employed continuously, however silly or futile the work. There was much growling from the men, for the pitiless rain and the chafe of knees on the deck were ruining our oilskins long before the time for their supreme test further south.

When the whole poop had been scoured, the job was started all over again for the second time. As if doing penance for our sins, we spent those cold, wet days down on our knees, rubbing the planks until they had assumed what seemed to us an unnecessary whiteness. For we knew the poop deck would be oiled later, when the ship had reached fine weather once more on the other side of the Horn.

The ship had passed through the Roaring Forties and was now away down in the tempestuous Fifties, in the great sweep of the west wind and its accompanying high seas. With the yards nearly square, she drove southward and eastward—rolling, rolling rails under without the lateral steadying effect of fore-and-aft canvas or of sharp-braced yards.

And all this time I was still running around in my bare feet, although the weather had grown so bitterly cold. Often the mate, looking down at my feet, purple from the cold, would remark: "B' Jesus, I couldn't go around like that—and I've been a good many years at sea!"

This procedure of mine was due to no hardcase ambitions on my part. A horrible truth had dawned on me shortly before, when it was too late to do anything about it. Owing to my practice of being barefooted at all times aboard ship, my feet had spread enormously; it was only with the greatest difficulty that my leather seaboots could be forced on. And once on, they almost crippled me.

There was apparently no remedy, for the few pairs of seaboots in the captain's 'slop chest' had been snapped up by the new hands signed on in Sydney. At last a little incident, apart from the growing cold, decided that some foot covering would have to be worn.

It was a black, wind-filled night, the ship running heavily under fores'l and tops'ls. The mate stood by the man at the wheel. The dim, flickering light in the binnacle played faintly on his fine tanned face and on that of the helmsman, tensed to his task of holding the ship to her course as she yawed wildly in the big following sea.

Suddenly a fierce squall broke upon us, tearing from its lashings the long canvas cover of the cabin skylight. We boys were setting tight the lashings again when the bulk of the captain came hurtling from the chart-room door. With eyes as yet unused to the inky darkness, he blundered against me, trampling my bare feet with his heavy sea boots. Though I knew who it was, the agony made me cry out a curse. He ignored me and my remark entirely, his thoughts absorbed by his hard-pressed ship.

The idea came to me: if the boots are too small to be worn with socks or stockings, perhaps they can be worn *without*. So it was my bare feet were greased with tallow, and the boots *hammered* on to them. For three weeks those heavy leather boots never left my feet. Like the poor, they were always with me; like an over-ardent lover, they accompanied me every time I went to bed. . . .

* * *

The barque had scarcely reached the latitude of 50 degrees when one of those easterly gales of great ferocity, which are sometimes met in the winter months, overpowered her.

Little time was given the tired crew to shorten sail. All hands toiled through the hours in soaked clothing, stripping the canvas from the yards. The wind, raging directly against the run of the high sea from the westward, soon raised a fiendish turmoil; the water climbed unceasingly aboard the ship. She pitched and rolled madly—rolling between thirty and forty degrees, almost wresting us from our frozen hold on footrope and jackstay.

When at last our work aloft was done, the vessel was hove-to under main and mizen lower topsails and foretopmast staysail. The fore lower topsail had been furled in an endeavour to force the barque closer to the wind. As she lay there, her whole weather rail was continuously invaded by the tormented sea, until the main deck was nothing less than a terrifying maelstrom of deep, surging water.

The off-duty watch (is one ever off duty in a sailing ship?) was permitted to go below for a couple of hours. Soaked to the skin in spite of oilskins, worn and weary, we stretched out uneasily until the call would come again. It was impossible to sleep, for the outcry of the straining ship and the roar of the maddened elements would have awakened the dead. Moreover, six inches of water swirled about the deck of our dismal domain, swamping noisily and with rude disdain the seachests and the lower bunks. Our dripping clothing just had to dry on our bodies, for there was no other means of doing it.

And then, at a quarter to midnight, we were called on deck again. Throughout that long winter night we stood on the poop, shivering incessantly, waiting for whatever emergency our battered ship might impose upon us. With helm hard-down, under the three little rags of sail, she was riding out the gale.

The motion was so violent that it seemed to us a miracle she did not heave the long steel masts right overboard. The film of oil, dribbling from the for'ad closet-pipes, appeared to have little effect on the pyramidal seas which surrounded the barque.

The next day, Sunday, dawned with the ship still rolling and pitching wildly in that horrible sea, the deck awash with hundreds of tons of water. The daylight came late beneath the lowering sky. When it came at last, we were set to the dangerous task of unravelling a hopeless mess of running rigging. Every rope had been torn from its allotted pin. Braces, leechlines, buntlines were intermingled in a snakelike maze. Some of the ropes had been washed over the side, and streamed forlornly their full length outside the ship. Jumping into the rigging or scrambling hastily on to the midship house at frequent intervals, we cleared the confusion at the risk of our lives.

When we returned to the comparative safety of the poop, the mate called to me to go down to his room to see if all was well down there. In that miserable damp hole—a poor den indeed for an officer—I found the rough log lying open in the bunk. A trite entry in it told me of the official record of that wild night: "Gale of hurricane force. Ship labouring heavily in high confused sea, and shipping heavy water continuously. Vessel rolling 35 degrees. . . . Barometer reading at 2 a.m., 28.46 inches. . . ."

That was surely a phenomenally low glass. And I knew it was a correct reading, for I had seen the madly swinging mercurial barometer in the chart-room while relighting the binnacle lamps. Never again in all my experience at sea have I seen such a low glass.

*　*　*

When the west wind came again, the ship drove far down into the Fifties. That scourge of the windjammer now made its dread appearance. Hideous boils broke out amongst us, so badly that some were wellnigh crippled. Wherever there was chafe—at neck and wrists where oilskin lashings irritated the skin—there foul boils made their unwelcome presence known.

And we had to suffer them, for no cure was at hand. The everlasting briny diet and the continuous living and sleeping in sea-soaked clothing and bedding were having their effect. My wrists and forearms were festered with the pestilential things; at times the pain was so intense that only by the greatest effort could I get aloft.

All this time the days were growing shorter, and the sun was rarely seen. For sixteen hours out of the twenty-four, darkness lay over ship and sea. The long, black nights were, of course, the worst. Some of them seemed like interminable nightmares.

*　*　*

We were almost down to the high latitude of the Horn. In a great wind-blown watery waste the ship flew on, eastward, ever eastward, with a little southing in her course. One grey desolate day, when all but the foresail and the three lower topsails had been furled, the ship was running like a frightened hare—harried, pursued, hunted by the majestic might of the wild west wind and its ravenous satellites, the great rolling seas which bore down on her in endless procession.

The fore upper topsail was threatening to blow adrift from its gaskets. Three of us were told off to go aloft to lash the sail to the yard. Leaving the security of the poop, we plunged into the surging water which swirled about the main deck.

As we made our slow and dangerous way for'ad, great caution was necessary to avoid being washed overboard. The high, seething seas, overrunning the ship, toppled aboard on both sides with thunderous sound. The water was often more than waist-deep, for the mournfully-clanging ports had no time to clear the deck. It was only by clinging to the lifeline, the angry water tearing at us, that we reached the safety of the fore rigging. The main deck, like a submerged rock, had grown a treacherous slime from its continuous wetting for many days.

Then came the climb aloft, the wind screaming and grasping at us, the icy rigging almost *searing* our hands with its coldness. Once on the footrope, we rode the long, swaying yard like a trio of broncho-busters, retaining with difficulty our foothold on the slippery wire. With some fathoms of gasket-stuff we literally frapped the sail to the yard.

The job completed, my companions left me there. In spite of the intense cold and the sleet-laden squalls which frequently beat down on the ship, I lingered on—to watch a scene the like of which my eyes had never beheld before.

The barque was doing easily fourteen knots in the squalls—rolling, staggering, yawing as she ran. The view from that yard was something immensely savage and grand, and a little frightening for a youngster so fresh from home.

Overhead the lowering sky menaced the ship, dimming the wan winter daylight of our little world so that we moved in a sickly, eerie half-light. Ragged wisps of storm-wrack flew low past the trucks, pointing jeeringly, derisively, with jagged, windtorn fingers as they passed.

But it was the sea which grasped my attention. From the west, from a wilderness of angered waters, came that great cavalcade of enormous, striding seas, stately and towering in their orderly procession.   Far as the eye could see stretched that lonely, wind-maddened waste of water—great valleys bounded by swiftly-moving, roaring surf-clad peaks which leaped hungrily upon the barque.

Ever and anon a monstrous roller, a giant amongst its fellows, could be seen approaching in its isolated grandeur. It would seem that the ship could never lift to such a mighty cliff of water. And then it would be on her; and when it looked as if that roaring crest would sweep the ship from end to end, she lifted bravely, if a little tiredly. Nothing more than a few inches of creaming water foamed over the poop before the torrent tumbled from each side on to the main deck.

Shelley, tragic poet, who surely loved the sea which claimed him in the end, must have thought of such a scene when he wrote the following lines:

> "With the solid darkness black
> Closing round his vessel's track;
> Whilst above the sunless sky,
> Big with clouds hangs heavily,
> And behind the tempest fleet,
> Riving sail, and cord, and plank,
> Till the ship has almost drank
> Death from the o'er-brimming deep."

At the quayside in Cape Town and Sydney the barque had been big and powerful. Here she had shrunk unbelievably as the weather worsened, until she had become but a puny plaything of the gods.

Below me, tugging bladder-full with the force of the gale, reared the great foresail. Like the cleft in the buttocks of a colossus, the heavy double forestay bit deeply into the hard, grey canvas. Looking aft again, I watched the ship in that eerie half-light. Two men were at the wheel, for one helmsman could never hold her in such a sea. With the master and mate standing near them, they struggled to keep her somewhere near her course.

Our barque carried no wheel-house, those who steered her standing unprotected on gratings in the most exposed part of the ship. As each greybeard rolled ponderously but swiftly from astern the courage of those helmsmen was taxed to the utmost. Just when each great breaker—for they were breakers though we were in hundreds of fathoms of water—gathered itself to sweep aboard, the poop soared skywards, plunging the long spike jibboom into that deep valley ahead. Fresh impetus was given to the ship that moment, but she faltered in her stride. The shattered crest of the monster sea, split by the ship's stern, rushed for'ad on each side, to rumble into the waist, filling it with a deadening load. Bursting over the deck-houses, washing the running rigging into a tangled mass of rope, it tossed off their feet like match-sticks the unfortunate men who worked down there.

Seen from where I swung, the main deck was never free from swirling white water. The long, lean hull appeared incapable at times of carrying that great load and the enormous weight of her four tall masts and broadspread yards. With dismal dirge the clanging washports strove to clear the deck. Before their work was half done, another leaping sea had filled her up again. . . .

Though no other ship was in sight, it would be wrong to say that we were alone on that tempestuous flight to the east. For two of the People of the South—two great Wandering Albatrosses—accompanied us on our stormy way, cheering me, at least, by their presence there.

Ever a-wing, for it was inconceivable that they could rest or even alight on those troubled waters, they hovered near the ship, sailing with a brave nonchalance strangely out of keeping with the turmoil around. Every now and then they passed me close, those two splendid birds, as I swung precariously on that footrope. Their beady eyes, in which was neither fear nor dismay, gazed calmly into mine as they drew abreast of my lofty perch.

With an ease which defied the understanding of the human mind they rode the gale. Sometimes they fell a little astern; and then, at lightning speed, they passed a mile ahead of the barque. 'Bracing sharp up,' they came back again to meet us. Snug in their snowy-breasted coats, they appeared to feel no cold or discomfort such as I was suffering.

*   *   *

The night which followed will long be remembered by me, for it was the worst of the many long black nights through which we passed on that winter rounding of the Horn.

At eight bells, 4 p.m., the short, grey daylight done, conditions were such as to strike fear into any first voyager's heart. The weather had worsened appreciably, and it was obvious that we were facing sixteen hours of dread darkness before the wan light would seep through those lowering clouds again. Though prudence must have urged him to heave-to for the night, before the sea became even more dangerous and prevented him from doing so, the captain still held his plunging, reeling ship on her course.

At 8 p.m. those of us who had been below to re-lash oilskins, in preparation for whatever might lie ahead, emerged from the half-deck door. At that moment a hoarse, warning cry reached us from the mate at the break of the poop.   It came too late.   With a thunderous roar an immense sea literally swamped the deck from both sides.

It lifted me off my feet, helplessly, like a match-stick. My head, within its sou'wester, came into violent contact with the underside of the after boatskids, over seven feet above the deck, That wild torrent took several of the others and myself for'ad, floundering all the time in vain as we attempted to get hold of something solid.

The ship took a heavier roll, sending the whole deck-load of tumbling water towards the side on which I floated. In a frightened frenzy I realised the water, pouring over the lee rail, would take me clean over the high t' gallant bulwarks.

My clutching hands grasped at last the main royal backstay, to which I clung desperately, the strength of fear in my arms. Eventually the life-line, stretched along the main deck, took us back to the poop, where our other shipmates, a sorry lot of drowned rats, were nursing their sores and literally licking their wounds.

For hours we stood on the wind- and sleet-swept poop, shivering in our sea-soaked clothing because there was nothing dry left into which to change. And had the necessary things been ours, the first visit to that flooded main deck would immediately have saturated us once more.

At first there was little to do but watch the dim form of our half-drowned ship storming through the night. Two bulky, oilskin-clad figures stood to windward, steadying themselves against the jigger rigging—the master and mate, both tried warriors of the sea who had been brought up from childhood to this manly game, had indeed never known any other.

The darkness was filled with the roaring of the pursuing seas and the thunder and scream of the gale. Every backstay had its different note, but above all else was the strident voice of the great West Wind in the cavities of the black, iron-hard topsails, tearing aloft at sheet and shackle.

When the night was yet young, while many hours of darkness lay before us, the usual trouble raised its dangerous head. The binnacle lights started going out. As quickly as one was re-lit, the other expired.

The mate called me to stand near the wheel, where two of the best helmsmen toiled as the ship yawed and wallowed in her flight. As soon as one of the miserable lights went out I whipped it from its socket, and ran to the chart-room to rekindle the spluttering flame.

The mate came with me, cursing, blaspheming, scratching damp matches on an even damper box with his clumsy fingers.

This was repeated, time after time, until the mate's blasphemies and obscenities had become a little monotonous in their repetition.

The climax was reached in a vicious sleet-squall which overtook the barque in a flurry of fury. There was a sudden cry of fear from the helmsmen as *both* binnacle lights went out.

Oh, but you had your torches, some intelligent reader will remark. No, we had no electric torches such as are supplied so plentifully to the pampered modern voyager. The only torches with which we went to sea in the old square-riggers were the heavenly lamps of God's bright stars and the moon. And if those blessings were denied us, as on the wild night of which I write, all that was left to us was the flickering, fitful flame of those treacherous colza lights. . . .

On the deck in the chart-room we crouched, the mate and myself, rasping nervously at two pulpy boxes of matches, while the helmsmen aft cried out in vain for light.

"Christ! This bloody ship will be lost through these goddam lights!" raved the mate as he rasped at his box. "She'll broach-to any minute now!"

When we returned to the wheel, the damp wicks spluttering feebly once more, we found that Johansen, the unconquerable blood of the Vikings in his veins, had torn the sou'wester from his head. Somehow, from the feel of the ice-cold wind on the back of his skull, the old sea-warrior had kept the ship as near her course as might be. . . .

Half way through the night the young third mate was sent for'ad to see how things were going at that end of the ship. He disappeared down on to the main deck; it was some time before he returned—to report, of course, that the sidelights had gone out, and that a number of robands on the head of the foresail had parted, so that the sail might blow away if not attended to immediately.

"Never mind the sidelights!" roared the Old Man. "God help us and anything that comes between us and the east to-night! But take some hands aloft, and secure the head of the fores'l."

Once through the maelstrom of the main deck, that hazardous journey accomplished, we stood on the footrope facing the difficult job before us. In three or four places the head of the sail stood far away from the jackstay, the crescent-shaped cavities placing a tremendous strain on the head-earrings and on the remaining robands. Clinging there with numbed fingers, we worked for several hours, slowly gaining, inch by inch, a little on those yawning gaps.

It was bitter-cold, dismal work, but it had to be done to save the sail, one of the most important of all. We got no help whatever from the booming, snorting monster which we were striving to make secure. For the gale was almost aft, and there was not one lull throughout the time we spent aloft. On our descent, the job done to the best of our ability, we found the main hatch tarpaulins required attention and re-wedging. Thoroughly tired out and frozen to the bone, we eventually reached the poor safety of the poop.

I realised then that relations were a little strained between the captain and mate. Snatches of their shouted conversation reached me. Apparently the mate had had the temerity to pass the remark that it would have been better if the ship had been hove-to for the night, before daylight had left us.

The skipper turned savagely on him. All the pent up anxiety he was suffering seemed to come out in his answer: "Heave-to for the night! Yes, that's fine for you, mister!

"What the hell's a man to do anyway?" he went on bitterly. "Lie-to, and you've got some knock-kneed pen-pusher ashore saying sarcastically 'You've made rather a long passage, Captain!' Drive her through it, day and night, and you're cursed by everyone aboard for risking their lives!" . . . .

SWINGING ALOFT 'TWIXT SEA AND SKY

Penso

No further words reached me, for a shrieking sleet squall bore down on the ship, literally tearing the tops off the great rearing seas astern, and hurling their spray and spume the full length of the barque. . . .

The master never left his post on the poop that seemingly endless night. The wind was nearly aft, so that the scanty weather-cloth in the jigger rigging offered him poor shelter from the freezing blast.

The winter dawn was long a-coming in those high latitudes. The chill, wan light was slow in seeping through the leaden clouds and the welter of salt-laden air and spume and spindrift in which the ship flew eastward, ever eastward. And when it came at last it lit faintly, gigantically, unreally, the huge spars and dark, straining sails. As it grew, the outline of the harried ship took shape, moving swiftly in that waste of water. Her jibboom showed up last—dimly, distantly, soaring and falling like some gaunt finger pointing the way.

The skipper lurched over to the chart-room. He was body weary, mind weary, from the strain of many hours. He examined the wildly swinging barometer on the bulkhead. He smiled tiredly as he noted the convexity of the rising mercury. Flayed by the bitter wind and sleet, and the driving spray, his face showed up the colour of raw beef.

Out on deck he made his way again. Looking aft, he noted the long streaming wake of the fleeting ship, stretching far away into the ragged hills and deep valleys astern. A chuckle escaped him as he realised how his bolting barque had eaten up the miles which now lay to the westward.

Aloft, in drumming, faithfully hand-sewn sails and straining rigging, the west wind sang its triumphant, age-old song, bearing on its bosom the sorely-tried ship and valiant man who was daring all to 'make a passage.'

* * *

We crossed the meridian of the dreaded Horn at 2 a.m. one morning, as nearly as could be computed by dead reckoning, for the sun had not been seen for days.

The gale had blown itself out, but the great swell still rolled up sullenly from the west. The pale sun rose to give us some small measure of cheer, though there was no warmth in its fitful rays.

H

The wind had veered to the nor'east, a dead muzzler. Sail was piled on the ship in the lull; she stood away close-hauled to the south-east.

Somebody cried out that a sail was in sight to windward. All hands crowded the weather rail, for there is no more comforting sight than another vessel in those lonely latitudes. She was a big four-masted skysail-yard barque, with everything set up to the royals.

"That's the *Oweenee*!" half a dozen voices called out. This ship had been with us in Sydney. Though too far off to signal in the haze, she made a splendid picture as she plunged and rolled majestically in the long, high swell.

At noon that day a watery sun gave us our latitude. The pallid orb clung shyly to the northern horizon at an altitude of about twelve degrees, bluntly informing us that we were almost as far down as 58 south. We had thus passed many miles to the s'uth'ard of Cape Horn; many miles to the s'uth'ard, too, of the Diego Ramirez rocks, whose grim fangs have torn to pieces many a fine ship.

CHAPTER VIII.

NORTHWARD

So it was the ship passed from the stormy, misnamed Pacific into the South Atlantic Ocean. Contrary winds delayed her there; it appeared as if all hope of a good passage home had vanished. For the forty-eighth day out had been reached before we cleared the Horn.

With the sheltering South American continent to the westward, sea and weather conditions improved so much that we were able to take some interest in our personal appearance again. Gladly, with the worst of the bad weather astern, I parted company with my unpleasant bedfellows—the heavy seaboots.

And for the first time in weeks we had a wash all over, and took the opportunity of cleaning out our quarters. Behind the sea-chests, lashed to the bunk stanchions, a sodden foul medley of odds and ends was discovered—pulpy biscuits, ruined garments, scraps of putrifying food. When the purifying process was complete the place smelt sweeter, and we resembled less a body of young cut-throats. With the ship standing up to the nor'east, the corner had really been turned at last.

The coming of the better weather was the signal for the commencement of the extensive spring cleaning customary aboard the homeward bound sailing ship. All the way up the Atlantic this activity would be continued, alow and aloft. In many ships it was the practice for the afternoon watch below to be robbed of their four hours' leisure, these being spent instead on deck while all hands continued their labours together. We, however, were not treated so harshly though we were forced to work hard while on watch on deck, the eagle eye of the mate ever upon us. So strict was the discipline that whistling and singing while one worked were not permitted, other than the official chanties which were always encouraged when sail was handled. Smoking was strictly prohibited, and never, even by the refractory hands, did I see any attempt to break this rule. This unpopular restriction may have been responsible for the perhaps too frequent visits to the lavatory for'ad. One one occasion, when the mate went along to dislodge a hand from his snug retreat, the man, a notorious sea-lawyer, came out protesting loudly that the Board of Trade had prescribed in one of its Acts seven minutes as the time necessary for the daily relief of nature.

"Seven minutes!" roared the mate, as he chased the man back to his work. "I'll give you seven minutes, you damned sea-lawyer! Skulking in there smoking your pipe while others do your work! Get back to your job at once, or I'll give you enough jollip to keep you in there for a week, never mind seven minutes, Act or no Act!"

* * *

The barque had now been over two months at sea. We were growing a little weary of one another. Living in close confinement, no vestige of privacy in our steel deck-house, it would have been nothing short of a miracle if bitter little feuds had not developed. Open warfare was reached one afternoon.

It was a fight to the finish between Mulock and Dobson, the latter a much more heavily built lad than his opponent. But Mulock fought pluckily though knocked down repeatedly. The fight was already over, for poor Mulock was groggy and incapable of carrying on, when the captain rushed down off the poop to separate the boys. Dobson was henceforward regarded as the cock of the half-deck roost; for some days his antagonist's aristocratic features were completely marred.

We set about shifting every sail aloft just prior to entering the region of the south-east trades. The mates cunningly pitted one watch against the other to expedite the work, so that the spring cleaning of the ship could be resumed. Most well-found sailing ships were equipped with three suits of sails. Unlike a woman, a ship wears her oldest rags in the finest weather, conserving her best for the stormy latitudes.

A number of days were spent beating about against head winds, or lying becalmed. And then our cheeks were fanned by a breath from the south-east. Gradually it freshened, till we knew for sure the age-old, well-named trade wind had come to carry us joyously on our way.

Any windjammer man will look back with pleasure on the period he spent in the tropical belt of those grand winds. Those were the halcyon days of the whole passage. For many days and nights the brave wind drove the ship on her course, little attention

beyond an occasional 'sweat up' being required by well-filled sails
or rigging. Criss-crossing the shearing bow, down in the depths of
the bluest of sea, swiftly swam albacore, bonito and dolphin, while
the dainty flying-fish scurried from our hurrying forefoot.

Many hours of our watch below were spent out on the jib-boom
fishing for some change from the eternal salty fare. It was never
my lot to drag a struggling fish to the empty sack which awaited
our haul. But sometimes a lovely bonito would be caught by some
more fortunate shipmate as his flicking rag danced the seas.

It has always been a matter for wonderment to me how one's
skill and personality can be transmitted down some yards of line
to the hook which lures the lurking fish. Perhaps it is good fishermen, like good helmsmen, are born, not made. Mulock, who had
by now recovered from his blackened eyes and battered face, was
our star turn. His first bonito was hooked with the greatest ease.
Fried with onions, it made a delicious change on our monotonous
menu. And when Slushy the cook demanded the greater portion
of our week's whack of butter for the frying there was none who
said him nay. The flesh, rather dark and not unlike the tenderest
of steak, was the finest fare we had tasted for months.

It was not surprising that my efforts were never rewarded and
that my hook went empty. For my eyes kept straying from the
dancing bait to the deep blue sea around, to the bluer sky above,
and to the beautiful ship which was flying towards us.

There were times when the most of my free dog watch would
be spent out on the tip of that finger spar—alone, while the others
filled in the leisure hour with the customary sociability and relaxation of that watch. On such occasions my thoughts would turn
to the bank and that queer old gink who used to pinch my cheeks.
Had he been with me then he would have found more than roses
there, for I seldom wore a hat or cap of any sort, and my face
was burnt almost black by tropic heat and salt-laden wind.

How fortunate had been my release, ere it was too late; how
narrow had become that fast closing gap of escapement before I
had passed through—to this! Instead of those dismal walls, mine
was the freedom of the seas; the wholesome, limitless sea which
cares nothing for the tin-pot affairs of men; the good clean wind
and the deep blue of the faultless sky. Though no warbling song-
bird by nature, I sang at the thought of it all, sang loudly and

exultingly, for there were none but the leaping, rollicking fish below me to cavil at the discord of my notes.

*   *   *

We had not proceeded far into the warmer weather when the fly in the ointment made its appearance. But it wasn't a fly. It was a far more fearsome entomological matter than a mere fly which concerned us. It was, in one loathsome word, BUGS! Yes, bugs, those nasty little brown-jacketed fellows who persistently make their home in the majority of ships.

Prior to this we had, of course, been aware that our domain was shared, though not obtrusively up to then, by others. Shortly after joining the ship something had tickled my face as I lay in the darkness. Rubbing the spot with a finger, my nostrils were filled for the first time with that disgusting, unmistakable odour.

As has been mentioned before, the half-deck was fitted with steel tube bunks which were supposed to discourage the habitation of vermin. A recent article in the *Nautical Magazine,* based on extensive investigation, refutes this theory, maintaining that hollow metal tubes are even more congenial to bugs than the old-fashioned wood. The vermin apparently penetrate deeply into the pipes to lay their eggs in places which are practically inaccessible.

For months the Little Boys in Brown had been hibernating. Once the warm southern tropics were reached, out they came from their hidden lairs, accompanied by the numerous progeny they had begat despite the period of hibernation. Laughing at futile applications of turpentine and paraffin—the only poor remedies we had at hand—they fiercely attacked and devoured us in the night watches. And we had to suffer these savage raids, until finally we were driven from our home to seek rest upon the bare main hatch. The Little Boys in Brown had won the Battle of the Bunks!

This seemed at first a hardship and an ignominious defeat. But soon I grew to love those hours out on the hatch, the hardness of our sleeping quarters unfelt by our resilient young bodies. Those few minutes between wakefulness and sleep, how delicious they were, as we lay there watching the sway of the lofty trucks against the starlit dome overhead. All around us, outside the ship, it seemed as if the sea were some vast living thing, breathing slowly and deeply in the night.

*   *   *

It was inconceivable to me that the mate should be so restless and so ill at ease on such a lovely night. He paced the poop, muttering blasphemously to himself as I stood at the wheel.

The full moon had risen shortly; its path lay like a silver band across the water, paling the sky and the stars above. For me, steering the ship in the second dog watch, it was a night for peace, contentment, and goodwill towards all men. The ship, being now 'by the wind,' was steering easily, the great sensitive fabric responding to the slightest movement of the wheel. And though I was supposed to watch the royals, there was actually no great reason for me to crane my neck uncomfortably.

The little squealing cry of the sheave of the royal sheet at the mizen t'gallant yardarm (had Chips been neglecting his oiling duties?) gave me sufficient warning of bringing the ship too close to the wind, and thus incurring a volley of abuse from the mate. The binnacle was turned away, blinding my view of the compass —a common practice applied to the less experienced helmsmen when the ship was steering 'by the wind.' For me there was, that night, a guiding star of the first magnitude, hanging like a lantern in line with the fore yardarm.

So peaceful was the barque's passage through the water that the voices of the men on the fore hatch reached aft clearly. From the half-deck the gramophone was grinding out the sugary notes of some dreamy, sensuous waltz.

In spite of the beauty of ship and moonlit night through which she sailed, the mate was obviously ill at ease, pacing the poop with a restlessness inconsistent with the tranquillity of the scene. He stood by me at the wheel muttering incoherently as he stared aloft at the weather clew of the mizen royal. He looked into the averted bowl of the compass, threw up his head and sniffed the wind. Then, turning to me, he asked in all seriousness: "Have you ever had anything to do with a Kanaka girl?"

It was an odd question to put to a youngster fresh from home. In the religious atmosphere of the manse Kanaka girls had never been discussed, except perhaps in the light of their possibility as a field for further missionary endeavour.

"No, sir," I answered dutifully. And then the little warning squeal came from aloft. A spoke or two of the wheel cured that, and the mate went on: "One of those nice, light-skinned South

Sea island girls and a bottle of whisky—the finest combination in the world."

He walked to the fore-end of the poop and stood there a few minutes before returning to the wheel. Then he spoke again. "Some years ago I was trading to the islands. It was a good life too. . . . You might call those girls niggers, but they're the finest in the world. . . ."

He sighed and muttered as he gazed reminiscently around the lonely sea. . . . "But I could forget them all if only I had a drink. The Old Man's got plenty down below, but he won't give me a drop. . . ." His voice tailed off as the captain stepped from the chart-room and called imperiously to him.

*　*　*

It was no great hardship to be forced to spend two hours on lookout duty on the fo'c'sle head that morning, while the ship shouldered the North Atlantic on the last lap of the passage. The weather was mild, and the down-draught from the great foresail pleasantly cool as it played upon me, my bare feet making no sound as I paced the deck.

In the east a pearly greyness was growing, spreading slowly across the broad bosom of the sea, gradually dispelling the darkness which lay there. That greyness had not yet given place to the rosiness of the nearby dawn when I spied the ship right ahead. At first there was but a suspicion of a break in the dim circle of the horizon. And then, as the light grew slightly, I knew it was a square-rigger which was there.

"Sail right ahead!" I called out lustily. "Aye, aye!" came the answer from the poop.

With that black oblong in our path slowly assuming definite shape as the day was born, I fell to wondering over the daily, age-old miracle of the dawn. How many millions of the world's population lay stuffily a-bed while that miracle was achieved? There must surely be a great multitude who never see the fairy wand of the rising sun calling to life their world again.

The colouring that morning was magnificent. The delicate, ever-changing pastel tinting of the sky and sea would have taxed a limner's art. And on that immense, sensitive canvas of nature a man-made ship was taking form, her sails gradually turning from the pearly-grey of early dawn to the rose and gold of the almost-risen sun.

Presently the mate came on to the fo'c'sle head, glasses in hand. "What do you make of her?" he asked, peering through the binoculars.

Before long it was obvious we were gaining on the vessel ahead. At noon she was but a couple of miles in the lead. Our ship had borne off a little, to pass to leeward of the stranger. For some time our ensign and numbers had been flying, as if to challenge the other ship to further effort.

The day was beautiful, the sea a deep blue like the sky, the breeze strong and true. A few big, white billowy clouds drifted overhead, like stately frigates passing on their way. Both ships leaned steeply to the sturdy wind as they tossed the spray from their bows, rolling and pitching with an easy grace and grandeur which no steam-ship ever knew.

The master and mate stood on the poop, signal book at hand, some of us boys nearby to tend the bunting in the usual interchange of silent speech. Our flags, standing out boldly as they whipped the wind, were now visible to the other ship. In response, the handsome flag of Norway and her numbers crept aloft on her gaff. All this time her counter had been in deep shadow so that, so far, her identity had not been disclosed.

Busy with the long glass, signal book and Lloyd's Register before him, the captain remarked, "It's the *Euphrosyne*," and then went on a little bitterly, "She was British until a year ago. Another of our fine ships gone. The same story every time—poor dividends, or no dividends at all—and then sold foreign!"

The International Code of signals lay on the skylight, open at the middling, heavy, green tape from which all signals were easily picked out. The captain, one hand spread over the pages, guarded the leaves against the flirting of the playful wind.

Four little flashes of colour soared to the gaff of the *Euphrosyne*. The Old Man thumbed the book as the mate roared out, "ARTC, Sir." "ARTC . . . . ARTC . . ." muttered the skipper as he turned the leaves in haste. And then, coming to the right page, he ran his big forefinger down the column. "ARTC . . . ARTC . . . ARSN . . . ARSX . . . ARTC—Port Victoria! Up with that answering pennant, lads—lively now!"

The four little bits of bunting descended, to be replaced by three this time. The Old Man's stubby forefinger was busy again . . . "CNO . . . CNO—To. Up with the pennant, me sons!"

Then followed another geographical signal, easily recognised as such by the four-flag group, with either A or B uppermost. AFWS —Queenstown— the same destination as our own. After she had given us the number of days out it was our turn. The bunting, handled quickly, rose and fell sufficiently smartly to earn for us the grudging satisfaction of our master and mate.

* * *

By now the two ships— four-masted barque and full-rigged ship were almost abeam, truly a lovely sight which was not lost to even the most soulless aboard. Our ship, only half a mile to looard, was slowly drawing past the three-master, whose black-painted hull was deeply laden like our own. While we were carrying every stitch of canvas possible, she had no cro'jack set; the watch had gone aloft to paint that naked spar. Already the newly spread paint glistened wetly on the yard.

But that did not deter the sailorlike Norsemen from accepting the challenge of our flaunting flags and slow overhaul. As we gave particulars of our passage, we saw the hands coming down from aloft. When we were abeam, two gipsies of the Horn curtsying to each other in the brave wind and the *scend* of the sea, a line of men passed aft along the deck of the other vessel. On their shoulders they carried something which closely resembled a long, thin white sausage.

It was an old cro'jack; they were about to bend the sail; they had accepted our challenge, in spite of the paint glistening wetly on the yard.

* * *

We had watched closely every detail of the bending of that sail. Slowly it had swayed aloft, to be stretched each side from bunt to head-earring. On each yardarm perched a man, poised nonchalantly to the roll and pitch of the ship. The long-drawn, musical cries of those fine Norwegians came down-wind clearly to us.

"There are not many real sailors left now," the Old Man remarked a little sadly to the mate, "and those Scandinavians are amongst the finest." He had looked on with interest and a certain amount of admiration at the way in which the big sail had been handled.

This valiant, sporting effort availed nothing, for our ship continued to draw ahead. Later in the afternoon, when I took the wheel for my two hours' spell there, the mate came to me, calling down upon my head all the plagues of Egypt should I fail to watch my steering. "If you let her come up on us—I'll twist your skinny neck . . ." he threatened sinisterly.

The barque was steering sweetly, requiring little attention beyond a spoke or two of the wheel on either side to keep her 'full and by'. There was for me a grand exhilaration in standing at the helm of that great sensitive fabric which responded so docilely to my slightest touch as she plunged and rolled along with a queenly stateliness. In spite of the mate's dire warning, my eyes kept turning repeatedly to the other ship, well abaft the beam by now. Every one of her sails was cleanly full, the sun-bleached, snow-white of the rounded bunts merging gradually into the shadowed greyness of the straining clews as the *Euphrosyne* tore after us with a foaming bone in her teeth.

No doubt, from her decks our ship must have been an equally magnificent sight. Such titanic sailing had never been seen even by Cowes, and many of those playtime sailors there would have given much to have seen those two great, yachtlike ships that day in the North Atlantic.

When it was definitely established that we were showing the *Euphrosyne* a clean pair of heels, our last two signals soared to the gaff. "HPZ—Goodbye", and "TDL—Wish you a pleasant passage." A little disgruntled, perhaps, she answered shortly, "XOR—Thank you."

Later, when darkness came, two little pin-points of colour—red and green—and a dim shadow in the night were all that was left of the other ship. At daylight next morning she was a small, slightly-tilted oblong on the far rim of the horizon . . . .

Reaching Queenstown four days after our arrival there, this fine old ship was soon to meet her doom. Her tragic end came suddenly several months later, when she had just commenced her outward passage from Hull to Santos.

It was a fine, clear moonlight night. no danger other than steamships, deadly enemies of sail, lay over the peaceful sea. There could have been no excuse for such a mishap on such a night. Nevertheless, the blundering steamer *Dallington* crashed into her, wounding her so mortally that she sank in a few minutes, with barely time for the crew to get clear before she took the final plunge.

So passed another of the irreplaceable ships of 'the sticks and strings'. The thought of them all brings back, to some of us at least, many happy memories of those brave old square-riggers who wooed, yes, and on occasion stoutly fought, the wholesome wind which was their only motive power.

*   *   *

The northern summer that year was particularly fine and windless over the entire North Atlantic. When the trades breathed their last and vanished, our progress was slow and tiresome. Four months after leaving Sydney we found ourselves several hundred miles—but a fair day's sailing—from Fastnet Light, at the southwest corner of Ireland.

Here the wind failed us almost entirely for a number of days, the ship lolling about lazily in the long, low swell. We were right in the steamship track to and from the United States. Many of them passed us close, flaunting their whirling propellers at us as they went on their disdainful way. Some of the largest liners, their captains, no doubt, old square-rigged men, altered course to give their passengers a close view of our barque. Their decks packed with people who lined the rails, gazing with interest at the becalmed windjammer, they tore past, leaving us rolling in their queenly wake.

By this time we were getting short of some supplies. The water in the remaining unfinished tank came up red with rust and unpalatable to the taste. No cigarettes were left aboard, and even the meaty plug for our pipes was becoming scarce. Tea leaves, dried after use in the pot, were tried as a substitute without much success.

Slowly, in company with three or four other sailing vessels, we worked in towards the Irish coast. It was exasperating—well we knew by the skipper's bad temper—to have such bad luck in the way of wind. Instead of that succession of beautiful, calm days what we prayed for was a sou'westerly gale to storm us on our way.

The steam trawler *Swansea Castle* kindly gave us the bearing of and distance off Fastnet Light one afternoon. "East by North, 20 miles," her skipper roared through an immense megaphone. It was a pity he did not extend his kindness further by passing aboard us a bag of fish, for food like everything else was growing scarce. The hideous boils with which I had been troubled since before we passed the Horn were still unhealed, and the blood of all of us craved for fresh food and green vegetables.

An hour later the Emerald Isle was sighted. Mizen Head was passed, and Fastnet itself showed up ahead. The light wind was now heading us, the ship breaking off so much that it was obvious we could not weather Fastnet on that tack. Standing close in, the ship was put about, heading off-shore to the s'uth'ard.

There lay my native land, bearing on its shoulders the mantle of its proverbial greenness. Though the coast was not actually to windward we became aware of the delightful scent of the land as we swung away on the port tack. Over the water crept the sweet fragrance of ploughed fields, of fresh, green meadowlands, of flowering hedgerows, of new-mown hay. All that is delicious perfume in the nostrils of the sailor, a little weary, perhaps, of four months' sea and salt-laden food.

But somehow the coast looked intensely dreary as we bore away. Characteristically, the only prominent building in view other than the lighthouse was a sombre-looking Martello tower. These towers, which dot the Irish coast, were built, as most people know, at that other period of Britain's dire peril, when Napolean was contemplating the invasion of the British Isles.

Compared with his foul, would-be imitator, Napoleon might almost be regarded as a benign gentleman. He never crossed that guarding strip of water to reach the proud shores of Albion; to pillage and lay waste that peaceful land. Hitler, using the tactics of the thug, made a dastardly attempt to do the same—and failed.

* * *

Next morning we cleared Fastnet, standing along the coast to the Eastward with a freeing wind. At noon a tug was sighted ahead, racing towards us with a great plume of smoke. Ignoring the full-rigged ship in whose company we sailed, the tug *Blackcock* ranged up on our quarter, scenting in our big barque a prize more valuable than the smaller vessel. Greetings were shouted across the water from the tug, while we made our way for Queenstown.

But the wind was fair now, and the ship slipping easily along. Queenstown lay but 20 miles ahead, and our Old Man was not the one, under such favourable circumstances, to waste good wind and his owners' money. The sailing pilot cutter *Star of the Sea* lay

hove-to awaiting us. Soon her boat was alongside, towing at the
mizen rigging while the portly pilot climbed aboard. The two men
in the boat called out repeatedly in their drawling, wheedling
voices for a little bit of baccy and a lump of salt pork, not leaving
us, though the ship was now sailing fast, until their needs had
been satisfied.

"Ye'd better take the tug, captain," the pilot advised the skipper
when he reached the poop. "There's a bit of fog hangin' round
ahead." The *Blackcock* passed her rope aboard; we set about the
task of furling all the canvas.

The pilot was right. We had scarcely gone aloft when the
swirling fog came down upon us, so that we were isolated in a
wraithlike veil in which the deck had disappeared.

Daunt Lightship was booming out its warning signal as we
slipped past. Then the fog suddenly lifted as we neared the
entrance. In the evening dusk the ship passed through the headlands. Already the lights were twinkling ashore as our two anchors
clattered down, making a running moor. When we manned the
windlass to settle the barque between her anchors the pilot
shouted: "Give us a song boys!" How we sang, marching like a
crowd of carefree schoolboys around the capstan.

Before darkness crept over the water we had time to note the
beautiful harbour. Here was a yachtsman's paradise reminding me,
though in a smaller way, of the magnificence of Sydney.

* * *

Next day three girls, amphibious like all the Queenstown
youngsters who were said to have been born in boats, rowed off
to the ship and climbed the rope-ladder on her side. With a delightful friendliness they followed us into the half-deck, sitting on
the sea-chests there while they chatted merrily without one trace
of embarrassment or uneasiness. Their soft, drawling tongues were
music in my ears as we devoured them with our eyes.

The ship's main deck, the following Saturday afternoon,
resembled the scene of a happy Irish fair. Men, women, girls,
children—they all were there dancing and singing to the lilting
music of the melodeons. The young girls, dolled up in their
Sunday finery, kept making eyes at the sun-bronzed boys who had
sailed so far across the sea. Do you remember that summer's day,
May? Do you remember that strangely silent boy to whom you

seemed drawn by some bond which was undefined, amongst that gathering where there were many other boys far more blithe than he?

Do you remember swinging lazily in a hammock with that strangely quiet boy, whispering sweet nothings to him while the melodeons cried out their sad, glad notes all around? And the hot afternoon sun beat down on the ship and peaceful harbour in which she had come to rest awhile. Do you remember how some churlish knave, creeping up unnoticed, swiftly severed the hammock lanyard with his keen sheath knife, precipitating you and that strangely silent boy painfully to the deck, while the happy throng roared out their merriment?

How have you fared, May, throughout the years since that far-off day? Shadow and sun! How dark has been the shadow, how bright has been the sun?

And then came the strident voice of the captain when he returned from the shore, calling angrily to the mate: "What's all this about, mister? Clear the ship of all these people!" His wife and family, newly come from Scotland, were with him.

Those happy Irish folk packed good humouredly into their boats and rowed across to the nearest ship—the Norwegian barque *Songvaar*, so recently British. Long after dark their merry laughter rang out from the ship of the more tolerant Norsemen, and the sad, glad notes of the melodeons still crept across the calm, dark water . . . .

* * *

A number of sea-stained gipsies of the Horn came in from the open sea while we lay there at anchor. First the *Naiad*, 147 days from Portland, Oregon, with wheat; the four-master *Oweenee*, which we had sighted off the Horn, with her mizen—t' gallant mast gone in the bad weather down there; the *Kildalton*, 112 days from Sydney. The *Ainsdale* made a beautiful picture as she sailed close past us without a tug, after a long passage of 146 days. And then the *East African* came in to anchor almost alongside us.

These were all British ships. A number of others, French and Norwegian, arrived during our stay in Queenstown. Our old friend, or rival, the *Euphrosyne*, came in four days after us.

One of our A.B.'s, Williams, who had once been a naval signalman, carried on a lengthy semaphore conversation with the

Kildalton. This fine barque experienced wild weather off the Horn, losing two of her boats in that vicinity.

Queenstown was a pleasant, peaceful interlude, though none of us but the four boat boys ever set foot ashore there. The town, a little dull and uninteresting as seen from the anchorage, was dominated, as is usual even in the villages of Ireland, by the huge Catholic cathedral which appeared far too imposing and ambitious for such a place.

At last the Captain came aboard with our orders. We were to proceed to Liverpool to discharge our cargo. Liverpool! And I had hoped it would be Dublin, where many a grain carrier took her load for the Irish mills. But the great Mersey port was surely the next best thing for me. Preparations for getting under way were made without delay.

Our friend the *Blackcock* had been hanging hungrily around amongst the windjammers in port, in the hope that some ship would be assigned to Liverpool, thus giving her the opportunity of returning to her home with something paying its way behind her. But there cannot have been any great profit in that tow for, so far as my memory serves me, the tug agreed to take us to the Mersey for £60—with the use of her tow-rope.

We bade farewell to peaceful Queenstown, drowsing quietly while the other sea-stained sailing ships still lay there awaiting orders; we bade farewell to those happy, amphibious girls and boys who had welcomed so many windjammers in from the storm-tossed sea; and had sped them on their way again, those kindly words of farewell enhanced by the soft drawl of that pleasant Irish brogue.

*   *   *

Once past Tuskar Rock, the task of the *Blackcock* became comparatively light. For a fine sou'westerly breeze sprang up. Staysails, jibs, topsails and foresail were spread to the favouring wind. The ship romped along with little weight on the tow-rope. There was, indeed, at one time, when the wind freshened strongly, some danger of the barque over-running the tug.

We rounded the coast of Anglesey, heading to the eastward for our port. The life of the great river stretched out towards us. A host of inward and outward vessels of all sorts, from the smallest to the greatest liners, surrounded us. The breeze had dropped in the hot summer sunshine and all sail was furled. Without any precise orders from the mate all hands felt a thrill of pride in putting a special harbour-stow on the smooth-rolled canvas on the yards.

The clanging river buoys were passed in the narrowing estuary, their melancholy tongues real music in our ears. The great city lay ahead, the unsightly New Brighton tower close to starboard. Presently we were among the criss-crossing ferries whose passengers, densely packed aboard, hurried about their sordid, town-fettered business. How those white-faced landsfolk stared as our big barque strode like some stately queen amongst them!

The smoke-grime of the city, creeping out across the sunlit water, enveloped our ship, fresh from the wholesome, wind-swept immensity of God's clean sea.

And so our homing port was won at last. . . . .

I

CHAPTER IX

IRISH INTERLUDE

THE ship hauled into the Wallasey Dock at Birkenhead. When she had tied up the mate cast his eyes aloft in a gesture which had become part of his life, and said quietly, "That'll do, men." Though it seemed so inadequate after the months of toil and danger which had been shared by all, this was the usual term of dismissal when a long voyage had ended. The men trooped for'ad to pack their meagre belongings.

The next day they and the other apprentices left the ship—and I alone remained to see her decks and paintwork, over which we had spent so much time and care, defiled by the hob-nailed boots and grimy hands of the dock lumpers who swarmed aboard to take from her hold the Australian grain.

The owners appeared to be under the impression that, my home being in South Africa, it was not my wish to leave the ship for a holiday. So it was I stood by aboard for some days, wandering around the teeming loneliness of Liverpool each night when the work of the day was done.

On my evening walk to Wallasey Ferry I happened to call in at a shop behind the counter of which stood a young, fluffy-headed girl. Fresh from a passage of over four months, any girl is desirable to a sailor home from the sea. And Bessie looked particularly desirable as she smiled at me, my small purchases completed. With the blight of loneliness gnawing at me, I plucked up sufficient courage to ask her to come for a walk the following evening. She readily consented, filling my heart with a great elation.

* * *

Bessie nestled up in a friendly way as we left the shop. She was a coquettish little thing, pretty too, with her fair curls peeping out from under the brim of her hat. She should have brought gladness to the heart of any sailor home from the sea. Instead, I found myself embarrassed and tongue-tied, and foolish enough to be overwhelmed by the thought that she was devoting a whole evening to me.

The girl chattered blithely like a happy tom-tit. Somehow, I could not respond to her mood, remaining so silent that she looked askance at me and lost some of her bright gaiety. Mentally I cursed myself as we walked along; I thought many hard, unkind things about the upbringing which had not made me man enough to rise to an occasion like this. What was the matter with me anyway? Was it those all-embracing walls of the manse of my early days— that lack of broadening outside associations, those friends of both sexes, contact with whom would have put me at my ease with this pretty girl?

We walked along the Seacombe waterfront; we sat imbibing the weak tea and eating the stale cakes of the usual cheap cafe. We walked back along the same waterfront. There was a brilliant moon casting its romantic light in a silver path across the river. But Bessie had lost her spontaneity completely—and I knew that I was the cause of her change of mood.

There were long silences between us now, for my life-long reserve could not overcome that night. My companion was obviously ready to respond to my slightest gesture, and I was home from the restraints and restrictions of a long passage. Yet the whole evening fell flat as a fluke.

It would be hypocrisy for me to say her proximity aroused no stirrings within me, but the inhibitions of my childhood, perhaps the pretext that I had 'just picked her up', robbed me of the pleasure of her company. We parted at the shop door, the girl having given me a half-hearted promise to meet me the following evening.

When we met next day Bessie stood regarding me as if I were a bit of dirt. "Aren't you coming out with me to-night?" I asked her. "No, I'm never coming out with you again!" she replied freezingly. And then she went on: "What's the use of coming out with you again anyway? You're too sanctimonious!"

After delivering this shattering broadside, the young minx turned from me, stuck her cheeky nose still higher in the air—and dashed into the shop. Too sanctimonious—that was a nasty one! Standing on the pavement there, I cursed roundly the whole universe, using good, solid cuss-words which, had she heard them, might have made the girl realise I wasn't so sanctimonious after all.

But Bessie was gone for ever. Obviously my tactics would have to be changed drastically if I were ever to be a success with the ladies. As the ferry took me disconsolately across the river, my thoughts turned to that last night in my father's study before I left home for the sea. While the grandfather clock ticked ponderously outside the door, he had briefly handled the perplexing matter of sex with those inadequate words: "Always treat women with the same respect you would show your own mother."

It does not take a youngster long to find out that in this imperfect world there are a lot of women who are not noticeably anxious to be treated with that particular brand of respect . . . .

*   *   *

The time seemed ripe to write to the owners telling them rather pointedly that a holiday would be both welcome and beneficial to me, though my home *was* in South Africa. My release came in a couple of days.

The clerk in the office of the steamship company told me there was a boat sailing that night. I took the cheapest fare they offered, paying five shillings for a deck passage across the Irish Sea to the North Wall, Dublin. The clerk, looking surprised, remarked: "Cabin class costs only a pound and is very comfortable."

On the passage from Australia I had successfully weathered four months of the direst discomfort, covering many thousands of miles for nothing. It would indeed be shameful waste to spend a precious pound on the journey of a handful of miles to my native land.

A number of my fellow passengers, practically all shawl-clad women, were standing dismally on the fore deck. The night had turned cold and gusty, a nor'westerly wind blustering in from the sea. Most of those wayfarers carried their poor possessions in bundles. It was obvious they were not looking forward with any relish to the stormy crossing of the water which lay before them. And I knew only too well what the Irish Sea could do when really annoyed.

We had long passed the Bar Light Vessel before I found that the words 'Deck Passage' on my ticket were being taken too literally. Most of the other passengers had disappeared, while I remained shivering on deck with the ship floundering into the rising wind and sea.

The lookout crouched unhappily behind his little dodger in the eyes of the ship. When I joined him there, we carried on a

desultory conversation, the poor shelter providing small protection
from the driving spray. "Why don't you go below?" he suddenly
asked me. "We're in for a dirty crossing." When he heard that I
was only a deck passenger he told me that did not matter—there
was a place provided even for such poor travellers.

* * *

The fo'c'sle had been set aside for the humbler ones like myself.
Its legitimate occupants, the sailors, had apparently been given
more comfortable quarters further aft. Going down the ladder, I
found myself in a bare compartment which smelt damp and musty.
Two tiers of bare, wooden bunks lined the sides of the V-shaped
place in the usual manner. The thunder of the sea on the ship's
bows filled the air with a deep, hollow booming sound.

Noticing the number of women who were stretched out
uneasily on the hard bunk boards, I felt my entry was in the
nature of an intrusion. But no 'Women Only' notice warned me
off, and no hostility was shown by those who lay there watching
my arrival.

There remained only one upper bunk. Into this I climbed,
throwing my suit case at one end to act as a somewhat uninviting
pillow. There was not even a 'donkey's breakfast' to temper the
harshness of those cold, damp boards. Sleep refused to come to me;
on the deck-head, directly above, the unfriendly light of a powerful
bulb glared down on my unprotected face.

The ship was feeling the full force of the gale. Her motion had
become uncomfortably lively, so lively indeed that the whole place
was filled with the moaning and groaning of those poor stricken
souls. Many were *in extremis*. Some of the women lay with white
faces, softly babbling prayers while they fumbled with their beads.
Others, their hair tousled and their faces lined with the intensity
of their travail, retched wholeheartedly and with the utmost
abandon over the sides of their cold, hard beds . . . .

Half-way through the night a young woman crawled from her
bunk to attend to her urgent needs on the bare, reeling deck. As
she staggered against the bunks on her return, she came to mine
and stopped, clinging there precariously. With almost closed eyes,
I lay feigning sleep. Her breath, laden with the sourness of her
sickness, played upon my face.

"Ye young divil, ye've been watchin' me," she said . . . "Ye
young divil, it's watchin' me ye've been doin'."

She lay down again. Through half-shut eyes I saw she was looking over at me; and I could hear her muttering, over and over again, "The young divil, he was watchin' me . . . the young divil, he was watchin' me . ."

When I quit feigning sleep and opened my eyes in her direction the poor wench smiled wanly but bravely at me, the throes of seasickness still torturing her vitals. And in that twisted smile I saw she had in her heart no enmity towards me.

* * *

The ship drew alongside the North Wall in the morning. The wind had dropped, for there was no venom in the elements that summer, but the heavy, lowering sky was weeping, weeping softly, sadly, broken-heartedly—as is so often its wont in Ireland.

The old, grey, smoke-stained buildings, the old, familiar, wetly-glistening streets gave me welcome home after eight years. "Home is the sailor, home from the sea," I quoted to the man at the gangway as I stepped ashore.

Nelson still stood poised on his lofty perch, gazing detachedly away over the smoky roofs. Clustered around the base of the Pillar were the same shawl-clad women, monotonously calling their wares: "Panny each thim nice juicy oringes an' limuns . . . panny each thim nice juicy oringes an' limuns . . . ."

The old grey city gave me glad welcome back again, but somewhere under that gladness was the tragic, brooding spirit of the Irish. Those people mourn the past, seeing in the present little which can comfort them; seeing in the future perhaps even less happiness than in the present.

Why is it that Ireland is so sad? Sadness mixed so closely with gladness; the merry laugh with the sob hidden in it; the lilting melody with a sweet melancholy which clutches at the heart—that is Ireland.

Is it what they call the Curse of Cromwell which sets them brooding by their firesides, nursing the wrongs of three hundred years ago? Three hundred years—that's surely an unconscionably long time to nurse a grievance! Perhaps none but the quaint yet lovable Irish would continue to peer so deeply into the past—unforgiving, unforgetting.

Could those hearts but be lifted up towards the sun, the shadow would fall automatically even further behind; could the hand of

real friendship but be extended—in forgiveness and forgetfulness—
across that narrow strip of water, their one-time foe might well be
ready and willing to return a clasp of friendly helpfulness.

Surely the soothing balm of three centuries of time should have
healed those erstwhile wounds; surely the hour has come when the
'Curse of Cromwell', with its crop of religious and racial hatreds,
might well be exorcised for ever from the Emerald Isle.

And so I passed along the streets of the city, seeing everywhere
old friends, not in the faces of the passers-by but in the shops and
soot-clad buildings. There was Lawrence's toy shop where we spent
our meagre shillings at Christmas time; there was Switzer's big
store—larger, more imposing—where I had often gone with my
mother as a boy. And through it all flowed the dear old Liffey—
muddy, sluggish, just the same, doing little to enliven the scene . . .

The kind friends with whom my holiday was to be spent were
camping on Howth Head. The electric tram took me there, along
the same route on which as a child I had wondered how those
trams were driven. My welcome was a joyous one, as the good
people ran down towards me among the whins and heather of the
hill. It was a little disconcerting at first to see the ladies clad only
in shirts and bloomers. That straw in the wind was but the opening
phase of the great emancipation of women which was soon to
sweep the world.

* * *

The evening was late when the iron gates of the manse stood
before me. The words of Thomas Hood's rather morbid poem,
learned at the nearby school, drummed in my ears.

The windows of the house where I was born were there all
right. But there was no sun peeping in, and no light of any sort
shone out. The big house stood staring blankly at me; no glow
from its windows welcomed me back from the sea. Later I learned
that my father's successor and his family had gone to the seaside
for a month.

It was a relief to find the house deserted. Seizing on the
opportunity to wander without let or hindrance around the well-
remembered grounds, I opened the gate and stepped within.

Close by stood the well-known holly tree. Running my hand
along its trunk, I felt the scars the years had partly healed. We boys
had wantonly stripped the bark from that bole. In the *Boys' Own*

Paper—the annual volume of that publication was the *pièce de resistance* of our Christmas presents from 1895 to 1906—we had read that bird-lime was made from holly-bark. The experiment was a dismal failure, but the evidence of our rude attack still remained on that unfortunate tree.

Through the little gate at the side of the house my footsteps took me, down to the end of the big back garden where we had laid old Major to rest. In the gathering dusk I searched, finding no trace whatever of his grave. Some vandal had torn up the name-board and had levelled the mound we had raised so laboriously to mark his resting place.

The rich harvest of the gnarled apple trees had been gathered; the currant and raspberry bushes were bare. The sycamores which lined the stone wall had grown much taller; the shrubbery where Major died was thicker; the bushes where our poor misguided servant had been wooed and won were denser too.

Walking around the church, I peered into the school playground where we had so often had our games of Hares and Hounds, frequently cutting our knees on the clinkers with which the place was so plentifully scattered. In front of the church was the little clearing between the trees where I had once caught a sparrow in a cruel brick trap, its trigger sprung by a long string. Unfortunately, the falling brick had broken the bird's wing instead of capturing it unhurt. The salty tears were recalled, shed over that poor sparrow which would inevitably fall prey to our cat, prowling in the offing.

* * *

There was, at the time of my return to my mother city, a school friend from Stellenbosch studying medicine there. On my first visit to him he hailed me with delight.

"Come with me," he said, "I'll show you a sight you have never seen before, and probably will never see again." He took me through the spacious grounds till we stood before a door over which were inscribed the words: "Dedicated to those who have given their bodies to the cause of science."

"Where are we bound for now?" I asked him.

"You'll soon see," he replied, "but be ready to clear out quickly when I give you the tip."

We went inside together. Before my eyes had grasped what lay before me, I became conscious of an all-embracing mustiness. The room contained a number of slabs set at a convenient height. Around each slab hovered several young men—and every one of those slabs bore upon it a human body.

There they lay—man, woman, child—their naked remains proclaiming to heaven that their bodies had been dedicated to the cause of science.

Once the initial shock had passed, the scene before me was one of the greatest interest. The nearest slab was occupied by an old grey-headed woman. Broad on her back she lay, her face with its tightly-closed eyes serene in death. No lines of suffering marred those fine old features. The woman slept on—utterly oblivious to the fact that her whole abdominal cavity had been laid open, exposing the entire contents. Two students, their books propped up at impertinent angles, nonchalantly examined the intricacies of the old lady's 'innards'.

We passed through the room, from slab to slab. Man, woman, child, they were all there, mutely submitting their naked bodies to the sacred cause of science. And what better use could they have been put to? Far better so than that slow mouldering for years in the damp ground. Far better so than to be lost to the needs of science in the intensity of the crematorium's flame.

No notice had been taken of my presence by the students. But suddenly my friend said to me, "Get out quickly. Here's old Buggalugs!" I retreated hastily, the stern eye of old Buggalugs already on me. Passing through the door I turned to read again: Dedicated to those . . .!

Who were those poor souls whose naked husks remained within, I wondered? How came they there?

* * *

As if a surfeit of corpses had not already been mine, someone invited me next day to see the famous centuries-old bodies entombed beneath St. Michan's Church. A garrulous guide showed us round, leading us through dark passages into the bowels of the earth.

The soil upon which St. Michan's stands is reputed to contain powerful tannic properties. The appearance of those naked remains would seem to bear this out. Though the skin is brown and leatherlike, the state of preservation is wonderful when one realises that these bodies have lain there for hundreds of years. The hair on head and body is apparently unchanged by the passing of the centuries.

As we walked through the church on our way out, the care-taker pointed proudly to a large, shining brass plate, remarking, "Look at that! Shure it hasn't been polished for months!"

What we had seen below were undoubtedly genuine exhibits but, knowing only too well the dampness of the Dublin air, it was difficult for us not to question the veracity of his last remark.

* * *

That idyllic holiday at Howth is one of my happiest memories. Never shall I forget the green vegetables, for which my blood craved so much after over four months of salt tack. When those kind friends, only too eager to please me, used to ask, "What would you like for dinner?" my invariable reply would be, "I don't mind what we have as long as there's cabbage."

The weather was ideal, almost tropical, during those three weeks of my stay at Howth. Scarcely a cloud marred the blue sky, and the sun shone as brilliantly as in South Africa.

My ability to run barefooted over the hill, through the gorse and whin bushes and over sharp cobble stones, caused a great deal of interest amongst my friends and the local inhabitants. The months at sea during which my feet had always been uncovered, except in the coldest weather, had toughened the soles so much that the freedom from shoes was most enjoyable. Those were, indeed, irksome and uncomfortable when they had to be worn on visits to the city.

Howth Hill never looked more beautiful than that summer, and delicious mushrooms grew in profusion in the fields. We collected basketfuls for breakfast while the refreshing dew still lay heavy in the grass, before the warming sun had dried the blades.

* * *

That holiday passed all too soon. The summons to rejoin the ship arrived, and I was forced to say good-bye to those good friends who had done so much to make up for the absence of my home and people.

On the last day I roamed alone over the Hill, making my way to the cliffs overlooking the Baily Lighthouse. So blue was the sea that it might well have been the famous ultramarine of the Mediterranean. (Incidentally, on many occasions I have seen that Midland Lake intensely grey and drab and dreary.)

Lying alone there in the brilliant sunshine full length on the warm rocks, the sweet sad murmur of the flowing tide came up to me, caressing my ears, attuned to its soft lullaby. Far below, the brown-sailed fishing smacks went quietly on their way, the only sound of their passing the melancholy cries of the gulls which followed them, arguing greedily over the scattered offal thrown overboard.

* * *

Just before leaving Dublin an unhappy little experience came my way, though I had been warned. "Boys like you shouldn't walk on the post office side of Sackville Street after dark." Those were the words of a woman who knew her Dublin well.

It was not even dark when I passed down Sackville Street. A pretty, rosy-cheeked girl approached and spoke, addressing me in a modification of the words of the lady in Proverbs 7. Telling her curtly to leave me alone, I hurried on.

But she did not leave me alone, increasing her pace instead until she drew abeam and fell into step with me. Then, finding me too young or too blind to appreciate the seductive wares she had to offer, she dropped a little astern to give me the length of her harsh tongue. It seemed there was a great deal of truth in the words of the bard: "Hell hath no fury like a woman scorned."

That brazen colleen followed me half-way down the street, telling me all sorts of nasty, untruthful things about my parents and myself. It was amazing that so young a girl should have so free a flow of foul invective. Hating at all times a scene of any sort, feeling hot and embarrassed, especially as a number of onlookers were enjoying the fun, I walked on without replying.

The climax of my confusion was reached when some Irish wit, approaching me, called out loudly for all to hear, "B' all the howly saints in hivin, why don't ye pay the poor divil av a girl!"

* * *

The return trip to Liverpool was made as cheaply as possible aboard one of the cattle boats. Nevertheless, it was more comfortable than my previous crossing. For the night was fine and clear and almost windless. But a beam swell kept the ship fretting and rolling so heavily that the pitiful cries of the sheep and the cattle were continuous.

Half-way over, an enormous bullock fell and broke one of its hind legs. I wondered what action would be taken by the drovers as they approached the poor stricken beast. They lost no time in relieving its suffering—in their own rough way. A sling was passed around the sound hind leg; the winch rattled metallically as the great bulk rose from the deck, struggling violently. The bullock's struggles were short-lived. A razor-keen knife was passed across its throat, making me wince.

That river of blood was amazing. Rolling across the deck, it crimsoned the scuppers; it spread till it crimsoned the hooves of the other frightened cattle. They sniffed the deck, lowing their fear. That brilliant flood ran through the scuppers till the ship's wake, in the glow of the stern-light, was crimsoned too . . .

* * *

The *Elginshire* lay at the same moorings, riding high above the quay. Her sides were rusty, her yards pointing anyhow, and she looked like a towsle-headed, slatternly woman. Her decks were foul from the lumpers' hob-nailed boots; their grimy hands and dirty clothes had completely soiled the spotless white paint over which we had spent so much time and toil.

The ship was to tow over to Garston, across the river, there to load phosphate in bulk for Fremantle. That was a great stroke of luck. Australia again! Australia, promised land of the windjammer seafarer.

The minimum of ballast had been thrown down the hold—just enough to keep the ship upright while she crossed the river. It was filthy muck containing garbage and rubbish of all sorts. My first job after a delightful holiday was shovelling that filth into the wings of the hold.

The following day two friends from Dublin came aboard to visit me. Peering down the main hatch, they looked surprised to see me there, barefooted and grimy, trimming that ballast. Perhaps they had expected to find me bedecked in a brassbound uniform, strutting the poop with a telescope under my arm!

Naturally they thought very little of the half-deck, which was in its usual state of wild disorder. One of them had travelled extensively. It was he who remarked disparagingly, "It's hardly as good as fourth class in a passenger steamer—if there is such a class." As they went ashore the other one enquired, staring aloft at our masts and yards, "Do you have to go right up there?" My reply was, "Yes, day and night—but mostly at night, for a squall always appears worse in the dark. And there are no arc-lamps or electric torches to show us the way."

The ship hauled out of the Wallasey Dock, and was shepherded over the muddy river by two tugs. Her tall, gaunt spars soared above the towering, empty hull. It would not have taken much of a squall to have capsized her.

Garston lies seven miles from Liverpool and possesses an up-to-date dock. We joined a goodly fleet of other sailing ships there, most of them, like ourselves, loading for far-off ports.

CHAPTER X

BACK TO SEA

WITH the exception of the captain, the whole after-guard had changed. My kind-faced friend the mate had gone, and in his place reigned a little shaggy Aberdonian, whose ungrammatical remarks caused much amusement among us boys, especially the young gentlemen from the training ship.

Three new apprentices had joined the ship on their first voyage. Our number was thus brought up to twelve, filling every bunk in the half-deck. It was a decided crush, and the pandemonium at meal times, when all were gathered together in port, was deafening.

The new second mate, an Irishman, had never before sailed in such a big ship, most of his time having been spent in coasting schooners. He was literally lost aboard the *Elginshire*, a little afraid of her size and heavy gear, and was never at home aboard her throughout the voyage.

The third mate turned out to be a young fellow from one of the other Shire Line ships which had just been sold. He was so fond of warbling the chanty 'Sally Brown' that he was immediately christened 'Sally'.

One of the new apprentices had served three years running out East in one of Paddy Henderson's passenger steamers. He was anxious to spend the last year of his time in a square-rigged vessel. It took guts to leave the comfort and good food of a passenger ship to sail in the bleak cheerlessness of a windjammer's half-deck, especially when one was thin and weak from the effects of fever. Jamie and I became pals from the start, and I tried in every way during the voyage to help him in his strange surroundings.

While the ship was loading in Garston we did not see a great deal of that grimy spot. Every evening when work was over we took the tram or train to Liverpool, returning to the ship somewhere about midnight.

The girls of Garston complained bitterly to us that none of the sailing ship boys spent the evening in their particular part of

Merseyside. On one or two occasions, when we were boarding a tram for the city, several of them grabbed us by the coat-tails, attempting to pull us off the tram. They called out to us repeatedly, a touch of significance in their voices, "Stay in Garston to-night . . there's plenty of fun for ye here!".

As the tram drew off the elderly conductor remarked sagely, "Them factory girls is as hot as hell!"

Unfortunately, or perhaps fortunately, we never found time to spend an evening in Garston to test the exact temperature of those forward wenches, or to learn to what type of fun they referred.

* * *

There were a number of fine square-riggers around us in the dock. Most of them towed out to sea and set sail for a far horizon before we were ready to leave.

We attended the farewell party of the next ship astern of us, the barque *Inveramsay,* which was to sail in the early hours next morning. It was an hilarious gathering, the hilarity being mostly fostered, it must be admitted, by the many bottles of port which were plentifully provided by the hosts.

In the small half-deck there was standing room only. The smoke from many pipes and cigarettes formed a blue fog which stung the eyes. Ribald songs were roared out lustily, bawdy stories told and re-told by the wits of the different ships, and the whole company was on the best of terms.

But the heady wine was seeping to my brain. And there were still some bottles to be opened. Inconspicuously, knowing what offence would be caused if discovered—I slipped out of the half-deck and on to the quay in the early hours of the morning.

A shadowy figure lurked by the mizen rigging of my ship. Pausing to watch its movements, I made out the shortish form of our new second mate. In the privacy of the night he was studying the running rigging of the big barque. Taking each rope off its allotted pin, he shook it, peering aloft in the imperfect light of the dockside to find out where it led.

He started when he saw me quietly approaching him. Then, feeling perhaps that some bond should exist between two Irishmen, he made a clean breast of his trouble. The ship was far too big—he was afraid of her, and the maze of running gear puzzled him intensely.

Shaking each rope as it was called by name, I showed him the orderly arrangement whereby the correct line could be found even on the darkest night. We parted at the half-deck door. Sounds of ribald revelry still floated from the *Inveramsay*. And then, before leaving me, he unburdened his soul still further: "Thim ould schooners never had anythin' like this aboard thim . . . an' thim boogery boys is always laffin' an' jokin' at me."

He was indeed a bit of a joke amongst the boys. But I was sorry for him, foreseeing a voyage in which no happiness would be his.

* * *

Outside of us, loaded and ready for sea, lay a fine barque about to sail for Punta Arenas. Her crew were a splendid lot of young fellows—flaxen-haired, bronzed, good-looking. We became very friendly with them before they set sail for their far-southern port.

One morning they commenced to bend sail. A hand was sent aloft with a gantline block hanging over his shoulder. What actually happened to him nobody ever knew. As the young fellow passed over the fore cross-trees he must have lost his hold, for he came hurtling to the deck in full view of us all. There can surely be no more terrible sound than a human body striking something hard after a fall from a height.

The ambulance arrived promptly. He was carried over our ship, a battered mass of quivering flesh and shattered bones. It was to the morgue they took him, not the hospital, for life had already left the poor boy's body.

* * *

The *Elginshire* completed loading at the end of October, hauled out into the river, and anchored close to the training ship *Conway*. Sail had still to be bent, and the vessel made ready for her long passage. The fine weather of that long summer had broken up, and there was every prospect of wild weather to come.

Many of the cadets came over from the training ship to watch us bend sail. They had played at the game of sailorising. This was the real thing, carried out in the teeth of a bitter, rising gale, with a new crew who were strange to the ship and still drink-sodden from their last hectic binge ashore.

For over a week the barque lay straining at her cable. The wind, icy cold, laden with the bite of snow, howled from nor'west to sou'west and back again. On 10th November the master decided to put to sea, fair weather or foul.

The *Stormcock* towed the ship to sea. The weather had moderated slightly, but was by no means settled. The tug had contracted to take the barque as far as Tuskar Rock.

Off New Brighton a huge, four-funnelled liner came sweeping in from the sea. She passed us very close, her vast bulk moving through the water with an effortless ease. Her lofty bow drew swiftly past us, a graceful jet in the shape of a plume rising where the shearing forefoot cut the water. Then she was abeam of us, dwarfing our ship with her bulk, robbing our high masts of their loftiness.

It was a pity none was there to capture that picture of those two beautiful ships— the old and the new. Here surely were the two extremes—symbolising the enormous advance in shipbuilding made in a few brief years. The *Mauretania's* rail—for it was that famous ship—was lined with passengers gazing down on the barque trailing to sea behind her tug. That floating hotel had accomplished her passage from New York in as many days as we might be months before our wind-blown gipsy of the sea had made her distant port.

These thoughts came to me as the *Mauretania* swept past, the disturbance of her wake setting the barque nodding and rolling gently.

* * *

The weather had become vile again. Once clear of the Anglesey coast, the ship was exposed to the full weight of the gale. The wind had worked into the SSW., a dead muzzler, so that no sail was of any use. With the yards hard on the backstays to reduce the enormous pressure aloft, the ship staggered on behind the tug, the gale roaring and tearing at us.

Hour after hour the game and aptly named *Stormcock* dragged us slowly to the s'uthard, the deep heavily-loaded ship straining wildly at the long tow-rope.

In the middle of a bitterly cold night we had reached Tuskar Light at last. The tug signalled for us to let go; she could not, indeed, have held us any longer, so bad had conditions become. Her whistle wailed out three long sad farewell blasts as she turned to scuttle for shelter.

And we, with the red glare of Tuskar dimly lighting the dreary scene, set to the difficult task of getting sail on the ship. The

K

blocks were stiff from their lengthy period of inactivity in port, and the crew still strange to their new ship.

Under six topsails and the foresail, we bore away to the south-east, the vessel wallowing along with decks awash as she attempted to fight to the south.

* * *

A week was spent in the narrow confines of St. George's Channel and the Irish Sea. The wind blew so hard all that time that only the shortest canvas could be shown to the gale. Wearily the ship zig-zagged across that narrow stretch of water. Every few hours it was necessary to wear ship; and each time she wore she lost valuable southing because she would not stay in such wild weather and under such small canvas.

Steadily she was driven northwards, losing all the ground so hardly won by the dogged efforts of the *Stormcock*. Ever present was the sailing ship man's deadly fear—a lee shore. We were nearly trapped and embayed in Cardigan Bay; how many times we sighted Bardsey Island Light it would be difficult to say, for it kept re-appearing with a tantalising monotony, and further to the south each time.

An even greater fear than a lee shore was always with us—the peril of being run down at night. The ship was right in the steamer lane, offering her broadside to every steamship that came blundering through the spindrift and darkness. Sometimes our wan side-lights were insufficient to warn them off, and bluelights were hurriedly set ablaze.

On one occasion a big steamer approached so closely at four bells in the middle watch that it seemed no action could save us from collision. The barque was close-hauled on the starboard tack, the yards hard on the backstays, giving her, according to the Rule of the Road at Sea, the right of way over all other craft on the seas, steam and sail, with the one exception of overtaken vessels.

That apparently meant nothing to the great steam-driven brute which blundered down on us, so closely it seemed nothing could save us.

"Down helm!" roared the skipper, as a last resort.

Sluggishly, with canvas thundering as the ship came slowly to the wind, she answered her helm. A blue light, flaring up from the poop, lit up the scene with eerie clarity, etching the maze of soaring rigging and the narrow dark strips of the rain- and spray-soaked lower topsails.

"Christ! She'll be aback in a minute!" the Old Man yelled out to the mate.

And then the steamer suddenly saw us. With boiling bow-wave she tore past us, her propeller flogging wildly at wind and sea as she lifted aft. Grabbing the big megaphone, the captain screamed out a volley of abuse as the snorting monster passed.

How we detested those steamships! There was always a sigh of relief when their well-defined tracks were left behind, and the ship far out on the lonely windjammer routes where no telltale smearing line of smoke marred the clean horizon. We always pictured them prowling around the ocean, dealing death and destruction to sailing vessels where and when they found them. They were never given any credit by us for keeping a proper lookout. The popular belief in sail was that steamship's officers lounged in comfort behind glass while on watch, puffing at gaspers instead of filling their pipes with good, meaty Fair Maid plug.

* * *

At the height of the gale, the heavy pin which held the fore upper topsail yard to its parrel sheared off. The yard had been renewed in Liverpool, but a flaw soon showed up when it was put to the test of storm and stress. Through the fault of some slipshod work ashore, we were now faced with the difficult task of securing that yard to its parrel (the big hoop on which it was hoisted or lowered on the mast) while the ship plunged and rolled in a heavy sea. After some hours of work aloft under the most trying conditions, the captain taking a most prominent part, the job was done—and done so well that no further trouble was experienced there on the passage to Australia.

When the captain must have seriously thought of giving up the struggle by squaring away to pass round the North of Ireland—the wind freed. With the bite of a knife-edge in its icy breath, it blew from the nor'west.

The glare of my old home town lit up the lowering night sky as we manned the braces for that fair wind. Baily Light, familiar friend, shone out across the jet-black water; Kish Light vessel drew abeam as the ship swung off upon her course.

Hoyle piped up with his long-drawn, eerie cry . . . "Wey, hey, hey - - Oh! Haley, haley, haley - - Ho! . . . ." The brace blocks cluttered merrily as we squared away for Australia; the great yards swung to the fair wind as the ship fell away to the s'uthard.

I thought of the *Mauretania*. She would take less time on her next outward passage than we had wasted in the Irish Sea. Perhaps there was something in steam after all. Practically the whole value of the *Stormcock's* valiant effort had been lost. And we had been forced to spend a dangerous and unpleasant week in waters far too narrow for such a big square-rigged ship.

Sailorlike, that was soon forgotten. Sail after sail was set to the bitterly cold wind till the ship was plunging and foaming on her way, making the first real progress in many days. When as much sail had been set as seemed prudent, all hands were called aft for a tot of grog to keep out the cold. And we youngsters, the second voyagers, drank ours as avidly as the old hands.

Later, with a long wake trailing the grey water astern, the barque passed Tuskar once more, running fleetly on the long trail which led to Australia. The Fremantle girls surely had hold of the tow-rope at last!

* * *

When the crew had settled down it was found we had been fortunate in securing quite a decent lot of men. The majority were Britishers, an unusual occurrence in the manning of the latter-day windjammers. The cook, perhaps the most important member of the ship's company and one who has to play a great part in the happiness of any deep-water vessel, was a frail little old man. On his temples the blue veins showed like cords; his pale blue eyes bore witness to his tiredness and resignation after a long life of thankless toil in the galleys of sailing ships.

His job was no sinecure, for he had to turn out every morning shortly after four. Then he would meekly ask the watch on deck to haul down the mizen topmast staysail until his galley fire was in full blast. Boiling hot coffee (of sorts) was always ready at 4.45 and the work of the day started at three bells, 5.30 a.m.

Jenkins, one of the A.B.'s, was an entertaining rolling stone with whom I became very pally before we had been many days at sea. He had drifted all round the world gathering, as he himself was the first to admit, very little moss on his wanderings. His lack of worldly possessions—he had come aboard with a very meagre ward-robe—caused him no loss of sleep. He was a cheery soul who was content to live from day to day, finding great amusement in the process. We were in the same watch, and I found myself drawn greatly to this good shipmate. As we worked together he told me many stories of his adventurous life.

He had been through the Boer War, having deserted his ship at Cape Town to become a soldier, like so many of his type. His experiences in that campaign would have filled a volume. One day as we worked together on a heavy wire splice I asked him what was the worst job he had ever tackled. He looked at me whimsically before replying. Then he answered as follows:

"The dirtiest, rottenest job I ever had was after the Boer War, before I went back to sea. A number of soldiers had been buried on an outlying farm where an engagement had taken place. Though they were doing no harm—poor devils, they were as dead as mutton, had been for several years—the whiskered old farmer objected to having those 'rooineks' planted in his soil. The authorities decided to exhume the soldiers and re-bury them in one of the town cemeteries.

"I had the job of uprooting those poor lads, with several niggers to help me. The bodies had been buried without coffins, just an army blanket around each battered corpse. The blankets had rotted—but they hadn't rotted half as much as the men!

"That was the lousiest job I ever had in my life. I smoked hard all day, the strongest Boer tobacco I could get. There was a bottle of Cape brandy always in my pocket— and I needed it too. What with the brandy, which I took neat, and the smoking, I got through with it—but it was hell!"

*   *   *

Tuskar Rock had been passed again, the ship foaming along with numbers flying, and 'Please report me to the owners' streaming from the halliards. They would probably cuss when that report got through to the dusty office in Glasgow. Masters of sailing ships were apparently expected to have some divine gift of governing the elements, and it would give the owners a jar to find we had progressed so little on our way.

The fair wind took us far out into the Atlantic until the north-east trades came along to speed us south. The sun shone brightly on us, and the wild experience of the last few days was soon forgotten.

It is surprising how close to the British Isles the sun may be found, shining with a brilliancy rarely known in those rain-drenched islands. Each day brought better weather as the ship moved south. Soaked clothing and bedding littered the hatches. There was, however, little fresh water available for washing clothes or our persons. The Board of Trade daily 'whack' of one gallon per head was rigidly enforced, the pump being rigged at the mizen fife-rail at 4 p.m. each day. The third mate superintended strictly the issue of water.

The twelve of us boys received six two-gallon buckets as our ration. Of these, four buckets were demanded by the cook and carried along by us to his tank in the galley. The other two bucketfuls were placed in the half-deck tank—our entire supply for 24 hours for drinking and cleaning ourselves. In hot weather, or when we were employed on particularly exhausting tasks such as the continual bracing of the yards in the doldrums, we would drink the whole supply, leaving none for washing.

Occasionally a small amount might be spared for cleansing face and hands, the senior boys performing their limited ablutions first, the younger ones having to be content with the dirty leavings after they had been used a number of times. The red-letter days were those when it rained heavily. Then every available receptacle was filled with the precious gift from heaven, and an orgy of clothes' washing indulged in. Mother-naked, we stood under that gigantic shower-bath as the tropic rain beat down on the deck.

My stock of clothing had all become soiled and wet long before we reached the fine weather. I had resorted to the futile practice of turning my shirt inside out when the captain noticed my grubby condition. He examined me carefully and then remarked drily: "It's about time you put on a clean shirt before you find yourself lousy."

On this particular passage the ship was fortunate in experiencing little delay in the doldrums, where sailing vessels frequently lay practically motionless for days. Most people know that the "Doldrums" is that calm belt between the southern limit of the north-east trades and the northern edge of the south-east trade wind. It extends, roughly, over ten degrees of latitude, shifting somewhat with the seasons. For the sake of the uninitiated it might be mentioned that ten degrees represent a distance of six hundred miles.

Many a splendid passage has been spoiled completely by long delay in this region. On the other hand, cases have been known when ships have run almost directly from one trade wind into the other. That, however, was unusual, and to most old salts the name of this part of the ocean will recall the heartbreaking, almost continuous pully-hauly work on the heavy braces in the intense, humid heat.

Day after day the ship wooed the most fitful airs; frequent torrential rain and violent thunder storms beat down upon her; at times fierce squalls, of short duration but capable of dismasting an unwary vessel, swept across the water. Every favourable breath of wind had to be taken advantage of. The exhausting work of hauling the heavy yards from one tack on to the other went on continuously. It was the most trying period of the whole voyage, the sweltering heat not being conducive to good tempers.

It is here that the sailing ships were collected by the protracted calm. From the fore royal yard I counted one day no less than over twenty sail, all square-rigged vessels with the exception of two or three schooners. Truly, although I had left my going to sea almost too late, the age of sail was not entirely dead.

One afternoon, just prior to picking up the good south-east trades, we had an illustration of the danger of assuming that, because there is apparently nothing in sight, no other vessel is in the vicinity. The weather was of the usual unsettled nature; squalls were gathering and dispersing or passing clear of the ship. And then a particularly ugly one was noticed bearing hotfoot down upon us.

That squall almost caught us aback. The royals had already been lowered, and we were about to do the same to the t'gan'sls when the fore and main split from head to foot. The ship slowly paid off and started flying close-hauled to the s'uthard, while a torrential down-pour almost blinded us.

And then, running swiftly before the wind in the midst of the squall, came a full-rigged ship which passed very close. The first sound we heard of her approach was the seething of her bow-wave and the flogging of her royals and t'gan'sls, which had been

hauled up clumsily in their gear. Before we had seen her name—
Asuncion—we knew she was a foreigner by the strange, unfamiliar
cries which rang out across the water from her crew as they
tended the braces. That Italian ship vanished as quickly as she had
come.

*   *   *

On this, my second voyage, I found my status had been considerably enhanced. I was now taking a regular wheel, fair weather
and foul, doing exactly the same work as the A.B.'s with, of
course, as was customary, any other unpleasant tasks which were
considered the boys' work. The loosing and furling of the royals
was invariably done by the youngsters of each watch, who also
frequently made fast the t'gan'sls unaided by any of the men.

Any praise we received was given grudgingly. We were usually
referred to simply as 'them bloody boys', except for the second
mate, who had his own little pet name for us to which I have
referred before. Our position, like that of all apprentices in sail,
was an invidious one, for we were neither officers nor men. One
or two of the latter, less friendly than the others, used to refer to
us disparagingly as 'officers' toe-rags'.

But amongst those men before the mast there was a rough
kindness which helped me greatly in my tyro days at sea. All the
sailorising such as splicing, making knots and mats and the many
types of sennit and fancy work was learned from them. It annoys
me intensely to find in books of the sea written by superior persons
many derogatory remarks about the deep sea warriors who drove
the square-rigged ships around the world. They have been called
all sorts of foul names—gaol birds, ignorant rapscallions, diseased
wastrels—and many other unkind terms. One writer makes the
following statement: "They were traditionally classed with gaol
birds . . . their knowledge of the various countries they visited
was confined to the public houses and brothels of the sea ports. . ."

That may be true about a number of them, but it is most unfair
to sweepingly describe all as such. And, now that the despised and
displaced sailing ship has been succeeded by the lordly steam- and
motor-vessel, one does not exactly hear of the public houses and
brothels closing down through lack of business.

Some of these men undoubtedly were diseased—because nobody
ever cared a damn whether they got cured or not. Many were

very ignorant, poor devils, but on the other hand some of them were very fine fellows with whom it was a pleasure to be shipmates. There were some, too, who read books, good books, which made me ashamed of the literary rubbish I habitually absorbed at that time.

One old man stands out in my mind above all others, a tough old shellback who carried his years amazingly well considering the long life he had spent surrounded by the hardships of sail. He knew his art from A to Z. I can see him now, sitting on deck skilfully patching his clothes, a battered pair of spectacles perched loosely on his nose. He was full of kindly counsel for us boys. As he stitched the words of wisdom dropped like pearls from his tobacco-stained lips.

Good old Dad Wilson, I have you and others of your kind to thank for much of what I learned at sea!

The truth is, of course, that these men were more sinned against than sinning. They were, in the days of which I write, exploited to the utmost by the shipowner. They were forced to live in damp quarters where no comfort of any sort existed. Their food was of the coarsest and poorest. It is hardly to be wondered at that they sometimes kicked over the traces when they got ashore.

* * *

There is in my apprentice's Indenture (it lies before me as I write) a clause which reads as follows:

"In consideration whereof, the said Master hereby covenants with the said Apprentice that during the said term he, the said Master, his Executors, Administrators, and Assigns, will and shall use all proper means to teach the said Apprentice, or cause him to be taught, the business of a seaman."

It all sounds very fine but the average sailing ship master lost no sleep over the commitments apparently contained therein. He considered, quite rightly, he had enough to do for his poor salary looking after the owner's ship without being obliged to play the part of schoolmaster too.

We were very fortunate in having a fine man as captain of our barque. The above clause, which appeared in every apprentice's Indenture, must have been imprinted somewhere in the back of his mind. He paid us an almost daily visit to the half-deck. Sitting on one of the sea-chests, he would propound a few of the axioms

of the sea. Sometimes in the dog watch of a clear moonless night
he would call us, one or two at a time, on to the poop to point
out the different planets and major constellations.

Those stars became trusty friends to me in later years when I
was navigating officer in steamships. Even to this day, when my
eyes are turned at night to the great celestial concave, the scene
on the poop of that ship so long ago comes back with startling
vividness; the huge dark sails rearing towards those selfsame stars
which bejewelled the blue-black sky; the dim light of the binnacle
as it played on the intent features of the helmsman, and the fairy
song of the wind as it caressed sail and spar, driving the tall ship
on her way . . . .

*   *   *

The third mate's Big Joke fell flat— flat as a fluke! The usual
fun of the dog watch was in full swing, and we were singing
lustily to the time of the half-deck foo-foo band when his big,
fatuous red face came perring in.

"Come and see the Queer Fellah," he said, grinning broadly.
"He's gone daft—stark, staring mad!"

We made our way out on deck. The ship, leaning close-hauled
to the urge of the fresh wind, was sailing sweetly and swiftly,
requiring no immediate attention from the watch on deck. On the
poop the master and mate, apparently deep in conversation, paced
fore and aft the length of the deck, as was the manner of the
windjammer men.

Synchronising our entry with the after-end perambulation of
the two, we passed inside the poop alleyway, halting at the door
of the room shared by the second and third mates. Though a
vast improvement on the bare half-deck quarters, it was a mean
little place.

"Have a look at him," the third mate whispered. "He's gone
dilly—daft as a coot!"

The little room was feebly lit by the downturned bulkhead oil
lamp. The port was open, for the weather was mild. On the deck,
kneeling in front of the bottom bunk, we saw the short, stocky
form of the second mate.

His head was bowed over the bunk board, his body swayed
slowly to the motion of the ship as she rolled and pitched easily.
From the open port a little backdraught fluttered his dark curly

hair. Above the murmur of the wind without, and the soft gurgle of the ship's passage through the water, came the babble of his prayer.

Though he must have known that we stood gaping there, no recognition of our presence was given by our second mate. The quiet intonation of his prayers went on, blending somehow, it seemed to me, with the great, eternal voice of the dark, nightclad, everlasting sea outside.

Looking over my shoulder, his hot breath playing against my neck, the third mate sniggered. "What do you think of him, the daft — — —?" he enquired obscenely in a hoarse whisper.

There was not another there who sniggered, even smiled or laughed. We turned from the door and tiptoed along the alleyway, synchronising our exit from the poop door with the heavy-footed tramp of our lords and masters above.

Out on deck again, the third mate came amongst us. "What do you think of him?" he asked, grinning broadly, his big white teeth showing clearly in the darkness. "Didn't I tell you he was daft?"

Something within me rebelled at that; some glimmer of the religious training which had been imbibed with my mother's milk. "Daft," I said . . . "no, he's not daft. It's you that's daft . . . and I wish to God I had the guts to get down on my hunkers and do in the half-deck what he is doing in there!"

The third mate slunk away, returning to his post on the lee side of the poop. And we trooped into our deck-house again, to resume our music and song once more. But there was no song in my heart, for my thoughts kept turning to that lonely soul aft there who sought some solace from his Maker, while the ship drove on through the darkness of the night and the sea . . . .

* * *

Eight bells had rung out on the for'ard bell which always answered the after one throughout the night. The watch had been relieved, and the second mate had taken over from the mate.

I walked to the weather rail and stood looking out to windward. A moon almost at the full hung high in a flawless sky, bathing in its brilliant light the ship from delicate, fluttering royals to waterline. With no immediate duty other than keeping handy, an intense longing for sleep possessed me. That was the bug-bear of sailing-ship life—lack of continuous sleep throughout a long passage of months. The weather looked so settled that I decided to snatch a little unofficial shut-eye. Curling up on the lee side of the main hatch, I was soon dead to the world.

I awoke with a jar to find that something had precipitated me suddenly and painfully from the hatch to the deck. Picking myself up hurriedly, I made for the lee poop ladder. The ship was lying over at a tremendously steep angle, so steep that in my still sleepy condition I had some difficulty in negotiating the ladder.

The change in the weather in the short space since midnight was unbelievable. A heavy pall of inky cloud had blotted out the moon, and the wind howled as it drove with it a heavy rain which immediately soaked me to the skin.

The din aloft was indescribable as my way was made to where the second mate stood at the fore end of the poop. There was sufficient light to see that he was clutching the rail like a man paralysed with fear. Below the break of the poop was clustered the watch, waiting for the orders which should ere this have come from him.

But no word left his lips. This sudden fierce squall, coming out of a moonlit sky, had left him speechless; the emergency which had arisen so suddenly had overwhelmed him.

The ship was pressed down until the lee rail was awash, the water surging on to the deck. She flew along like a mad thing. The wind screamed in the tortured backstays and thundered in her canvas; with all sail on her she groaned and complained in every rope and rivet.

We wondered how long it would be before the whole of her top-hamper came crashing down about our ears. We wondered, too, why the skipper did not come. How was it he did not wake with all that racket above and about us?

And then he came hurtling from the lee chart-room door, a blasphemous, pyjama-clad fury. "What the hell are you doing with the — — — ship?" he roared, among other things, at the frightened second mate. "Lower away royals and t'gan'sls!" To the man at the wheel, "Look out there, or you'll have her aback!"

The helmsman, one of the best in the ship, had been trying, without orders, to 'shake it out of her'. Away aloft in the darkness the weather clews of the royals and t'gan'sls were pounding and hammering furiously.

The captain stood up to windward, sniffing the wind, gauging the weight of the squall. The wind strengthened even more, and the barque shuddered from truck to keel as she buried her rail in a smother of foam. The sails came down the masts slatting and thrashing like wild things against the curbing buntlines and clew-lines.

"Shall I send the hands aloft to make them fast?" the second mate enquired timidly. The captain gave him a curt negative, and then blazed up at the unfortunate officer. "You get away for'ad, you useless article! Get away for'ad and . . . and . . . PICK FLOWERS! That's all you're bloody-well good for—picking flowers."

The ship was still hard pressed and smoking through the water at great speed. Standing watching the weather horizon, his pyjamas plastered to his sturdy body by wind and rain, he had seen a thin line of silver underneath the angry, ragged cloud. Soon the blue-black dome of the moonlit sky appeared again as the dark mass wheeled overhead.

A little later, away down to looard, a black wisp of cloud, no bigger than a man's hand, hurried over the horizon. As we hoisted sail again, the canvas dark-stained with rain, the ship sailed steadily through the beautiful moonlit night once more. . . .

* * *

Down in the Roaring Forties the ship made excellent sailing, topping the 300 nautical miles per day on several occasions. On the long, lonely, empty trail between the Cape and Cape Leeuwin we sighted only one ship—the full-rigged British *Inveravon,* running eastwards like ourselves before the gale under foresail and topsails.

When New Year's Day broke with a vague grey horizon and roaring wind and spindrift flying, we picked her up almost right ahead. We gained on her so much that several of us were able to photograph her in spite of the weather conditions. How that ship rolled! She was in ballast, and at times seemed determined to throw the sticks over the side. She altered course to cross ahead of us, hauling to the nor'ard to make a more quartering wind of it, probably in an attempt to minimise that frightful rolling.

My diary mentions that on that day the skipper, good man,

passed two bottles of port wine into the half-deck with which to wet the baby head of the new-born year.

Fremantle was reached on the eighty-second day out from Tuskar. Shortly before midnight we hove to outside Rottnest Island. Hoyle's wailing cry rang along the deck as we eagerly backed the main yard to await the tug. By breakfast time we had berthed alongside the north bank of the river.

Our stay in Fremantle was no whit less enjoyable than that at Sydney, on the other side of the great continent. Our ship, the finest windjammer in port, was much admired by the sea-loving Australians who flocked aboard at week-ends. She made a brave show, too, with a brand-new house flag and ensign flying aloft, the colourful, quartered M.M.S.A. banner streaming from the jigger truck. Proud were we indeed of her neatly-trimmed yards and freshly-painted hull with its vivid black ports on their snowy band of white.

The cargo of phosphate was discharged, and we loaded grain for home in the same berth, a grand stroke of luck which made us regard our big barque as one of Fortune's favourites. On moorings, further up the river, lay the pathetic sight of the once beautiful *Samuel Plimsoll*, now a coal-hulk supplying the needs of her ruthless steam-driven successors. The *Thornliebank* was there too, and several other fine old vessels which, shorn of their lofty spars, seemed to mourn the unhappy end which had come to them.

The usual calf love flourished between those good-hearted Australian girls and ourselves. I was more or less adopted by a friendly couple with three cheery daughters aged sixteen to nineteen. Their home was mine during our stay at Fremantle, and we had many week-end picnics at Cottesloe Beach, and also up the Swan River. The local youths resented somewhat our friendship with their sisters. One particularly illustrative case of this comes to mind.

It was Saturday afternoon; we were washing decks preparatory to knocking off for the week-end. Four or five larrikins sat indolently on the wharf, their long legs hanging over the edge between ship and quay. In the hot sun they loafed, lazily picking their teeth as they watched our efforts to get finished. While we worked we chaffed one another good-humouredly. A girl's name was mentioned in connection with one of our number.

Suddenly one of those lazy larrikins came to life. Hoisting himself on to the quay, he marched aboard the ship, the nasty glint of battle in his eye.

Facing the youngster who had been the butt of our unfortunate humour, he addressed him thus: "So you're the goddam lime-juicer who's been chasing around after my sister. Well, I'll just tell you this—you keep away from that girl if you don't want those nice white teeth bashed right down your throat."

Though, in reality, any lovemaking with those girls was innocent enough—what are a few squeezes and a few snatched kisses when one is young?—the warning of that big cornstalk made an impression on us for a few days, and we walked a little more warily than usual.

Before we sailed a new apprentice, a local lad, joined us, swelling our ranks in the half-deck to the unlucky thirteen. He was allotted a bunk in the tiny, so-called hospital which was situated in the same deck-house. The evening he came aboard we were all having supper in the mess-room. His big, well-built form suddenly filled the after door as we sat there. Smiling broadly and good-humouredly, he called out cheerily: "Hello, all you bastards!" There was such good humour in his big smile, such *bonhomie* in his happy salutation, that none but the most fastidious could take exception to his choice of greeting.

The leader of the Training-ship Trio rose from the bench, positively bristling with indignation. "Hey, you!" he shouted angrily, "you can't come here calling us that!"

The smile never left our new shipmate's face. Leaning carelessly against the door-frame, he replied to the indignant one: "That's all right, friend. Don't get so excited. We call everybody that in Australia. There's really no harm in it at all."

That big Aussie proved a stout fellah and a good shipmate to the end.

The homeward passage was made by the westerly route, as was usually the case from West Australia, thus avoiding the stormy rounding of the Horn.

The Cape of Good Hope and, later, Table Mountain were in sight throughout a whole afternoon. Two valuable hours of sleep were lost to me, sitting on the fore cross-trees, scanning the familiar scene through a powerful telescope. So near and yet so far! How I wished something would happen to necessitate our putting into Table Bay.

In a few days St. Helena too was sighted—a gloomy mass of rock. Though we were by then in the tropical belt, the day was grey and dreary. As the ship sailed past at a distance of seven miles, the island looked intensely forbidding, its beetling cliffs clad in a lowering, sombre mantle of heavy cloud. If it always looked like that no wonder Napoleon, unhappy wretch, died of a broken heart in that isolated, sea-girt spot, brooding, like him, under its melancholy load of cloud.

*　*　*

The afternoon was perfect, the sky cloudless, the lightly-whipped sea a deep blue. Leaning to the steady breeze, the ship had every sail set. But there was a strange restlessness about the captain. Every now and then he passed from the weather side of the poop to stare fixedly to leeward. Head up, gazing apparently at nothing, he made me think of some wild animal who had sensed approaching danger. No land was nearer to us than some hundreds of miles.

He was joined by the mate. A few words passed between the two of them. Then the mate clattered down the poop ladder, shouting as he ran: "All hands on deck!" The order had an electrifying effect on the crew. The watch on deck looked at the mate as if they thought he had gone mad. The watch below turned out of fo'c'sle and half-deck, half clad and grumbling fiercely as they came. "All hands!" could be expected any time in unsettled weather, but what was it all about now, with the day so fine? "Clew up royals and t'gan'sls!" ordered the mate.

When the sails had been lowered and snugged up in their gear, the ship looked strangely naked aloft in the brilliant sunshine. I noticed then that the westerly wind was falling away, and that the ship scarcely had steerage way on her.

"Up aloft and make them fast!" the mate roared at us, an order which fully convinced the men that the skipper and he had both lost their senses. We jumped into the rigging and made our way aloft.

As I reached the cross-trees I became aware of a low, eerie moaning sound away out on the lee bow. Looking towards the distant horizon, I saw a ragged line of wind-torn water advancing

THE PRAYA, BAHIA, BRAZIL.

(Note the whiplike unstayed masts of the local craft — referred to on page 172)

Photo by the author

towards us. At that moment the excited voice of the mate reached us from the deck, yelling for all hands to come down from aloft. Sliding down the backstays, we were just in time to man the braces to haul the yards right round before the white squall leaped upon us.

There was no gradual increase in the strength of the wind; it struck the ship a solid blow. The chain topsail-sheets clanged bar-tight with a jar which shook the barque. With no way on her, she lay down like a stricken thing of life, the water surging through the scuppers and welling up towards the lee hatch-coamings.

And then she started to seethe through the water, the solid wall of the wind screaming and tearing at her. The captain stood by the man at the wheel. "Up helm!" he had ordered, running the ship off to ease the pressure. Under a cloudless sky, with no previous hint of danger, the ship stormed along at over fourteen knots for twenty minutes.

Later I stood at the wheel. The wind was back in its old quarter, the ship had everything set again. The master plodded up and down the poop. He came and stood before me, looking into the compass and then aloft to see how the sails were pulling. I thought he was about to find fault with the steering. But when he turned to looked at me there was no fault-finding in his keen blue eyes.

"Sonny," he said, "if you are ever master of a sailing ship—watch her like a mother watching her child. Watch her from the time you drop the tug until the other end of the passage. When I was a young man a 'white' squall like that came on us unawares. The ship was caught aback and lost her sticks . . . you've got to nurse a ship if you want to keep the masts in her—nurse her all the time."

He turned to continue his pacing of the poop. Mine was a tremendous admiration and respect for the man. On his shoulders rested a responsibility even greater than that of the commander of a steam-driven, so-called luxury liner. His course was strewn with many snares and pitfalls, his ship, in spite of her seeming strength, a sensitive, fragile thing.

Many a time I have seen him in bad weather, standing to windward on the poop—watching his ship. With no shelter of any

L

description he often stood thus for may hours of daylight and dark, his face flayed by wind and spray. His keen eyes missed nothing. Every little change in the wind, the slightest alteration in the cloud formation, had some meaning for him. And when such signs were absent, some uncanny sixth sense led him aright. Had that not been so, the white squall I had witnessed so recently would have dismasted the ship.

*   *   *

The coast of the Emerald Isle stretched once more along the port beam, with Queenstown not far ahead. We youngsters were looking forward to visiting again that friendly anchorage. But that was not to be.

The sailing pilot-boat lay awaiting us, hove-to. A tubby dinghy left her to grapple our mizen rigging, towing alongside while the pilot made his way to the poop to see the Old Man. "I've got your orders, Captain," he said. "You're to proceed to Barry Dock to discharge."

There was some disappointment when it went around the decks that ours was a Welsh port. Soon every sail was set to the fine sou'west wind as we romped away for the Bristol Channel.

CHAPTER XI

A CHANGE OF SHIPS

THERE was, at the time of our arrival at Barry Dock, another "Shire" line vessel, the full-rigged ship *Arctic Stream,* lying at Cardiff, a few miles up the Bristol Channel. This was a vessel in which I was particularly interested, for her captain was one of the best of T. Law's masters—an up-to-date man who was reputed to give his apprentices a better time than was the custom of most of the sailing ship skippers of the day.

Our old man had made his last voyage in sail. The owners had offered him command of one of their newly acquired steamers; he had decided to 'give up going to sea and go in steam'. His successor being as yet unknown to us, I wrote to ask the owners to permit me to transfer to the *Arctic Stream* as I was anxious to sail with Captain Dixon.

The crew had been paid off and the apprentices sent away to their homes. As at Liverpool, my release from the ship was the last to come.

* * *

Once more I trod the streets of Dublin, finding there a pressing invitation from my two aunts to visit them in Tipperary.

My return to my homeland coincided with the intense wave of nationalism which was just then sweeping Ireland. In the streets men were putting up the Erse nameboards at the corners. All the bright young things were industriously and patriotically learning the Irish language, which was considered 'the thing'.

These were not the only signs of the changing heart of Ireland. That year that great social gathering, the annual Horse Show, promised to be more brilliant than ever. When my friends took me there on opening day, the flower of the equine and human world were collected in the spacious grounds.

The great crowd waited silent and expectant. An open carriage came swiftly past, drawn by four splendid, milk-white, postillioned horses. In it sat a little grey man and a much larger woman. To some they represented the sovereignty and the splendour of the King across the water; to many others their presence there was not so welcome or so pleasing.

As the band struck up 'God save the King', a little sibilant sound reached us, above the clamour of the music. It came from somewhere—and yet from nowhere—creeping through the hot summer air like the hiss of a snake. When the band stopped playing, it was some time before that unpleasant sound subsided.

The Lord-Lieutenant assisted his Lady to the ground, his set face betraying no sign of emotion. Up the carpeted steps they made their way to the Vice-regal box, accompanied by their aides-de-camp and lackeys and flunkeys. What were the thoughts that day inside the head of the little grey man? Foreboding must have been within his very heart as he took his seat to watch the brilliant pageant unfold before him.

*　*　*

My aunts met me at Roscrea station. Between the shafts of their handsome dog-cart fretted a fine mare. And then we were off, scattering the fluttering fowls of the village street until we reached the quiet country road. My aunts, both masterly horsewomen, urged the eager mare to her utmost; there was something strangely exhilarating in her swift passage along the peaceful rural road.

Those two aunts of mine were brave women, for they lived in a big, lonely house with only, at night, the help and faithful companionship of their cheery, good-hearted, jack-of-all-trades Irish maidservant.

Ireland had known unrest for many, many years, but a new and more dangerous and insidious unrest was creeping over that fair land; creeping furtively until it reached its climax in the tragic rebellion of Easter week in 1916.

This fact, of course, was not unnoticed by my aunts. But they refused to give up their home to seek the comparative safety of Dublin. The elder of the two complained bitterly to me that the attitude of the peasantry towards 'the gentry' had changed greatly, and that the latter were not now treated with the same respect and regard which had been theirs from time immemorial. On one occasion there was obvious proof of this. While out driving we came to a gate across the road.

An ill-clad labourer was standing nearby, watching sullenly, morosely, our approach. My aunt spoke to him, requesting him to open the gate. He completely ignored her, so that I jumped down to let us through. The good woman was deeply incensed. "Do you see that?" she asked me. "That is the New Ireland! Not so long ago that man would gladly have opened the gate and stood respectfully, cap in hand, while we passed through."

Clicking her tongue angrily at Gipsy, she urged the animal once more into its long, swift stride.

* * *

The spacious grounds of the house butted on to three counties. From the front door one of my aunts pointed out the junction of King's County, Queen's County, and Tipperary.

We had many lovely drives behind Gipsy, that spanking mare who graciously permitted me to see much of the country around. One such drive stands out as vividly as if it were but yesterday. It was a bright, clear, sunny day, a spice of keenness in the air, for the summer was already spent. It may be that this particular drive remains so clearly in my mind because it was the occasion of a most unfortunate *faux pas* committed by me.

The mare was travelling fast, with a moderate wind which headed us, giving my elder aunt an exaggerated idea of its strength. Turning to me she remarked: "I suppose at sea you would say there's half a gale blowing."

Then came that dreadful *faux pas* which led to my hot, embarrassed discomfiture a moment later. "Oh, no," I said, "there's really very little wind. Gipsy is making the most of it as she goes along."

Believe it or not, Gipsy, saucy jade, must have heard me. Raising her tail jauntily at that precise moment, she gave vent to her feelings, loudly and longly—*a tergo*!

My aunt turned to me disapprovingly; I could imagine on her lips the words: "Is this some crude, vulgar sailor's joke?" Crimsoned to the ears, I turned away from her, unable to meet that stern gaze. And then she removed the whip from its socket to give the mare an admonishing cut, an indignity which the horse was rarely forced to suffer.

The wind whistled more shrilly in our ears, but an unhappy silence fell between us for a while . . . .

* * *

The summons to end my holiday had reached me. Leaving those two brave, lonely women, I went back to Dublin. The owners had agreed to my transfer to the *Arctic Stream*. She was loading at Cardiff—'black diamonds' for Bahia in Brazil.

My new ship was under the coal tips when an ancient, foul-smelling growler took me down to the docks. As the coal thundered into the hold, the dust rose all around like a black, impenetrable fog. A fine-looking elderly man met me at the gangway. His kindly eyes, from which he kept wiping the dust with a filthy handkerchief, gazed at me grotesquely from his blackened face.

"You're the boy from the *Elginshire?*" he inquired. "I'm the mate. Get into your working clothes and give them a hand aloft."

In ten minutes my crumpled dungarees had been dragged from the sea-bag, and I was aloft on the main t'gallant yard. Three or four boys were gathered there with a rather immature A.B., bending the sail.

My feet had scarcely set upon the footrope when it became plain to me that there was something wrong with that t'gans'l. Rather, there was nothing wrong with the sail, but there was something decidedly wrong about the manner in which it was being bent. For it was being stretched along the jackstay *back to front*, to use an un-nautical term. My new shipmates took it all in good part when this was pointed out. The job was soon completed, and we made our way down the rigging for our supper.

And then I received the shock of my young life. The coal tips had ceased their thunder, the black fog of dust had cleared. And on the poop, taking the evening air as he paced fore and aft, marched the figure of a man I had no wish to see there—the grizzled mate of the *Elginshire,* puffing at a long cigar.

"What's that old so-and-so doing there?" I asked one of the others.

"He's been promoted here," he replied, "and Dixon has gone to the *Elginshire.*"

It had never occurred to me that Dixon would leave the ship he loved and had sailed so successfully for so long. My feelings were indescribable; I felt like kicking myself good and hard. But it was too late to do anything about it.

*   *   *

The ship hauled out to the moorings in the dock. A dinghy was lowered to establish contact between ship and quay. After work I sculled many times around the ship, admiring her from every angle. With her smart painted ports and gracefully-raked masts she looked indeed a queen.

She was a beautiful, yacht-like vessel, built in 1885 in the semi-clipper era before the inexorable competition of steam had forced the British ship owner to produce the boxlike, heavy carrier of the last days of sail. This is what Basil Lubbock has to say about her: "She was a most beautifully proportioned vessel. I am certain not one of Russell's many 1885-built vessels excelled the *Arctic Stream* for model, looks or speed. She was undoubtedly one of the finest models ever built by Russell & Co. . . ."

The crew straggled aboard one evening in the usual drunken manner of sailors bound for the sea. I was standing idly around (for the day's work was over) when the first arrived. He was truly a strange figure, clad only in shirt and trousers, in spite of the chill of the autumn evening. He was hatless, and his dome-shaped head entirely innocent of hair but for a little patch over each ear. One hand held a large, bulging, red-spotted handkerchief which apparently held all his worldly possessions. The other was continually occupied in tricing up his braces to the apex of his narrow, bottle shoulders—a curious little habit which kept him permanently wriggling himself.

Wishing to find out what capacity he filled, I came from the overhang of the poop and hailed him: "Who are you, old man?" I called out. Putting down his bundle on the deck, he came unsteadily towards me. I saw that his hands were curled up with half a century's hauling on ropes, for he must have been long past sixty. Before he had reached me, the strong, unmistakable stench of rum tickled my nostrils. "Who are you?" I asked again, putting out a hand to steady him.

Carefully spreading his feet, keeping up the continuous swaying and hitching up of his braces, he raised a pair of faded blue eyes. In them I saw a look of drink-sodden incredulity as he asked: "Sonny, do you mean to say you don't know who I am?"

He was obviously injured; having learned that it is often unwise to hurt the feelings of a drunken man, I expressed my regret but, honestly, I didn't know him from Adam.

"All right, sonny," he went on. "Come here and I'll tell you who I am." Drawing me behind the scanty shelter of the mizen mast, he fumbled in one of his trouser pockets, produced a bottle, and demanded that we should drink each other's health. Tilting the bottle, I mouthed a thimbleful of the liquor, after which he threw back his head and drained the remainder, the fiery, undiluted stuff bringing tears to his bloodshot eyes.

"Now, young man, I'm going to tell you who I am. You can't have been at sea long or you'd know all about me. I'm Old Sails, and for nearly fifty years, boy and man, I've been making the white wings for ships like this, aye, and finer ones too, long ago when them things were considered a joke."

He pointed scornfully across the dock to a steamer, spitting vigorously on the deck at the same time, as though the sight of her was too much for his stomach.

*   *   *

I was busy on the poop in the early morning, filling with a bucket the captain's w.c. tank. (How we used to anathematise that lavatory! Its thirst was insatiable. Many a time we called callously on heaven to afflict our skipper with chronic constipation!)

A hail reached me from the quayside. A well dressed man was standing there, smartly clad in neat blue suit, hard hat, and carrying a neatly folded paper in his hand. He looked the typical owner's marine superintendent, or perhaps even the owner himself. Hastening to bring such an important person aboard, I hurriedly unhitched the dinghy and sculled to the quayside. On reaching the gangway he said, "Thank you, boy." And then, as he passed aboard, he leant over and remarked quietly: "By the way, I'm the Cook." Slushy the cook! And I had made my obeisance to him as though he were the owner himself.

Later I was to learn that, in spite of his gentlemanly appearance and advanced age, that cook was one of the most libidinous individuals it has been my lot to sail with. It was my misfortune to be forced to spend my off-duty and sleeping hours in a tiny six-by-seven foot box of a room with him while our ship wandered the world.

*   *   *

The *Arctic Stream*, instead of the *Elginshire's* unlucky thirteen, carried seven apprentices, the senior one acting as third mate. All were berthed in a deck-house abaft the fore-mast—a wet spot in any ship. My home was in the cubby-hole on the starboard side which I shared with the cook. A similar little room on the port side housed Old Sails. This he had to himself, the carpenter preferring to live in his workshop at the fore-end of the deck-house. The partition between Old Sail's room and mine was of thin planking; often he sang, for he was a cheery soul. Many a time my slumbers were disturbed by his voice, singing loudly some catchy ditty of many years ago.

*　　*　　*

At last the ship hauled out of the dock. In the outer lock she remained for a few minutes. As was the case on so many similar occasions, it was a grey drizzling day. A small cluster of depressed men and women, bedraggled in the chilly rain, had gathered to see us off. Our morose, half-muzzy crew were in no mood for pleasantries, and took little or no notice of their attempts at jocularity.

Two other square-riggers hauled out on the same tide—the *Marthe II* and the fine, full-rigged ship *Largiemore,* British until the previous year but now flying the Norwegian flag.

Practically all the clearing up and sail making, after the tug dropped us, fell to the mates and apprentices. For the men were still drink-besotted and unfit for work aloft. When all sail was set, we had been on our feet for almost twenty-four hours.

It took a week to rid the ship of her greasy coating of Welsh coal dust, and even longer to limber up the blocks of the running rigging, clogged and stiff from the inactivity of a lengthy spell in port. Our skipper was lucky in getting a fine slant which carried him far towards the north-east trades. He was greatly elated, pacing the poop as he everlastingly smoked the long, rank cigars which he apparently considered the insignia of his new high office. He had a smart ship under him, he was in command once more, and would soon show them what he could do.

My first two hours at the wheel convinced me that my new ship was easy to steer and a much faster sailer than the other. Doing nine or ten knots, she made far less fuss than the *Elginshire*, and in light airs had an uncanny way of 'ghosting along' which was quite unknown to the bigger vessel.

We had not proceeded far, however, before I bitterly regretted my transfer. The mate, to make matters worse, continually sang the praises of Captain Dixon. The third mate, who had been three years in the ship, told us newcomers sinister tales of the main deck filled up with heavy water every time she ran into bad weather.

That came later; many a time our deck-house echoed the onslaught of solid seas thundering over it. The iron door of the tiny domain of the cook and myself had been warped by such a sea; the chilly ocean often came pouring in around its ill-fitting edges.

* * *

Our crew included a number of Irishmen—some from Queenstown, some from Youghal. There was incessant rivalry between these two factions, and sometimes such forceful argument that heavy blows were struck. Amongst the lot there were but two foreigners—two 'dagoes' who, in spite of their cut-throat appearance, were the most docile men aboard.

The Greek carpenter, a shaggy, unkempt bear of a man, had a heart of gold inside the grubby shirt which covered his great, broad chest. The Turk, a tall thin man, possessed a tremendous hooked nose of which any Jew would have been proud. 'Chips' had a comical habit, when addressed, of looking at you, one puzzled eyebrow elevated, while he remarked enquiringly: "What-ee you?" This came from his lips repeatedly throughout the day, but nobody ever really succeeded in finding out what was meant by him.

This lack of English was not quite so pronounced in the case of the Turk. Wishing, no doubt, to improve his knowledge of the language, he was the first to repeat each order given by the mate. "Haul aft the main sheet!" the mate would roar. "Haul aft the men shet, Sir!" would answer dutifully the Terrible Turk who was not so terrible at all.

These two men, whose countries were locked in deadly warfare at the time, frequently held long and heated arguments in the carpenter's shop, using the mediums of Greek and Italian to press their points. Chips would often become so excited that nothing but English suited his needs. With flashing eyes he would finally shout: "Greekie man go BOOM! Turcoman all finish!"

As though to emphasise the total annihilation of the Turkish forces, he would lean down, distend his cheeks to their utmost—and blow vigorously the accumulated chips from his work-bench.

* * *

A number of windjammers were sighted that passage, for sail was not entirely dead. Two days out, on a grey, boisterous afternoon, a glimpse had been caught of the *Largiemore*. It was blowing hard and she was under a press of canvas, plunging and rolling with an immense grandeur in the high sea.

Some others were passed and then, when the nor'east trades had petered out, we found ourselves in close company with half a dozen sailing vessels. It is truly amazing how a protracted calm or persistent head winds will bunch ships together on the wide ocean. For a number of days we drifted about in the Doldrums. The huge British four-masted barque *Balasore* was close to us, with two of A. D. Bordes' four-masters not far from her. Several other three-masters loitered about, taking advantage, like ourselves, of every fitful breath of wind.

We were nearly ten days in that tiresome region. That tardy period completely spoilt our passage, and the skipper knew no record would be his. At last the south-east trades gripped us in their friendly clasp; we romped away for Bahia.

At dawn on the thirty-sixth day out we sighted the coast of Brazil, a low, sandy shore with picturesque palms waving on the yellow sand. Dozens of crazy-looking catamarans sailed about, manned by negro fishermen. They seemed frail craft indeed in which to venture so far off shore. All day we skirted the land, arriving off San Antonio lighthouse at 3 p.m. To our disappointment, the captain, apparently nervous at the close approach to his port, decided it would be rash to attempt to make the bay after dark with a falling, on-shore wind. The ship was consequently braced sharp-up, and stood slowly off the land.

Before daylight we headed in for the coast again. Later the lighthouse was passed, and the ship entered the beautiful Reconcavo, or gulf which stretches for miles inland. The master was moving about the poop in great excitement, for no pilot had come off and no pilot-boat was to be seen on its customary station.

We dropped anchor off Fort do Mar, not far from the full-rigged ship *Malete,* which flew the green flag of Brazil. While we were aloft stowing sail a steam-launch came alongside towing a smart cutter, in which sat a number of white-clad sailors and several extravagantly-brassbound officials.

The mate sent me into the saloon on some errand an hour later. The two officials were arguing hotly with the Old Man, who had gone so far in his attempt to pacify them as to draw the cork of one of his precious bottles of Scotch. This unprecedented

generosity had apparently not had the desired effect. It turned out
that we had anchored in a prohibited area. Next day, under easy
canvas, we moved further in, coming to rest near two barques,
one of which was the Britisher *Conway Castle.*

Ashore, and on the coasting vessels, flew the unfamiliar flag
of Brazil.   On its green field, around the twirling orb of the
world, was emblazoned the somewhat grandiloquent caption:
"Ordem e progresso". We had not been long in port before we
decided that caption should read: "Mañana e mas tardi". The
procrastinative nature of these people was soon obvious to us all.

*   *   *

Bahia is situated on a lovely inland sea, behind the further
shores of which lies a hinterland of wonderful fertility. The trade
of this great gulf was, at the time of my visit, carried on by a fleet
of fast sailing craft. A curious feature of these vessels which I have
never seen elsewhere was an entire absence of stays or shrouds on
the masts. With their unsupported masts bending whiplike under
the pressure of their big sails, they raced busily over the sun-
kissed water. All these craft loaded and discharged their freight
at the Praya, a dirty stone quay which stretched along the bay
for a distance of four miles. It was at this busy place that we put
ashore our skipper every morning after breakfast.

I was fortunate enough to be chosen for one of the boat boys
during our stay at Bahia. Two of the other three were fine hefty
lads from the Thames training-ship *Worcester.*   They were a
pleasant contrast to the rather uppish youngsters from the
Liverpool training-ship whom we had in the *Elginshire,* for they
suffered from no superiority complex such as is affected by some
of these boys.

In clean shirts and well-washed dungarees the four of us rowed
the captain to the landing place a number of times every day.
Usually he dismissed us there with a curt order to return
to the ship. This always meant the donning again of our dirty
working clothes for some hours' toil on our filthy cargo, until it
was time for us to bring the skipper aboard for his dinner.

There were times when he told us to await at the quayside his
return. One such day we waited for hours, watching the colourful,
somewhat smelly scene around us. Every shade of colour was
represented there—for the population of Brazil varies from jet-
black to a sort of dingy white.

Some hours passed, it was long past dinner time, and our Captain had not come. Growing a little anxious, two of us set out to find him. Our search led us unsuccessfully around the town. And then, noticing a small crowd collected at the door of a church, we made our way hurriedly in that direction. The vague fears which had entered our minds were well founded.

Pushing through the noisy throng, we peered within the church. And there, with feet well spread, swaying as though he rode the poop of his ship in a heavy seaway, stood our worthy lord and master. His seedy hat sat well back upon his grizzled head, between his lips was clutched the inevitable cheap cigar, its fumes rising like some foul incense towards those sacred rafters.

Two or three habit-clad ecclesiastics angrily remonstrated with him. So far as we could gather, our timely arrival had saved the skipper by the skin of his teeth from lynching, pole-axing, or whatever dire fate the Brazilians reserve for such flagrant irreverence. Shepherding him through the angry crowd, we led our well-oiled captain down to the boat.

* * *

The ship lay nearly six weeks at Bahia, the crew grudgingly shovelling the cargo, as was the windjammer custom at the time. The delay, however, was not entirely theirs. No tug being available, the big lighters were sailed to and from the ship. When the wind failed they were propelled by long sweeps, a tedious process when the lighters were deeply loaded on their shoreward way.

Bahia is an interesting old Portuguese city. From the Praya, or waterfront, it rises steeply 250 feet to the upper town. This cliff is vivid with the greenery of exotic tropical plants; waving palms fill the spaces between the stone houses perched on the cliff. On a number of occasions while awaiting the captain's often tardy return, I scaled tiresomely the many flights of stone steps to the summit. From that height the *Arctic Stream* resembled a little fairy, toylike ship far out on the rippling water.

Our deep sea warriors were allowed a day's leave, one watch at a time. We rowed them ashore in the early morning, happy in their anticipation of a few hours' freedom from the restrictions of the ship.

They went ashore laughing, singing happily; they returned

inflamed by the white rum which was so absurdly cheap in Bahia. Fighting drunk, some with blackened eyes and cut faces, they were rowed off in the evening. Every one had acquired at the Praya for a few pence a green Brazilian parrot. The boat that night resembled a weird madhouse, the sailors arguing and fighting angrily, the parrots screeching their alarm.

Once aboard, the parrots were tethered with ropeyarns to belaying pins or any other convenient anchor. And then the men turned their attention to the settlement of long-smouldering feuds, their minds poisoned by the quantity of crude liquor they had drunk. Pandemonium broke loose on the fore deck; so alarmed became the parrots by the uproar that they soon parted their insecure bonds and flew overboard, though their wings had been partially clipped.

In the dusk we boys manned the boat to rescue those poor birds struggling in the water. Most of them were drowned before they could be reached.

* * *

In spite of a grim rumour that an apprentice from a British sailing ship had recently had one of his legs bitten off by a shark, we bathed regularly from the ship. One day I swam alone about half a mile to a schooner anchored up the bay. Arriving aboard there rather tired, I found myself amongst a convivial party busily drinking the potent white cane spirit of Brazil. They forced their hospitality on the young *marinero ingles* who had come out of the sea. Not realising how powerful was that spirit, I swallowed more than was good for me, plunged over the side, and struck out for the ship.

Before getting half-way I was completely befuddled, and became the victim of all sorts of fears. Thoughts of the boy who had lost his leg filled my mind fearfully; then came the idea that I would tire and drown before reaching the ship. Every shadow on the water became an enormous shark making for me and, though there was nobody to help me had help been needed, it was only with the greatest effort that I refrained from crying out.

Eventually I climbed on to the gangway, actually more frightened than tired, cursing those Brazilians for their ill-timed hospitality and myself for having accepted it so lavishly. Had my father been there he would have shaken his head sadly and said: "The curse of drink! I warned you, my son."

One afternoon a large turtle was captured from the boat. When it was handed over to the cook, all hands looked forward to a delicious change from the cheap, stringy meat which was issued to us. Everybody was bitterly disappointed, for the preparation of that savoury flesh was entirely beyond whatever poor culinary art Old Slushy possessed. He served up to us a hideous mess of what looked like chunks of evil-smelling india-rubber floating in a greasy, green liquor. Few of us could eat it; for days after, in spite of many washings, that terrible stink clung persistently to my enamelled plate and knife and fork.

The port in which we lay is called in full *Bahia dos todos Santos* —the Bay of all Saints, a name which the people there delight to live up to. Nearly every day brought the celebration of some saint or other. Crackers banged ashore, squibs fizzed fussily, and rockets soared to the sky.

All South Americans, east and west, dearly love fireworks, and one hears them continually popping off. Curiously enough, the hours of daylight are considered quite as suitable as those of darkness for a firework display.

* * *

At length all our coal had been discharged, its place being taken by three mounds—seven or eight hundred tons—of very wet sand, for we were to sail in ballast.

No tug was available, but we were soon passing down the bay under easy canvas. The gloomy Fort do Mar drew abeam, the sunlit waters of the beautiful Reconcavo lay astern. The town drowsed lazily on its cliff, amidst its wealth of tropic greenery. None of us were sorry to leave, for amongst those waving palms, in the heart of all that luxuriant verdure, along the smelly Praya, it seemed to us there lurked the evil seeds of Yellow Jack.

The ship passed San Antonio. Before her lay the sea, the clean, wholesome open sea—the great, broad highway which was to take her to Australia, to Cape Borda for orders.

We had not proceeded far, sailing close-hauled all the time, before we found that a great deal of our sand ballast consisted of water. This, of course, gradually drained into the lee bilges, leaving the ship dangerously under-ballasted. Many a fine sailing vessel has been lost by capsizing through this cause.

The pumps were manned, and we toilfully drew off the water.

Then the wash-deck tub was rigged and hundreds of buckets of seawater thrown down the hatches on the slowly drying piles of sand. This process was repeated over and over again, particularly during the warmer weather.

Soon after leaving Cardiff it had been decided by the crew that the Old Man was no sail carrier. He had a fine, smart ship under him, and a bunch of men and boys in no way inferior to the majority of latter-day sailing ship crews. Yet somehow our ship was never given her head. Often, like some restive, sensitive animal, she fretted under the curb when he would not let her go.

With the Cape of Good Hope 350 miles to the northward, the great windblown Southern Ocean lay ahead of us. Here was the sailing ship's own domain, that vast stretch of stormy sea where most of the record passages of sail had been won. We of fo'c'sle and half-deck hoped that now had come our smart ship's chance of showing her paces.

The list of the daily runs of that passage before me, I search in vain for any outstanding run from noon to noon. 294 miles is the best that my search reveals. Our wary skipper never ventured further south than 42½ degrees although summer lay over the southern ocean. In spite of advancing years our ship could have been driven—for there was wind enough, even on the fringe of the Roaring Forties.

There were times, usually before daylight had faded from the dull, grey sky, when the unexpected order rang along the deck: "Lower away fore and mizen tops'ls!"

Some of the older hands who had served in ships which had been *sailed* would gaze quizzingly at sea and sky, in which they read no immediate menace or enmity. Then, before tackling the job in hand, one of them would turn to his fellows to remark sagely and sourly: "Is that old bastard aft there going to *sail* this ship to Australia—or *drift* her there?"

It became a standing joke amongst the crew that our Old Man was determined to polish the topmasts with the parrels by repeated lowering and hoisting of the topsail yards.

There were, of course, occasions when the boldest of skippers would have been forced to shorten sail. One such evening we had stowed the fore and mizen upper topsails, and were busy furling the main, swinging on the footropes in the wind-filled, rain-laden

THE FINGER SPAR OF THE JIB-BOOM, POINTING THE WAY AHEAD

Penso

STORMING ALONG WITH A BONE IN HER TEETH

Penso

dusk when a big east-bound steamer appeared close to our port beam. Under lower topsails and foresail, we were running fast as the steamer drew alongside, her overhaul of our fleet ship almost imperceptible. Her passengers lined the rail, gazing across at the windjammer flying to the eastward.

We, too, had ample time to regard the other vessel as she crawled past us, our lofty vantage point giving us a magnificent view of the plunging, rolling steamer. Already her decks glowed with many cheery, shining lights; rows of gleaming ports lit up the angry, windtorn water between the two ships.

As we clawed at the No. O canvas, pounding far over the yard my neighbour on the footrope turned to me. "Look at that," he said. "Look at the comfort there; nice hot food; dry clothes; the company of laughing girls . . . Why the hell did we come to this?"

That plunging, rolling steamer nearly cost me my life that grey evening. As I tugged at the gasket, the slack unnoticed under the over-riding turn, the line suddenly loosened and threw me back from the yard. Had the Turk not noticed my predicament and acted quickly I should have fallen to the hard deck below or to the angry waiting sea which foamed around the ship. Grabbing my arm and exerting all his strength, he hauled me back to the safety of the jackstay. . .

The steamer gradually drew ahead. When night had fallen, she faded into the darkling east, her bobbing stern light dimmed by spray and spindrift as it winked disdainfully at us while we made our way down from aloft.

*   *   *

It was during this passage that I came to see my room-mate, the elderly cook, in his true perspective. His mind was dominated by two obsessions—reading and women. Seeing that, far out on the infinity of the lonely ocean, women were a thing apart and totally unobtainable, he devoted all his leisure to reading. From this statement it might be imagined that he studied and gained inspiration from the classics. Nothing could be further from the truth. What he termed reading was actually the rapid, superficial absorption, through the bulging lenses of his glasses, of a mass of trashy rubbish which was avidly devoured by him throughout the day.

His arrival aboard at Cardiff has been described earlier in this

M

book. It was not mentioned, however, that his baggage had included two heavy, brown-paper parcels which had seemed at first to contain tracts. When those parcels were opened they disclosed not tracts but literally scores of 'Pansy', 'Violet', and other florally named penny paper-backed novelettes.

You know the kind of thing. The silly tripe beloved of sex-starved and love-lorn nursemaids. There was usually an illustration on the cover depicting the hero, with sharply-pointed, waxed moustache and 3-inch choker threatening to strangle him, making rather aggressive love to the heroine, wide-eyed, wasp-waisted, and more than a little alarmed at the hero's impetuosity.

One could perhaps understand tender and inexperienced nurse-maids finding in such stories some amatory titillation, but it was little less than ludicrous to see Old Slushy poring with the utmost concentration over those penny rags. With his beloved, richly-coloured meerschaum bowl-in-claw pipe jutting from under his shaggy, discoloured grey moustache, he spent all his spare time steadily demolishing that immense pile of paper-backs.

In fine weather he sat on a box outside the galley door, oblivious of the beautiful white sails aloft and the endless vista of blue sea around. When it was cold and wet he remained inside his little overheated domain, sitting before the glowing stove on which bubbled the big pots of salt pork or salt 'horse'.

At night he turned in early, for he had to rise just after four every morning. No lights were permitted after one bell—8.30 p.m. —so that he was unable to read in his bunk, turning, instead, his attention to his other absorbing hobby—women.

He was well on the way to sixty; he had wooed and won and sailed away in every seaport in the world. His fund of experience was consequently inexhaustible; the recounting of his amorous adventures covered that long voyage of ours round the world. And when we had finally docked at Leith it was by no means completed.

On alternate nights it was my watch below from 8 p.m. to midnight. That was the cook's golden opportunity to pin me down. My entry into the little dog-hole we shared would be hailed hilariously and with good-natured obscenity. The picture became so clearly etched upon my mind that it lives to this day, undimmed by the long passage of the years. . . .

Slushy is already in his bunk—the lower one—his greasy head upon the dirty pillow. He is clad in what he always refers to as his "panjamas", for he does not turn in carelessly in his soiled underclothing like those grubby sailors for'ard. Over the edge of his bunk projects the bowl of his cherished pipe; the little place reeks of the pungent fumes of 'Fair Maid' plug. Hastily throwing off coat and trousers, I climb into the upper berth, settling down on the comfortless thin straw mattress which scarcely covers the hard bunk boards. . . .

The dim smoky oil-lamp has been extinguished, and the tiny room is in darkness, except for the recurring glow of my companion's pipe.

The ship is sailing fast in the dark night, a hundred and one little sounds accompanying her swift passage through the water. There is, however, no throb and jar, no whirr and vibration from an engine-room's machinery. Far up aloft every sail is doing its work, silently but for the fairy song of the wind on distended canvas.

The truss of the foreyard, almost directly overhead, groans slightly as the ship rolls easily; the thin planking of the inner walls of the room creaks and squeaks faintly; the bowl of the cook's pipe gurgles softly as the glow of the tobacco grows and fades. . . .

I am hoping to edge off to sleep—for the call to go on deck again will come all too soon—before some fresh encounter with the fair sex flits into the memory of the man below.

And then his voice breaks the quietness . . . . "Did I tell you about that judy in South Shields . . . I must tell you about her, sonny, before you go to sleep. . . . She was a looker, she was, and the finest figure, stripped or dressed, I've ever seen on any girl. . . . "

His words have become an indistinct murmur in my ears . . . . and Morpheus has claimed me before I have even heard the name of that fascinating 'judy' . . . .

It was perhaps a pity that sleep in my young life of those days was a far greater urgency than women. Had it not been so, no doubt that grizzled Lothario would have imparted to me some, at least, of the irresistible technique which had apparently, from his own account, been so successful during his long women-raddled career.

* * *

On the fifty-seventh day out from Bahia we sighted Kangaroo Island. It was, however, too late to communicate with the shore. The only morse lamp the ship possessed, a crude, oil-burning contraption with a heavy awkward shutter, was useless for signalling beyond a ship's length. The night must pass before we could learn our loading port. The main yard was backed; under shortened canvas the ship lay hove-to throughout the hours of darkness.

Shortly before daylight came again, we stood in for Cape Borda. All the hopes, the anticipation, of the passage were crowded into the next hour or two. In the clear morning light the bare shaft of the lighthouse showed up the flagstaff nearby. Already our ensign and numbers stood out boldly in the breeze.

Any square-rigged man who reads these words will understand the excitement which prevailed aboard. Our future, for many months at least, rested not on the throw of the dice but on four little splashes of colour which would presently rise on that staff ashore.

The watch on deck, keyed up as they waited for the verdict, stood handy on the afterdeck; the watch below, half clad, lined the rail for'ad on the shoreward side. Would it be Sydney, or some other grain port—to load for home; or would it be Newcastle, thus condemning us all to the endless toil and monotony of the West Coast of South America?

On the poop the Old Man had the open signal book before him. The mate stood by, long glass in hand, while we youngsters already fingered the signal halliards. There was silence but for the soft purling of the ship's passage through the water. As we waited there the words of the poet came to me:

> *"Where lies the land to which the ship would go?*
> *Far, far ahead, is all the seamen know.*
> *And where the land she travels from? Away,*
> *Far, far behind, is all that they can say."*

Already we knew the one and only signal we wished to see hoisted ashore—ASKB, SYDNEY—learned by a furtive glance at the International Code the previous day while master and mate were at dinner.

The ship swung to the east a little, to display fully her numbers to those watchers ashore. To them, who had seen so many fine ships pass by, white sails crowding, it was a common occurrence to sight another standing close in to receive orders for her loading port. They could not have known how impatiently we awaited our fate—how futilely we damned their tardy handling of the hoists.

The answering pennant fluttered aloft on the white staff ashore, informing us our name had been received.

A 'geographical' signal was slowly crawling up, replacing the pennant which had been hauled down. The mate stiffened while he steadied the powerful glass against the mizen royal backstay. As the flags flew out from the hands of the men ashore he called out: "A . . . . S . . . ." There was a slight delay while the third flag of the hoist was cleared. We all waited in suspense. Would the next two flags be KB? The mate's eye had not left the telescope for a second. Presently the complete signal soared out clearly— ASML. It was repeated by the Old Man, "ASML . . . ASML . . . Newcastle, New South Wales!"

There was a groan from the young third mate. "Hell!" he muttered, "another cargo of coal—and then that damned West Coast!"

The news spread rapidly for'ad; the half-clad watch below disappeared grumblingly into the fo'c'sle. Even the master and mate could not disguise their disappointment. Snapping the big book shut, the Old Man turned to the mate. "That's that, mister," he said. "Set the royals."

The mate sprang into activity, roaring at us, "Up aloft and loose the royals, you boys! Stand by fore royal halliards, you men!"

Under all sail the ship gathered speed to the south-east, the shattered hopes of those aboard showing clearly in the continuous muttered curses of the men as they went about their work. The only one in all that crew to whom it seemed a matter of indifference was Old Sails. All trails were the same to that cheery sea vagabond. No home ties were his, the ocean his happy hunting ground. What cared he when or where the ship made port? His wild yodelling cry put fresh heart into the crowd as we mast-headed and stretched those royals. . . . .

Fourteen days later, for, with the exception of one day's run of 263 miles in Bass Strait, our rounding of the coast had been tardy, at five in the morning we sighted Nobby Head light. The previous night, soon after eleven p.m., the lights of Sydney had beckoned mockingly to us. Close abeam, that great friendly glare in the western sky had filled me with a futile yearning. Part of my watch below was foolishly wasted as I gazed longingly but impotently at the dim outline of those rugged heads which passed so swiftly by.

A tug picked us up without delay. While we towed in the masts of a fleet of sail could be seen above the low shore. At 8.30 a.m. the anchor was dropped in the Hunter River.

CHAPTER XII

NEWCASTLE, N.S.W.—FOR W.C.S.A.

MANY a time had I read, in the tiny print of Lloyd's Weekly List of shipping, the name of some well-known sailing vessel with the above terse addition to that name. Now I was about to realise fully the meaning of those letters.

The Australian Newcastle, like its namesake in England, had for a number of years been engaged principally in the export of coal. The number of windjammers transporting British 'black diamonds' along the stormy sea trail around the Horn was dwindling. But this humble yet so important cargo, at one time despised by the better class ships, did much to delay the banishment of white sails from the blue rim of the horizon.

The long west coast of South America, stretching from the equator right down to the distant southern latitudes of the 'Furious Fifties', had great need of this commodity. Newcastle, New South Wales, was the nearest source of supply for Peru and Chili, offering to the east-bound ships a passage where strong favourable winds could be relied on.

So it was this trade remained in the hands of windjammers to the last, scorned for the time being by the lordly steamship employed on more lucrative business on the high seas. It was one of the crumbs of commerce which fell from the rich man's table of the steamers.

* * *

We found in that port on the Hunter River a hospitality and friendliness in no way inferior to that of Sydney and Fremantle. At first, as is usual, the Mission to Seamen was the hub of our after-work universe. There the padre, Mr. Hare, assisted by his good wife and their charming young daughter, took the sailing ship apprentices under their wing. The daughter of 16 was undoubtedly a great attraction. She must have been admired and probably ogled by hundreds of youngsters who passed through the port.

Many evenings were spent under the banner of the Flying Angel. Concerts were organised, and the talent of the various ships encouraged to perform. Few of the men went there, preferring the pubs while their money lasted. One night Old Sails was prevailed upon to mount the stage. With comical face contortions and his customary wriggling of shoulders, this whimsical old fellow sang several songs. A perspiring pianist attempted vainly to accompany him, eventually being forced to give up the hopeless task. Nevertheless, Old Sail's turn was literally a howling success which brought down the house.

Our ship had been moved to 'Siberia', on the Stockton side of the river, to discharge her ballast. For years many thousands of tons of foreign soil from distant lands had been dumped there. We, too, gave our small contribution of Brazil to swell the already over large continent of Australia.

Our wheezy steam donkey hoisted the baskets of sand from the hold. Each basket was lowered on to a small trolley pulled by a horse which drew its load along lines leading inland to the dumping ground. All the work was, of course, done by the crew, even the navigation of the horse. Tommy Wallis, one of the younger apprentices, was detailed for this important part of the work. His knowledge of the ways of horses being absolutely nil, his antics to control the wayward movements of that nag kept those of us on deck in roars of laughter.

Every evening saw us making our way past the packed sailing vessels along the river bank to the Stockton ferry. I, like the others, imagined there was nothing to do at Stockton until I was more or less adopted by a family there—and thus met Molly.

On our walk to the ferry we had often noticed a stout, motherly woman sitting with a girl on the verandah of one of the houses. Then came one evening when some delay kept me aboard after the others had left the ship. As I passed her house alone, this woman spoke to me, inviting me on to the verandah. After introducing me to her daughter Molly, she asked me about my ship, showing, like all those good Australians whose forebears had come from over the water, a lively interest in ships and the sea life.

That was the first of many visits at that house. Faithless me, the Flying Angel was soon forgotten, yes, even the fair Miss Hare. For Molly was a happy young lady of 18 with that easy, inborn friendliness characteristic of the Australian girl. We had many walks together in the evenings, and her people gave me the freedom of their house.

One evening stands out very clearly in my mind. Molly and I were sitting on the verandah overlooking the river. The moon, hanging low as yet in the eastern sky, silvered brilliantly the sleeping water and showed up vividly the lofty spars of the many ships in harbour.

We were talking quietly about those brave old square-riggers; about the sad day not far distant when they would be driven off the seas. And then, almost noiselessly another such ship crept in behind her tug, fresh from the open, windblown sea. It was the big British four-masted barque *Crocodile*. Her anchor rattled down and the vessel came to rest in the river.

Presently we saw the little, dark shapes of her hands climbing the rigging to harbour-stow the canvas, hanging in its gear. On the foreyard they lay out along the footropes. To us came the musical voice of the leading chantyman singing the solo part of a fine old chanty.

The splendid voice of the soloist finished; the great, swelling chorus swept to us across the silent water. There was something indescribably beautiful about the scene before us; something so indefinably moving in that harmonious song that I was constrained to turn my head to kiss that not unwilling girl beside me.

The anti-climax came suddenly, shatteringly. From somewhere behind us overhead, giggles and derisive little cries reached our ears. A row of small faces peered down at us over the end wall of the verandah.

"We'll tell Mother you kissed our Molly! We'll tell Mother you kissed our Molly!" those shrill voices chanted together.

Presently they climbed down from their perch, came around to us, and loudly demanded from me the price of their silence. All Molly's little brothers and sisters were there—and their parents were a fairly prolific pair. Those kids made a combined raid on my pockets, drawing from them all the small change they could find with which to buy 'lollies'. That determined plundering made a big inroad into my weekly income of five shillings. But without probing unduly into the subject of relative values—I decided the kiss was worth the cost.

* * *

We were still lying at Siberia when disaster almost overtook the ship.

The process of discharging ballast had been slow. Our steam donkey, under the willing but somewhat bewildered care of the Greek carpenter, frequently refused duty. That Aussie mustang, too, gave Wally considerable trouble, persisting in going astern when he particularly wanted it to go ahead.

At length, however, the margin of safety, and scarcely that, had been reached. The ship rode gaunt and high in the muddy water of the river, just sufficient ballast remaining in the hold to keep her upright. She was now ready to receive her 'stiffening' of coal before the last of the Brazilian sand was taken from her.

That night I woke suddenly to find pandemonium let loose about us. It was pitch dark in that little room, but I knew the ship was lying over steeply, with the wind roaring and tearing at her murderously.

In the inky darkness the cook was calling out in fear while he fumbled at the door. At first for a moment I thought we were at sea again, for the mate was on deck with shrilling whistle, bawling out "All hands on deck!", a call one does not usually expect to hear in port.

Clad only in pyjamas, for there was no time to dress, Slushy and I pushed open the heavy iron door against the incline of the ship. Up aloft, in the rigging and amongst the naked spars, the wind was howling and wailing like a host of banshees hotly pursued by a pack of ravening werewolves. Rain beat down upon us like a solid wall of water.

The mate was on the fo'c'sle head with those already out on deck. Every mooring line had parted, fore and aft, the ship being held solely by the big, heavy 'preventer' wire we had put ashore each end. (When this had been done one or two of the sea-lawyers had grumbled, "What the hell's this for? Are we going to stop here a year?")

There wasn't a moment to lose. Thrusting the end of a heaving line in my hand the mate shouted at me, above the infernal din, "Get ashore down that wire—QUICK!"

The ship was lying away from the dolphins which had held her off the river bank, lying over so far towards the river that the gangway had slipped from the shore. Grasping the wire, I started my perilous journey to the bank. That long wire was tautened like a bar of steel. With the strain of the leaning ship on it even the additional weight of my body might be enough to part it at any moment. Should that happen, the ship would capsize into the river in a few seconds.

The wind tore at me, the bitter cold rain plastered my thin pyjamas to my skin, but eventually the bollard was reached. Quickly I pulled the end of the line ashore. They had forgotten aboard to cut the frayed end of the rope. My knife was on its belt in the room. Those frayed ropeyarns baulked me repeatedly in the darkness as I tried to make a bowline. From the ship came the mate's foul blasphemies as he cursed me for my slowness.

And then the job was done and the line set up taut with the fo'c'sle head capstan. Other lines followed, while the second mate aft was busy on the same work.

Suddenly the wind dropped; the heavy, black pall of cloud swept away to looard, and the stars shone out again. The ship, upright now, slowly settled back alongside the bank once more slackening, of course, the lines we had so laboriously hove bar-taut. Nobody was permitted to go below until all those lines were set up tight again. And then all hands, soaked and shivering for hours, lay aft for a tot of rum, supplied by our not over-generous Aberdeen skipper, who had been urged by the mate to open his heart.

But for the grace of God ours had been the tragic fate of the fine four-masted ship *Andelana*. That vessel, waiting with open hatches to load grain at Tacoma some years before, had suddenly capsized in spite of the heavy ballast logs which supported her. All aboard perished that night, literally being drowned in their bunks before a finger could be lifted to save themselves.

* * *

Into the ointment of that pleasant stay at Newcastle buzzed the fly. Not an ordinary housefly, but what might, in fact, be termed a bluebottle of great dimensions.

We were strolling, Molly and myself, along the bank of the river one afternoon when that huge bluebottle made his unpleasant appearance in the shape of a tall, powerful young man clad in the traditional blue jumper and bell-bottom trousers of the Navy.

"Who's that?" I asked, as he bore down upon us. "He looks a nasty piece of work. What does he want with us anyway?"

"That's my brother. He's just come home from his ship in Sydney," answered Molly. "You leave him to me."

The long cornstalk marched right up to us, the glint of battle in his eye, his huge, ham-like fists itching for contact with what seemed to me would be my unfortunate dial. After glaring murderously at me, he turned to his sister. "Get away home, you little bitch!" he snarled at her. "And if I catch you out with this goddam 'light-the-binnacle' boy again there'll be trouble—proper trouble!"

Now, surely, was the time for me to show my manhood, to punch him good and hard right on the nose. Why the hell had my parents called me 'Isabel' for months before I was born!

Swelling with righteous indignation, my conscience entirely clear in the knowledge that the girl had suffered no harm from our association, I stepped up to the long slab of misery. But the girl was quicker. Pushing me on one side, she squared up, with blazing eyes, to her brother.

So thoroughly did she slate him that he turned and slunk away. Over his shoulder he hurled his final threat at Molly. "If ever you go out with that bloody 'limejuicer' again—I'll break his damned neck!"

"Nice, gentle, amiable sort of bloke, that brother of yours. Thanks, anyway, for saving my life," I remarked drily to the girl as we resumed our walk.

The attitude of that Aussie was typical of many of the local youths, not, in all candour, without reason. For some of the bold sailormen, in from the open sea, who were made welcome in Australian homes, betrayed the trust which had been placed in them. Sometimes the girls, to their sorrow later, became a little too fond of the windborne wanderers who called for a while at their ports.

In Newcastle there were a few young men who had deserted their ships to make honourable amend. Others, lesser clay, just loved . . . . and sailed away . . . .

One valiant soul became, during his stay, so enamoured of the place and, perchance, of one of its fair belles, that he jumped overboard and swam ashore as his ship was towing to sea past Nobby Head.

* * *

We were under the coal tips at last, loading for Pisco and Supe, two ports of sorts in Peru. A number of other British windjammers were also bound along that stormy, windblown waste of water called the South Pacific: *Milverton, Westgate, Crocodile, Castleton, Conway Castle,* and some others whose names have escaped me.

One ship particularly interested us—a great, ungainly soft-wood five-masted American schooner. While in ballast she had appeared to us *hogged;* when the coal tips had done their work of hurling some thousands of tons into her bowels, she had a decided *sheer* and was hardly recognisable as the same vessel. It was as if she quailed under the deadening load of that tremendous burden.

The largest vessel amongst that fine fleet of sail was the powerful, four-masted barque *Arrow,* which had just been transferred from British to German registration. At the gaff-end from which the old Red Duster had fluttered so recently now flew an enormous black-white-red flag of the Fatherland. Few national emblems include black in their colour scheme, for it is usually associated with the trappings of death. There was something sinisterly bold and defiant in that huge banner of the *Arrow;* we often paused alongside to watch the Prussian precision with which the work of the ship was carried out.

* * *

We had just come down from aloft, having bent a brand-new main lower topsail— a fine piece of the stoutest canvas for the stormy latitudes ahead. The mate was standing aft, in conversation with a lay preacher from the Mission who had brought some religious pamphlets aboard.

The missioner had persuaded the mate to examine one of the leaflets before the latter decided to accept them for distribution aboard. Without a sign of interest the officer opened the pamphlet. Across the page before him toddled a bug! The sight of that Little Boy in Brown sent the mate stark, staring mad.

"Good God!" he raved at the startled missioner. "Haven't we enough bugs without you bringing more aboard? Here, take your damned tracts and get to hell ashore!"

Immediately, like the admonishing Voice of Heaven, came the 'S'utherly Buster'.

It struck the ship a solid blow, parting some of the moorings. It screamed and roared aloft. In thirty seconds it had blown that brand-new topsail clean out of the gaskets. The sail was pounding and banging and slatting, shaking the whole mainmast and threatening to thrash itself to pieces.

The Mission man slunk under the break of the poop for shelter. The mate came bawling along the deck, heedless of the blinding rain, "Up aloft and make that tops'l fast!" We sprang into the rigging to save that precious sail. Before the main top was reached our progress was halted by a bombardment of great, jagged hailstones. Every man was forced to place his hands over his head as a protection against that cruel attack, which cut and hacked our hands.

The hail passed, but the wind screamed and the rain still beat on us as we muzzled the sail. A few minutes later there wasn't a breath of wind and the decks steamed under the warm sun. Far away in the northern sky the ragged black clouds strode swiftly on their way before the demon wind.

These busters are a curious feature of south-eastern Australia. Though of such short duration they are the frequent cause of serious damage.

The mate had gone below for his dinner; the mission man still stood disconsolately under the poop overhang. He readily accepted my invitation to share the poor hospitality of my little room. Throwing off my saturated clothing, I wrapped a grubby towel around my waist before sitting down to dinner in that somewhat unconventional garb. Perched on the sea-chest opposite, my companion shared the meal of wet hash and potatoes, while he told me how saddened he was by the mate's rough words. "He's a hard, blasphemous man," he said repeatedly, "and he's not fit to be in charge of young men like you."

"Yes," I agreed, "he's a hard, blasphemous man, but under that seeming hardness and blasphemy lies a heart of gold. And, what's more, he's a real sailor and we like him."

Warmed by the glow of Slushy's steaming wet hash, he proceeded to treat me to a religious homily which I suffered in silence. And then sadly shaking his head, he made his way ashore, the bundle of tracts still under his arm.

The ship lay two days out at the 'farewell' buoys in the river while final preparations were made for sailing. Those last two nights particular care was taken that no boats came alongside. A shore watchman armed with a revolver guarded the ship to prevent any attempted desertion by members of the crew.

Our skipper made his final visit ashore. We picked him up late
at night at the steps under the great, squatting stern of the mighty
Arrow. Her lofty spars reared skywards so that they were almost
lost in the darkness overhead. Next morning the ship towed out
past Nobby Head—out to the open sea . . . .

It was good to be at sea again, white sails crowding, ship a-
leaning. Ports are demoralising places for the sailor. It is there one
becomes soft and effete and mildly contaminated by the touch of
the land. The land is for the landsman; the sea is for those who
have given their lives to it gladly, knowing full well that no great
material gain will ever be theirs; for those who love its grandeur
and greatness, which stretch almost to the edge of infinity. . . .

So it was good to be at sea again, although there were some who
gazed back longingly at that friendly shore fast fading as the
ship stood off the land. Our feet fresh spread to the heave of the
deck, we faced some thousands of miles of the stormiest ocean as
we headed down for the southern tip of New Zealand—with the
Roaring Forties beyond.

*   *   *

We were to the s'uthard of Stewart Island, the last land we
would see before sighting the Peruvian coast. Already the weather
was bleak and bitter, giving promise of worse to come, for the
southern winter was at hand.

That afternoon the ship, under full sail, was struck down by a
sudden, furious squall. The royal halliards were let fly. In the
excitement the young second mate threw off the pin the halliards
of the mizen t'gan's'l instead of those of the royal. The whole
weight of the t'gallant yard and sail was, of course, thrown upon
the royal sheets and the tie of the halliards. Under this strain the
royal yard snapped like a carrot. The sail, resembling a gull's
broken wing, thrashed and banged about, threatening to tear itself to ribbons.

The ship was pressed far down by the snarling squall. The rain
flung itself horizontally at her as she smoked through the water,
lying down to it with the rail awash. On the poop the Old Man
screamed foul abuse at the unfortunate second mate in between
the necessary orders for the safety of the ship.

Two of us, Jersey and myself, jumped into the rigging and ran
aloft to attempt to save the mizen royal from total ruin. In the

crosstrees we paused, for nothing could be done with that broken wing until the squall had eased off.

Standing there, far above the deck, the two of us witnessed a most amazing spectacle. It was as if the wrath of the gods were concentrated on our unfortunate ship. While the wind still screamed and screeched at us, a thunderstorm of frightening savagery and severity rolled over our mastheads with awesome cannonading.

It was the most stupendous electrical disturbance we had ever seen. The long tongues of fire from that mighty artillery of heaven crackled and fizzled all around us as we clung to the rigging, so close that it seemed we would be struck at any moment.

When the worst of the squall had passed, the thunder still rumbling near at hand, we got our broken wing down on deck. That unseamanlike mistake of the second mate's was fortunate indeed. Under its hard crust of repeated coats of paint the wooden yard was utterly rotten. It was a miracle it had not been carried away before—to throw one of us youngsters to his death far below. . . .

*   *   *

In 1520, when the saucy, tip-tilted jib-boom of Magellan's cock-eyed little ship poked its way out of the western end of the straits which he had discovered and which now bear his name, the weather must indeed have been propitious. Otherwise how could the man have been so deluded as to name 'Pacific' the vast ocean which faced him then.

Had he called it Terrific, Majestic, or some other appellation he would have been nearer the mark. Why, then, Pacific? We can only assume that those stalwart, early voyagers were the greatest optimists, viewing all they saw with the eye of romance and enchantment.

There was little enchantment for us on that passage through those stormy waters, for the ship bit down in to the high latitudes almost as far as 49 degrees south. That may seem strange to some, seeing that Newcastle lies in 33 South, and Pisco, whither we were bound, in but 14 South. It must, however, be remembered that a sailing vessel's greatest mission was to find *wind*, sometimes prolonging a passage by many miles to fulfil that quest. Then again, the Great Circle track across the Southern

Penso

"THE SUN'S RIM DIPS, THE STARS RUSH OUT: AT ONE STRIDE COMES THE DARK...."
(Coleridge's *Ancient Mariner*)

Ocean runs through the Roaring Forties.

The prosaic steamer, on the other hand, independent of the somewhat vagrant power of the sailer, a fair wind always embowelled in her engine room, worked more or less on the theory that the shortest distance between two points is a straight line.

Wind we had aplenty, and rain and cold, and the rude inroad of hundreds of tons of icy water sweeping the decks of our deeply loaded ship, causing us to live for weeks in the chill discomfort of oilskins and wet clothing. How she rolled, with the yards squared most of the time and the consequent lack of lateral pressure to steady her! It seemed at times she would tumble the sticks right overboard. She did, indeed, carry away several topmast backstays which required immediate attention before the others followed suit.

We were still some hundreds of miles from the West Coast, curving up to the northward to make our landfall when, one night, we ran into the phenomenon of the Milky Sea.

Towards the end of the first watch it was noticed that the sea was losing its familiar aspect. Under the half moon, the water ahead resembled a huge ice-field towards which the ship was sailing.

In the middle watch she was completely surrounded by the Milky Sea. It was an uncanny experience. The ship, leaning slightly under all sail, for the wind was light, pushed her way through the dead-white water which stretched as far as eye could see.

Under the impression that we were passing over the scene of some submarine disturbance, I asked the mate the cause of this unusual occurrence. He peered around the horizon, turned to me and curtly remarked, "B' Jesus, I don't know what's gone wrong with the sea."

The ignorance and indifference of this type of old sea warrior often amazed me. For my father, particularly when he realised my heart was set upon the sea, had often read to us the words of Psalm 107: They that go down to the sea in ships, that do business in great waters; these see the works of the Lord, and His wonders in the deep. . . . .

This grey-haired man had gone down to the sea in ships for

many years . . . had seen His wonders in the deep, yet had been blind to the works of the Lord. . .

When my relief came to the wheel I decided to investigate matters for myself by drawing a bucket of water from over the side. On striking a match the water appeared perfectly normal; but when the light went out the contents of the bucket, in the pale moonlight, regained their dull white colour.

The idea of a submarine upheaval was discounted by the smoothness of the sea. The ship was sailing slowly and almost silently. It was almost as if she were frozen, slightly listed, in an immense, solid field of ice. This strange condition is, I believe, produced by billions of animalculae whose minute bodies are invisible to the naked eye.

Three or four hours later the sea had assumed again its normal appearance.

* * *

Before reaching the coast I became so ill that I was forced to take to my bunk for several days. It was a severe chill on the stomach, caught one night through a 'hard case' two hours at the wheel, spent there in bare feet and the thinnest of clothing. The captain told me he could do nothing for me, for he had no chlorodyne. The cook's best effort for my relief was to feed me thin arrowroot, made with water.

On the third day Old Sails arrived in my little room, a tape measure in his hand, a piece of heavy canvas under his arm. With a big chew of tobacco bulging chunkily in his cheek, he gravely proceeded to measure me as I lay in my bunk. His faded blue eyes twinkled as he remarked with exaggerated seriousness, "Yes, that piece of No. 1 is just the thing . . . I'll sew you up nice and snug, sonny . . . the last stitch always goes through the nose to make things shipshape. . ." He made a motion as though he were driving his beloved sail needle through something particularly tough. . .

That rough humour did more than anything else to get me out of my bunk and on my feet again. And then, to make matters worse, while I was still weak and ill, several days later, the biggest and strongest youngster aboard picked a quarrel with me. We had been fighting only a few minutes when he gave me a crippling kidney punch. The mate, arriving at that moment, cuffed both our heads as he separated us.

This was as well, for the fight, for me, was over. That vicious blow kept me in agony for days. Lying restlessly in my bunk, the pain gave me no sleep in my watch below. To go aloft, which I was forced to do, was torture. My only consolation was the fact that my opponent never knew how cruelly he had injured me.

* * *

Out on deck in the early morning sunshine somebody was shouting "Land Ho! Land on the starboard bow!" In the next room Old Sails was singing loudly and cheerily as he prepared for his day's work:

> *"Has anyone seen my Mary Ann?*
> *She's gone with the Tingle-ary Man,*
> *Tingle-ary, hairy Mary, Tingle-ary Man!"*

Looking out through the door, I saw the dim shape of the coast. Out in the east, over that strange land, over the mighty Andes, the sun was slowly rearing itself.

On this coast the utmost caution was necessary to make one's landfall well to the southward of the port to which the ship was bound. The reason for this was two-fold. It was of such importance that it was clearly imprinted on the minds of those who sailed the ships relying solely on the wind for their motion.

The whole coast of Peru lies within the area of the south-east trades; the prevailing wind consequently blows up these shores. Moreover, the mariner is assisted or beset, according to whether he is bound north or south, by the cold Humboldt Current, which sweeps northward along the entire coast of Chili and Peru.

Many cases have been known of vessels which cut things too fine drifting helplessly past their port in the grip of the current when the wind fell lightly or temporarily failed. We had, therefore, made the land well to the s'uth'ard of our destination. Skirting the coast, we sailed to the north-westward. Our first impressions were not encouraging, for the land ran far ahead in a dull, dun-coloured line of seemingly inhospitable shore. Far behind, dim yet distinct, reared the everlasting peaks of the grand and mighty Andes.

In the afternoon, while our port still lay some miles ahead, a chilly fog crept over the water, blotting out the land. Before dark the ship was hove to on the off-shore tack, for it was unwise to proceed blindfold in such a dangerous vicinity.

It was an eerie sort of night which followed. Though the fog lay thick over the sleeping sea, enveloping ship from stem to stern, high overhead the full moon sailed serene and mist-free, turning into pearls the glistening drops of moisture which collected everywhere on rail and rigging.

The master scarcely left the poop that night. The dull rumble of the surf in the east was endless, and the strange cries of sea lions, which abound on this coast, came to us so clearly that it seemed the land was far too close at hand. Sometimes the menacing sound of the surf rose to an angry growl, setting the Old Man peering anxiously shorewards through the fog. For he was not sure of the ship's position, or of how that inexorable current was setting him. There are many parts of this coast where the land rises so steeply from the ocean bed that soundings are unobtainable until a vessel is practically ashore.

At dawn, with the wraithlike mist thinning slightly, the ship was headed in for the land. The skipper had come for'ad on to the fo'c'sle head, his glasses slung about his neck. Then suddenly, high above the now low-lying fog appeared the gloomy outline of a sombre menacing headland close at hand.

The Old Man, running aft, cried loudly as he ran, "Hard a-starboard! All hands t' th' braces!"

Like a curtain being drawn aside by the warming rays of the risen sun, the fog was swept away. In close proximity, the gaunt, rockbound heights of the Paracas Peninsula barred our way. The boiling surf climbing the cruel rocks seemed to clutch and roar at our ship.

She was slow at answering the helm, for in the early morning the wind was light. It appeared at first she was embayed. And then, foot by foot and yard by yard, she won out to the westward, the wind freshening a little with the growing day. Rounding the island of San Gallan later, we stood in with braced-up yards between the Ballesta Islands and the mainland.

Fresh from the immense freedom of the open ocean, the ship looked oddly out of place in such narrow waters. It was as if we were encompassed and engulfed by the menace of those frowning black rocks on which the high swell climbed and broke with noisy strife.

Under all sail, these dangers were passed, and after crossing the sunlit bay of Pisco the ship came to anchor with the last of the daylight at 7.30 p.m. She had been two months at sea, a disappointing effort for so smart a ship. The following day the consignees complained that the vessel was lying too far off shore. Under easy canvas, a little puffing billy called by courtesy a tug having proved unequal to the task, the ship was sailed to the inner anchorage.

We had reached that desolate, dreary land off whose coast we were destined to lie rolling in the everlasting swell for many, many weeks before bidding it a glad good-bye. A land of blazing sun and chilly mists; of endless booming surf; of innumerable warring sea-lions and sad-voiced seals; of myriads of wailing sea-birds so numerous that it is no idle exaggeration to say they darkened the sun as they flew across the sky.

It was these last who were to fill the hungry belly of our ship once the last cob of coal had been discharged. . . . . .

CHAPTER XIII

THE WEST COAST

IN the mind of a steamboat man exist thoughts of many West Coasts round the world. For the men who sailed the square-rigged ships there was but one—the lengthy western seaboard of Chili and Peru off which we had come to anchor.

Though the nature of the trade of this region did much to prolong the life of the windjammer, the 'West Coast' was detested by one and all. As has been said before, this dislike was partly fostered by the clause in the crew's agreement with the owners whereby the men bound themselves to work all cargoes in and out of the ship while on this coast.

The average seaman grumbles by tradition when employed solely on his work of sailorising; he grumbles ten-, twenty-fold, when he is forced to assume the role of coal heaver and guano delver.

So it was, putting aside temporarily the art of sailorising, we faced the dismal task of digging nearly twenty-four hundred tons of coal out of our ship.

A stage had been rigged between main hatch and ship's rail; from the outer edge of this angled a wooden chute, swung from the main yard. Our portable steam-donkey had been unearthed from its out-of-work lair in the fore 'tween decks, and we lived in hopes that it might be persuaded to snatch some, at least, of that cargo from the hold.

In close proximity stood the steam-donkey's deputy, a primitive hand-winch with a wooden barrel to which were attached two long handles. This contraption, humorously termed 'Armstrong's Patent', required the sweating, blasphemous efforts of four of us to hoist laboriously three bags of coal at a time.

The stage was set for the commencement of our discharge. The first lighter had just arrived to receive its bellyful of black diamonds. Though the sun shone brightly the air was cool—as yet. But before long that lonely ship and that desolate coast off which she lay would be scorching in the tropic heat.

The crew stood in the square of the hatch, shovels in hand. On the platform were gathered the second mate, the third mate, another apprentice who was 'tallying', and myself. Through the often dimming mist of over a quarter of a century that scene comes back to me clearly.

'Chips', muttering enigmatically and repeatedly "What-ee you", fussed about the donkey, endeavouring to tighten up leaky joints here and there from which steam came hissing noisily. One of the younger boys stood by to drive the engine. Already the machine was showing signs of disgust at the indignity of having its boiler defiled by salt water. Smears of dried salt appeared at every leaky spot. Fresh water was, of course, far too precious on that arid, rainless coast to use for such a purpose.

Later, its intestines festered by the continual use of salt water, the donkey frequently refused duty altogether. Then the torture rack of 'Armstrong's Patent' would be manned and the work carried on by hand.

The consignees had stipulated that all the coal must be bagged. Great bundles of brand-new sacks were already aboard. As our clothes wore out we found those sacks useful for making garments. Many pairs of skilfully cut trousers were fashioned from them. With a little care the central blue stripe could be persuaded to run along the outside of each leg, thus giving us the appearance of a band of sackcloth-clad, grotesque lifeguardsmen.

The bags were filled, sewn up, hoisted and weighed three at a time. The third mate and myself lifted them on to the scale which stood at the outer edge of the stage. I can say without exaggeration that I lifted every bit of that cargo, with the exception of a few tons, out of the ship. One of our boys tallied for the ship, while an olive-skinned effeminate young man from the shore looked after the interests of the consignees. Greasy-haired and spectacled, his knowledge of English was practically nil. Peering closely at the scale, he would mutter, "Una, dos, tres, cuatro . . . cinco . . ." After being weighed the bags were hurled, helter-skelter, down the chute into the waiting lighter.

We youngsters had imagined that we might obtain some relief from the monotony of this work through ferrying the Old Man between ship and shore. We were disappointed in this. For some reason the captain did not go ashore a great deal at Pisco, and he often used the agent's boat. It may be that he imagined his

presence aboard would expedite the discharge of the cargo.
Slouching about with his inevitable cigar, he would keep a
watchful eye on us all.

Occasionally he sauntered along the deck to the stage where we
stood. Without actually looking at us, almost as if he were
addressing the deep blue sky or the endless dun-coloured shore, he
would growl, "Put your foot on it—put your foot on it." Finding
later that the shore clerk, besides having no English, was a little
hard of hearing, he indulged more frequently in his little
Aberdonian joke, and his subtle suggestion, or command, would
come to us from where he leaned over the rail at the fore-end of
the poop.

So the days passed, days of uncongenial toil from 6 a.m. to 6
p.m., with a begrudged half hour for breakfast and forty-five
minutes for dinner. Though our anchorage was more sheltered
than many of the open roadsteads on this almost harbourless
coast, in spite of the small number of 'surf days', there were many
delays. As in Brazil, the doctrine of 'Mañana' and 'Mas tardi'
held sway over Peru, as is, indeed, the case throughout South
America.

Shortage of lighters and numerous 'fiestas' interfered seriously
with our discharge and prolonged unduly our stay at Pisco. Those
days of 'fiesta' were as numerous as at Bahia, punctuated by the
popping crackers and soaring rockets which were growing so
familiar to us.

No shore leave whatever was granted—I never set foot in Pisco
—but the mate had informed us that when we reached Supe,
further up the coast, we would be given a day's liberty ashore.
This close confinement to the ship intensified the grumbling and
discontent which had for some time been evident amongst our
unruly Irish crew. Treading the traditional Irish path of that
distressful country, they were ever 'agin the government'.

Fanned by the growlings of the bitterest of the malcontents,
this spirit broke out one morning into open hostility and mutiny.

The second mate, on the stage above the hatch, had shouted
down to the men below, "Hook on, down there! What's all the
delay about?"

Mike O'Brien stood in the square of the hatch, glaring
impudently up at the second mate. His shaggy moustache bristled

truculently as he called out to the officer, "Come down and hook on yer bloody self!"

The second mate quietly ordered the man up on deck, telling him he would soon find out who was going to do the hooking on. Throwing down their shovels, the whole lot came like ravening wolves from the hold, shouting blood-curdling threats as they climbed the ladder.

From aft the mate quickly made his way, scenting something amiss. "What's all this damned nonsense, men? Get back to your work!" he said. Refusing to do this, the men milled with brandished fists around the young second mate. The older officer, seeing that further argument was useless and a fight unavoidable, roared out, "Make a ring, men! Let's have fair play!"

A ragged ring was formed—the angry men on the fore side, we youngsters, the mate and the third mate on the after side. O'Brien, bombastic, cocksure, faced the second mate, fully convinced he was about to make mincemeat of that officer.

That fight was sheer delight to watch. (In my mind was registered the vow that if ever I had a son the boy would master the art of fisticuffs at an early age. Alas, that boy has nearly reached manhood without ever having handled the gloves.) Nobody had dreamed that the little, quiet, unassuming second mate could 'use himself' so well. He literally toyed with Mike, knocking him down repeatedly. But that Irishman had guts; he rose again and again, his face battered, his ragged singlet and hirsute chest covered with gore.

And then he cried out that he had had enough. That was the signal for a general melee, the men calling out, "Come on, boys, men against the officers!" The situation looked extremely ugly for a few minutes. Big Paddy O'Brien (there were two of that clan in the fo'c'sle) towered over me; I tensed myself for a shattering blow from his enormous fist. Before this took place the mate bawled out, "Play the game, men! It's been a fair fight. Get back to your work now!"

Their fists dropped to their sides, but they continued to curse us foully with their Irish tongues. And then, their braggart champion defeated, they all turned and walked for'ad, swearing by the Virgin Mary they would never do another hand's turn aboard the ship. After washing themselves and putting their clean clothes on, they sat about the fo'c'sle head wondering, no doubt, what would be the outcome of their foolish insurrection.

The boat had been dispatched hurriedly for the captain. On his arrival aboard, all hands were mustered aft. Many exaggerated statements were made by the men. They had been 'hazed', ill used and ill fed and had at last decided they would stand no more 'slave driving'. Their angry shouts rose in a confused roar as the captain stood looking down from the poop. One man dared the skipper to gaol him, swearing he would kill him if he did so.

Mike was in the forefront, his ugly battered face giving him a villainous appearance as he egged the others on. In spite of the Old Man's assurance that he was prepared to forget the incident if they turned to at once, they refused to resume work.

Once more the boat hastened ashore, while the urgent signal YN—Want Police—fluttered from our signal halliards.

Presently a boat brought off the *Capitan del Puerto,* the British vice-consul, and the Chief of Police, who carried a very large and much betasseled sword. With these dignitaries came five *vigilantes,* armed with swords and rifles. These five men lined up with much ceremony on the quarterdeck, and the crew were called aft once more.

Their names were read out and each was asked whether he would work or go to gaol. At mention of that unpleasant word the men grew so abusive that the five *vigilantes* were ordered by their officer to load their rifles. This was done with much impressive ostentation. The vice-consul, bored and no doubt peeved at the loss of his beloved afternoon *siesta,* listened almost disinterestedly to O'Brien's wandering harangue, from which one might have imagined our vessel to be a proper Yankee 'hell ship'.

Growing a little weary, the V-C ordered our men into the shore boat. At their blunt refusal to do this, he nodded to the police officer. That individual immediately drew his prettily-tasseled sword, and commenced to use its pursuasive power flatly on the rumps of our recalcitrant crew. This base indignity would never have been suffered by the proud Irish but for the grim, menacing muzzles of those five rifles.

As it was, at the risk of his life, O'Brien dashed clear, ran with a cry of rage towards young Le Mesurier, gripped him savagely by the throat, and gouged his fingers into Frenchy's windpipe.

The maddened Mike was hurled clear of his victim by half a dozen of us. As he was forced down the gangway he cried out that he would surely kill Frenchy on his return.

In the boat that wild Irishman refused to be subdued, calling the Chief of Police repeatedly a 'hoary headed old bastard'. His knowledge of English decidedly limited, that officer knew enough to sense the insult. Drawing his sword once more, he belaboured, with many sinister 'carambas', our unruly shipmate until some sort of submission had been obtained.

Of the crew, four had not joined the mutineers: the Turk, who was night watchman; one old man who was entirely inoffensive; another A.B. who was sick in his bunk, and Le Mesurier, or Frenchy, as he was always called. This last, a fine young fellow from the Channel Isles, hoped to sit for his ticket when he got home. He had taken no part in the disturbance, naturally being unwilling to risk his good discharge. He was very much upset over the affair, knowing well his life would be in danger when the men returned.

* * *

The outcome of this unfortunate incident was a sentence of six months in gaol for the ringleader, the others to be treated more leniently. A number of Peruvians came off from the shore to work the cargo with us.

Two days later we heard the men were coming back. Mike had been promised a free pardon if he could persuade the rest of the men to return to the ship. This had been done, and Frenchy knew he was 'for it'. Apparently those Peruvians had no overwhelming wish to entertain indefinitely, either in gaol or out, those turbulent Irishmen of ours.

We heard our deep sea warriors from afar as they were brought off in the police boat. The Old Man had foolishly been persuaded to give each of them two *sols*, an amount which afforded at that time in Peru ample scope for a glorious drunk. They stepped aboard inflamed, calling, before they had scaled the gangway, for Jersey's blood. Their sheath-knives had been returned to them on their release from gaol. With these they swore they would cut out the blackleg's heart. A drunken hue and cry was started for the unfortunate young man.

But he was nowhere in sight, having grabbed a few biscuits and

disappeared down the hold when he first heard his shipmates'
noisy approach. Finding they could not locate him, they wantonly
threw his clothing and other belongings overboard before crawling
into their bunks to sober up.

Next morning, slightly sobered but none the less bloodthirsty,
they renewed the search. But Frenchy had been up on deck before
them, slipping aboard the first lighter, where he hid for hours
under a piece of tarpaulin till he was taken ashore. He was
subsequently paid off and we never saw him again. Later in the
day the men turned to, sullen and morose.

*   *   *

We manned the windlass while it was still dark, and were under
way before the dawn had come. I stood at the wheel while sail
was piled upon the ship. It was good to see those lofty spars
clothed once more, to hear the gurgle of the parted water.

The sun had risen. It lit up the gloomy rocks of the Chincha
Islands as we passed close by. Those islands held my rapt attention.
Some years before going to sea I had read and re-read a book
entitled 'The Shellback, or at Sea in the Sixties'. In that book
was written a very vivid account of a visit to load guano at these
selfsame islands. In those far off days ships literally flocked here
to fill their holds with humble but extremely valuable bird
droppings.

It was about the early 'forties that the Peruvian government
first came to realise what immense wealth lay scattered broadcast
along its coast. For centuries these lonely, off-lying rocks had
been the home of numberless sea birds. Gradually their droppings
had formed a coating in some cases as much as 100 feet thick
over the islands. This guano, unthought of for so long, was found
to be a valuable fertiliser, rich in ammoniates, for in this rainless
climate nothing had been washed away or lost.

Here, at the front door of somewhat impecunious Peru, was
a veritable if somewhat smelly gold mine. At first, the Peruvians
being too indolent to engage themselves in such unpleasant work,
Chinese labour was imported to remove the initial deposit. Ships
waited sometimes months their turn to load, so densely were they
gathered at the Chinchas.

On that early morning on which we sailed from Pisco, the
malodorous glory of these islands had long departed, though their

annual yield, with that of the many other deposits, still employed
a goodly fleet of sail. As the ship drew past the Chinchas I noted,
instead of the thronging vessels which once lay there, a solitary
square-rigger, lonely and inconspicuous at anchor not far from
the foam-girt rocks from which the sea-lions roared their defiance.

As we passed Callao a big black ship stood out from that port,
bound off the land with everything set. Leaning to the breeze,
she made a magnificent picture, and might well have been the
inspiration of Robert Bridges' "Whither, O splendid ship, thy
white sails crowding . . . . ?"

It was but two hundred miles between our ports. But the wind
was light all the way, and it was almost dark on the third day
when we dropped anchor off the little town of Supe. We found
ourselves in a very different anchorage from that of the sheltered
bay of Pisco. The long, eternal swell fretted our ship day and
night, until at times she rolled as if she intended spewing her
masts overboard.

On many such 'surf days' work on the cargo had to be
suspended, and we gladly turned our attention to some more
sailorlike occupation than shovelling coal. The heavy, double
forestay was renewed, a job requiring the greatest nicety so that it
was set up at the correct tension by the throat seizings. Other
parts of the standing rigging were replaced, including the topmast
backstays which had carried away on our stormy passage over. In
all this work the old mate excelled, and I was proud indeed that
he chose me to take part in it.

A thirty-two foot log had been purchased to make a new mizen
royal yard, the loss of which had spoiled the symmetry and beauty
of the ship aloft. Chips turned to, with many incantations and
mutterings, to fashion the new spar, one or two of us youngsters
helping him. Soon a network of chalk lines appeared on the log
and the old Greek set to with adze alone to mould the yard. Any
remark or question from master or mate was brushed aside by
indignant and rebukingly enigmatic 'What-ee yous'. In the end he
made a very fine job of the spar and the ship regained her trim
appearance aloft.

*　　*　　*

Our captain had just returned from a friendly binge with some
of his cronies ashore. He was, indeed, what might be termed

'slightly under the influence'. When the Capitan del Puerto arrived aboard shortly afterwards to pay his respects our Old Man was in decidedly vainglorious mood.

Standing somewhat unsteadily at the fore end of the poop, our skipper greeted the port captain. We boys, enjoying a smoke in the half-deck after the pull from the jetty, heard every word which passed between them.

The preliminary greetings over, the Capitan del Puerto, by way of making conversation, remarked pleasantly, "You are lying a long way out, Captain." Our Old Man seemed to take offence at that. "A long way out, you say! My boys think nothing of it . . . (Don't they, from all of us, with one or two embellishments) . . . and they row it at least four times every day. Your crew can't be much good if they find it a heavy pull."

It was now the turn of the port captain to become a little heated. A long argument took place regarding the qualities of their respective boats' crews. This was exceedingly gratifying to us, for we had never before heard our Old Man say such nice things about us.

When the Capitan del Puerto went over the side we clearly heard his parting remark. "All right, Captain, on Tuesday we have the fiesta of San Pedro. We will have a regatta . . . your boys against my men."

We left the half-deck to peer over the rail. Already the boat was some distance off, rapidly covering the water with long, well timed strokes. "Holy smoke!" remarked somebody, "that old tyke aft there has surely let us in for something now."

The next morning the mate came along to tell us formally and officially that the port captain had challenged our skipper to a boat race over a course of three miles, the winning crew to receive a prize of two pounds. It must have nearly broken the Old Man's skinflint Aberdonian heart to risk his precious and carefully hoarded sovereigns on such a doubtful issue.

A day or two later he came down to the jetty, where we patiently awaited him. Hilariously he thrust into our hands a number of handbills of a particularly unpleasant hue of pink. Our knowledge of Spanish was scanty, but we had little difficulty in deciphering the purport of those bilious looking sheets.

They proclaimed to all and sundry that Tuesday was to see the celebration of the *fiesta* of San Pedro. There was to be a *Banda da Musicales* on the jetty to liven things up; there was to be, amongst many other attractions, a *Regatta*—the well known crew of the *Capitan del Puerto* against that of the *Marineros Ingleses*. We noticed the type announcing the *Regatta* was considerably heavier than that of the other items. Apparently, to our consternation, the race was to be an event of some importance.

On the way off to the ship the skipper, instead of cursing us for a lot of sogers, delivered himself of a little homily. He spoke a bit thickly, but every word bit home. . . "Sock it into them, or I won't carry you boys for ballast in my ship. . ." The youngster pulling stroke next to him answered only, "Aye, aye, Sir," gripped his oar tighter and increased the power of his stroke.

* * *

The second mate, a wiry Scotsman of small stature, offered to cox us. There was little time before the fiesta, so that we managed only one or two trial runs after working hours. These brought no great assurance when we thought of the other boat, its powerful crew in constant practice.

The day arrived, heralded by the usual firing of crackers, squibs, and rockets without which no South American saint can be appeased or honoured. On board we saw very little of the celebrations until the afternoon. Then the port captain's boat pulled off to the ship. In our heavy gig we set off for the starting point together.

We were filled with gloomy misgivings when we saw our opponents at close quarters. Every advantage seemed to be theirs except, perhaps, that as a crew they were a bit too weighty. Their boat was a lightly-built smooth-skinned one, while ours was the usual clincher, heavy-pulling gig supplied to sailing ships. The Peruvians, moreover, were four powerful men, stripped to the waist, the muscles rippling on their naked backs and arms as they pulled leisurely to the mark. A buoy had been moored some distance to the northward. The course from there to the jetty would take us close past the ship.

The south-east wind had freshened, promising a heavy pull of three miles almost dead to windward. It was a glorious afternoon, the brilliant sunshine flooding the sparkling sea. After all these years the picture remains vividly with me to this day.

To the eastward lay the barren, naked hills of the coast, gloomy and inhospitable even in that bright sunlight. Far behind, soared the mighty, inscrutable Andes, untamed, sublimely indifferent to the foolish antics of those microbes called men.

To the westward stretched limitlessly the sea, the everlasting sea, joyous in its freedom, unhampered by thousands of miles of almost landless space. Near at hand the water fretted under the urge of the long, south-easterly swell and was whipped to more than playfulness by the fresh trade wind.

And in the roadstead rolled our rusty yet yachtlike ship, nodding and swaying her trucks and tilting her yardarms, while the Red Ensign streamed out proudly from the monkey-gaff. . . .

There was the crack of a pistol shot, and we were off, pulling in the teeth of the freshening breeze.

Of the actual race I can tell you but little. Tugging at the bow oar, I was soon drenched by the spray which flew continuously over the fore part of the boat. The third mate was pulling stroke. Between him and me sat two hefty *Worcester* boys. After our long passage from Australia and our lack of boat work at Pisco, we were all out of practice. It seemed at first we would be badly left behind.

None of us had much recollection of that gruelling pull beyond the agony of cruelly strained muscles. The boat became a blur to me. In my brain the voice of the second mate kept hammering as he gave us the time.

We drew abreast of the ship. A great heartening cheer reached us, and I have a dim memory of the crew festooning the rigging, shouting hoarse encouragement. We dared not look around to see how fared the other boat.

* * *

When the jetty was still some distance ahead the second mate called out that we were gaining. Our stroke slightly increased its speed. But the pace was killing, and I longed for the moment when we could relax from that terrific strain.

Then we heard the cries of the spectators on the jetty. It seemed the whole population was there. The blare of the *Banda da Musicales* reached us and shouts of "Marineros Ingleses! Marineros Ingleses!"

At last the end arrived. Tossing our oars in man-of-war fashion, if somewhat groggily, we brought the boat alongside the jetty to victory. The Peruvians were two hundred yards astern, badly rowed out as, indeed, were we. As we mounted the steps of the jetty the *Banda* burst out once more into strident music. "That's 'Rule Britannia'," said Wilson. "Go on!" retorted the second mate, "who ever heard of a Dago playing 'Rule Britannia'?"

The port captain and our old worthy were arguing hotly at the end of the little pier. Evading them, we made our way shorewards. Olive-skinned, velvet-eyed *senoritas* smiled friendship and admiration at us as we passed, speaking soft insinuating words of Spanish to us. To our surprise, we found we were the heroes of the *fiesta*. San Pedro had indeed smiled benignly on us.

Gallons of *vino* were put before us, for which no payment would be taken. "Oh, for a glass of foaming English ale!" said the second mate, quaffing a flowing measure of wine.

We reached the boat a little fuddled by the generous hospitality of our new-found friends. The skipper arrived soon after, more fuddled than we. His dour Scots nature permitted him no unseemly levity or wild enthusiasm over our success. With the exaggerated gravity of one under the potent spell of alcohol, he shook hands all round, mumbling to each a few indistinct words of congratulation.

The wind had freshened considerably; our aching arms all but refused to pull those oars, and, of course, we had no sail. But no official heed was paid to our tardy progress as the boat drew slowly away from the jetty.

Aft, in the stern sheets, sat a grey-headed old man slumped over the tiller. "Good boys . . . . damn' good lads," he kept muttering thickly . . . . "good boys, alow and aloft . . . . an' pullin' a boat too. . ."

From that hard old man, who all his life had scorned to tread a steamship's deck, those words were reward enough for that long, exhausting pull. No mercenary thoughts of that, so far, visionary two quid were ours as we bent to our task.

* * *

Night was spreading over the darkening sea. Away out in the roadstead lay our ship, nodding and swaying her trucks in the swell. At the gaff-end the ensign still streamed out stiffly in the strong breeze . . . . proudly, perhaps a little arrogantly, as if she, too, considered she had been smiled upon by San Pedro.

Until a late hour rockets and crackers still lit the darkness. Oblivious of these tributes, four weary youngsters slept the sleep of fatigue-cum-vino as they lived in their dreams again that epic race.

* * *

A day's shore leave was granted at last, one watch at a time. After putting on our cleanest clothes and cramming our feet uncomfortably into shoes, we of the port watch were rowed ashore. On close acquaintance Supe proved a dreary place. The few stone and brick buildings were surrounded by rows of low, filthy huts and hovels. While the men sought out the grog shops, several of us boarded a strange little open tram drawn on railway lines by two lazy donkeys. This contraption took us at the pace of a snail to Barranca, a village two or three miles away, where we enjoyed a meal of fried eggs—a luxury we had not tasted for months—and the coarsest of bread.

On our return to Supe we found the novelty of being ashore was wearing off, and there were still some hours before the boat would come for us.

And then we discovered a small hall in which bioscope shows were occasionally held. A performance was just about to start. As we entered, the swarthy doorkeeper grinned broadly at us and mumbled something which sounded like, "Tricky-tracks. Muy bueno!" The first part of his remark meant nothing to us at the time.

The opening film, silent and wobbly in those early days, showed an exciting bull fight in which a number of valiant bulls were slain. The hall rang vociferously with the 'Carachos' and 'Carambas' of the onlookers. Then the lights went up and the crowd, men and women, passed out into the road. The doorkeeper grinned at us once more as he whispered his previous remark.

The crowd stood awkwardly and self-consciously for several minutes, and then the women, detaching themselves, walked slowly away. The men, looking a little sheepishly at one another, began to enter the building again. The doors were carefully shut, and on to the screen was thrown a foul product of *La Belle France*—a film of the most outrageous obscenity. It was amazing that performers could be found to enact such scenes.

Why didn't the police put a stop to it? some indignant reader will ask. Don't make me laugh, indignant reader. Sure, in the best seats, in full view of the onlookers, enjoying themselves immensely, sat the senior police officials, and what might in other circumstances be termed the elite of the town. The Peruvians like their smut laid on good and thick. . . .

While the others awaited the boat, I strolled alone away from the landing place. It was a lovely night; the stars hung limpidly in a velvet sky. The cool night air was doubly clean and sweet after that noisome show in the hall.

Above the everlasting rumble of the surf, the sound of music and gay laughter reached my ears from a low, humble building nearby. A *fandango* was in full swing, the barefooted couples dancing so vigorously that the dust from the earth floor rose and enveloped them in a cloud. Gladly they welcomed in the young 'marinero ingles,' placing drink before him.

But where were the twanging guitars and snapping castanets?

In one corner stood an ancient barrel-organ, strangely incongruous in such a setting, a sweating native grinding its handle. From its moth-eaten depths emerged, over and over again, the sad, haunting notes of 'Waves of the Danube.' Going over to it, I saw the little plate with the London maker's name on it. The pointer of the circular dial for the change of tunes remained unaltered. As I looked at this, the perspiring organist smiled broadly, held up one long finger, and shouted, *"Una! No mas!"*

So that dilapidated instrument sang on its one and only melody —its swan song—while the dust and the stench of sweat and cane spirit rose to the rafters. . . .

Returning close to the rumbling surf which shook the land beneath my feet, I pondered over that ancient organ. How many ragged London urchins had danced happily around it in its palmy days? How came it here, so far, to sing its last sad tune?

* * *

The ship, almost discharged, was taking in sand ballast. Flying light, she rolled so badly that the swinging slings of sand bags often charged us with the frenzy of a maddened bull. Taylor, one of the A.B.s, was struck and hurled down the main-hatch, from which he was hoisted so badly hurt that he did not work for many days.

There was a spot of unpleasantness aboard before we sailed from Supe. When the figures of our official ship's tally clerk informed us that fourteen hundred tons of coal had been discharged, there still remained a number of tons in the hold. The ship should have been empty except for the sand ballast which had been put in her. Instead, a hefty heap of coal still lay down below. While the pomaded, dandified shore tally clerk gazed in bewilderment at this, we stood about looking the picture of innocence.

That poor Peruvian spent hours going through his figures again and again . . . . *"Una, dos, tres, cuatro . . . . cinco. . . ."* Occasionally he threw down his books, let out a fiery curse, ran his skinny fingers through his greasy hair, and then raised his arms heavenwards, imploring some celestial aid. Hurling himself on to the scale repeatedly, he peered short-sightedly at the reading as he checked it by his own weight.

His and the ship's figures coincided exactly, showing clearly that fourteen hundred tons had been delivered to the consignees. But what about that hefty heap still down below? Distressed, dishevelled, distraught, he demanded to be rowed ashore. Later he returned with several important looking individuals who argued angrily with our skipper.

They were up against a stone wall. All they got out of him as he puffed ingenuously at his cigar was, "Ye've got yer fourteen hundred. That's all yer entitled to. Ye'll get nae mair." The men left the ship muttering sinister Spanish curses at all of us.

The remaining coal was bagged and put aboard a schooner. As the last sling swung out of the hold the skipper chuckled softly to himself. The ship then weighed and set sail for Macabi Island, a lonely rock at which she was to load guano for Leith.

* * *

We were still some distance from the anchorage at Macabi when we became painfully aware of the odoriferous nature of our future cargo. That ammoniacal stench would easily have out-stunk the Augean stables before Hercules did his great purifying trick.

Macabi Island lies in 7 degrees 49 minutes South latitude, six miles off the mainland. It is in reality two islands, for a narrow passage divides the north from the south. This gap is bridged by a wire carrying a box by means of which the *huaneros* pass from one portion to the other.

With the exception of the months of June, July, August and September, this lonely rock, an off-shore dot in the vast Pacific, is uninhabited. During that part of the year, however, anything up to one hundred labourers are brought from Callao to collect the deposit for shipment.

That first afternoon we were surprised to find so few birds hovering about the island. Later we learned something of the habits of that winged host, which left every morning for the feeding 'grounds,' returning regularly towards sunset every day. At these times the sun was literally darkened by the flight of countless pelicans, gannets, shad, and some other varieties which were not so plentiful. The strange wailing cries of the birds and the beating of their wings filled the air deafeningly as they left in the morning or returned at night. They swarmed over the island, encroaching even on the miserable encampment of the *huaneros*.

Fish abounds in these waters as, indeed, it must to support so many ravenous creatures. Often we saw the sea-lions wantonly mutilating fish which they did not actually want for food. The birds, too, took a terrible toll of the finny shoals. Diving like plummets from a great height, the gannets gorged themselves. The huge, ungainly pelicans chose other, more stately, tactics. Alighting on the water, they literally scooped their enormous bags full of fish.

The manure deposit on the island is, of course, mainly that of the night droppings; those of the day, except from the nesting birds, are lost entirely in the sea. This enormous but unavoidable loss must run into thousands of tons per year.

Macabi Island, fretted and battered by the everlasting swell, is honeycombed to its very core. In the reverberating caverns live many hundreds of seals and sea-lions which are rarely silent. The sad, almost lamblike cries of the youngsters and the fierce, challenging roars of the huge sea-lion males echo and re-echo day and night. Unending fights rage amongst the enormous bulls, on whose bodies hideous scars bear witness to the savage nature of those duels.

The method of loading the guano was simple, and has probably not changed to this day. It was, of course, like all other operations on this somnolent coast, intensely slow. After collection with picks and shovels, the bagged deposit was carried on the backs of the Peruvians to the wire down which it slid, several bags at a time, to the waiting boats below. A heavy anchor, laid out just beyond the line of the surf, held the lower end of the wire, the upper one being set up to a sturdy trestle on the cliff above.

As the bags, thirty at a time, were brought off to the ship they were hoisted aboard three at a time. The steam donkey's indignation over the continuous use of salt water often reached bursting point, and we were frequently forced to resort to the hand winch. On the stage above the hatch the mouths of the bags were opened and their contents shaken down the hold, the empty sacks being returned ashore for refilling.

It was all so hopelessly slow, as if we were filling the ship with a teaspoon. It seemed we were destined to spend months at Macabi, and all hands knew they would never set foot ashore until Leith had been reached.

There was much grumbling from the men, especially when they were in the hold, we youngsters along with them, trimming the cargo. Down there the smell of the guano was almost overpowering. At times the potent fumes caused nose bleeding. The manure, a brown, almost dry substance—for there is no rain on this coast —was mixed with feathers and literally crawled with vermin.

The captain, anxious, no doubt, to keep the men sweet in this lonely, inaccessible spot, gave orders for an issue of *pisco* every morning at eleven. Shortly before that hour the mate's red face appeared over the hatch coaming. "Smoke Oh! Lay aft and get your grog!" he would roar. From that reeking hold they gladly came, hiking the chews from their mouths and loosening the wet rags which covered their nostrils.

The Old Man had bought a supply of this fiery spirit at Pisco, whose name it bears and where the stuff was so ridiculously cheap. The gain to him, calculated in terms of goodwill and cheerfulness amongst his crew was in no way commensurate with the small outlay. It would have done some of those rabid prohibitionists good to have seen the way those unkempt sailormen downed their tot before returning to their unsavoury work with new life in them.

But the work was so monotonous that one of our temperamental Irishmen became so melancholy that he sought the Muse, bursting into verse, composing a long, sad poem which ran through many stanzas. Its opening lines are still clear in my memory, though my copy of that unique poem has been lost. This is how they ran:

> "We don't want the turds
> From thim dirty ould birds ..."

Weeks later, just before we sailed from the island, he finished this masterpiece with the following words:

> "Wid our cargo complete
> We are bound home to Leit! ..."

the terminal aitch being dropped in the inimitable manner of the Irish.

* * *

The first Sunday at the island the skipper let us have the boat to catch fish, on condition no attempt was made to land there or on the mainland, six miles away.

We pulled right round Macabi as close to the rocks as was safe. The whole place swarmed with seals and sea-lions. The huge bulls were obviously polygamists, for each enormous, battle-scarred warrior was surrounded by a number of docile wives and calves. As we shouted at them the whole "rookery" made a clumsy rush for the surf, plunging in as if they intended attacking us. Their clumsiness disappeared immediately they entered the water. It was an amazing sight to see hundreds of heads uplifted while they all studied that curious object, our boat.

On the southern end of the island the long surf broke with tremendous force. Yet here the animals were thickest, gambolling in the crashing rollers with the greatest ease where a strong swimmer would have been torn to pieces by the cruel rocks.

As an example of the intensity of maternal affection in a seal, the following may be of interest.

One day one of these creatures was seen near the ship with her baby, who was striking out manfully beside his mother. The little fellow was easily captured from the boat.

The mother remained near the ship all day, craning her neck for a glimpse of her offspring. On deck he flopped about, with an occasional dip in the wash-tub to freshen him up. Once, when his little, lamblike cry rang out, the mother swam at full speed directly towards the ship, battering her snout against the iron

plates so savagely that the water was tinged with her blood. She
was still there the following morning. When the little fellow
was thrown into the sea again she went through the motion of
fondling him, and the pair set off happily for the rocks.

With the exception of one or two visits of a tiny coasting
steamer bringing stores for the *huaneros,* and a small sailing
vessel which supplied the island with water from the mainland
(there was none on Macabi) we were almost completely isolated
from the rest of the world. Occasionally a P.S.N.C. steamer
passed disdainfully by without a glance at our lonely ship lying
there.

And then we had a little excitement with the sighting of an
approaching square-rigger to the s'uth'ard. She must have been
fully twenty miles away when her royals were first seen on the
rim of the horizon. Through the afternoon her progress was
slow, for the wind had fallen light. It was not until long after
dark that she neared the island. We had made her out to be a
deep-loaded, full-rigged ship bound apparently for some port to
the north of Macabi, steering a course to pass between it and the
mainland.

Every soul aboard our ship turned out to watch the stranger's
approach in the pale moonlight. Having seen us anchored there,
she hauled over towards the island to speak to us. When she had
drawn so close as to be little more than a stone's throw away, a
British voice hailed us clearly across the water: "What ship is
that?" "*Arctic Stream,* loading for Leith," shouted our Old Man
from the poop. Then came the answering hail, "This is the
Segura, Newcastle for Pacasmayo."

She was a truly magnificent sight, running with every stitch
of canvas set. To us came the little intimate sounds we knew so
well ourselves—the little sounds of a windjammer swinging her
joyous way along the trail that led to her destination. The steady
seething of the parted water at the forefoot; its gurgling sob
where it played upon the rudder; the musical drone of the night
wind as it embraced the towering fabrics of spars, rigging and
canvas; the soft patter of reef points as the ship pitched easily;
the little creaking protest of straining cordage.

Having spoken us, she ran off a trifle, making for her port
twenty miles up the coast. We heard the long, wailing cry of

her crew at the braces. And then she was gone, like a fairy sprite fading into the night. And we were alone again, alone as we lay off that desolate rock on which the surf boomed unceasingly, while the sea-lions and countless nestling birds quarreled noisily through the hours of darkness.

On our arrival home we heard that this beautiful ship was to be sold to the Norwegians as soon as she had completed the present voyage.

Even at this lonely spot the atmosphere of the *fiesta* must needs be observed. There were two consecutive days on which the workers ashore refused to bring off to us one bag of guano. On these occasions, before the ship had settled too deeply in the water, we put out stages over the side and erased with a fresh coat of paint the rusty scars of our stormy ocean passage.

Occasionally the Old Man made a trip to Malabrigo village by boat, pulled by half a dozen husky Peruvians. He usually returned with a great haunch of beef which kept us in fresh meat for several days.

But we did not fare too badly in between, for the sea abounded with fish. One day an immense shoal of mackerel surrounded the ship, biting so voraciously that even an unbaited hook secured a fish. Hundreds were caught—to be salted down for future use. And then, like a flash, for some unknown reason, they suddenly deserted us.

On our captain's last visit to the mainland he got soaked coming through the surf, arriving at the ship looking more seedy than ever. Nevertheless, he was in the best of spirits. For the ship was nearly ready for the homeward trail. Water was now her greatest need, that and the two tons of potatoes which were to reach us by schooner from Callao.

Our water came off from the mainland in big casks by sailing cutter. It seemed the puddles and cess-pools of Peru had been drained to supply us with the precious fluid. As we emptied the water into our tanks it stank—stank perniciously, openly and without subterfuge or apology. What it would be like before we reached Leith God alone knew. And we could but suffer it, hoping for the best, for no other water was available.

In vain we waited for those potatoes which meant so much to us. The horizon was scanned a hundred times for the vessel from Callao. And then the captain decided to sail the following morning—spuds or no spuds. This decision naturally caused consternation amongst our Irish crew. That was the last indignity of a long and trying voyage—three or four months at sea without so much as a bite of the national fruit of ould Ireland.

This objection was overcome to some extent by the captain's assurance that there were plenty of preserved potatoes aboard. This doubtful statement appeased in no great measure our Irish malcontents. Next day we put to sea, facing a long passage of nearly four months with a few tins of rubbery dried potatoes— a poor travesty indeed of the fresh tubers so essential to the Irish, whose staple diet they have been since the early seventeenth century.

So it was we faced the long trip home under the doubtful encouragement of a menu of salt horse, salt pork—and calavances, otherwise commonly known as beans...

We manned the windlass in the early morning. In spite of the absence of those spuds, there was more cheerfulness and enthusiasm than had been apparent for months. For we were homeward bound. At long last we were about to say good-bye to that dreary coast off which we had lain so long.

Already in the dawning light, that myriad of birds was astir, wheeling noisily about the ship and island before leaving for their feeding grounds.

"Call all hands to man the windlass,
    See your cables run down clear..."

The chanteyman sang the words of the well-known homeward bound song as we hove short. And the wailing cries and the beating wings of that flying host overhead were a strange accompaniment to the clanking pawls and our rough song.

The topsails were loosed and set, and we returned to the fo'c'sle head to weigh the anchor. It was unwilling to leave the snug spot where it had lain embedded for weeks. A score of *huaneros*, filthy and evil smelling, who had rowed off from the island, threw their weight on the bars. The anchor suddenly left the ground; the ship, with fore yards boxed to cast her, slowly gathered sternway.

And then the Old Man noticed we were setting down fast on the cutter which had brought off our water, lying astern. "Let go the anchor again!" he roared from the poop. This was done immediately, the heavy bower rumbling down once more in fifteen fathoms.

Somebody called out, "Where's old Bill?" The mate looked round us all as though mentally counting the hands. Then he said, his face anxious with fear, "Christ! I clean forgot him! He's down the locker still!"

Shouts brought no reply from the chain locker. Hurrying down the ladder into that gloomy pit, we found Bill lying on the rusty chain, bleeding profusely from the head. For days he lay in his bunk in the dim fo'c'sle until the mate, imagining he was exploiting his injuries in the absence of a doctor, hauled him out on deck by his moth-eaten beard.

* * *

Without further trouble the anchor was weighed again. Under her growing canvas the ship stood off the land. The filthy guano delvers, rewarded for their labour by a handful of ship's biscuit each, scrambled hurriedly into their towing boats. Our last link with this strange, forlorn land was parted. And there were no regrets, no sad hearts such as had been ours on leaving Australia. For now we were homeward bound, leaning close-hauled to the south-west under all sail.

Gradually the sad-tuned song of the everlasting surf, the monotonous roaring of the sea-lions, the harsh cries of the birds grew fainter . . .

And then they were no more, and the ship was alone, with the land receding. Out into the vast emptiness of the Pacific she sailed, bound for Cape Horn—and Home.

CHAPTER XIV

"WID OUR CARGO COMPLETE . . ."

A SQUARE-RIGGED vessel bound south for Cape Horn from the Peruvian coast was forced to sail what amounted virtually to two sides of a triangle. This lengthening of her passage was due to the broad belt of the south-east trade winds which pressed a ship far out into the Pacific before she reached the westerlies. The *Arctic Stream* was in almost 96 degrees west longitude before she could run away south and east for the southern tip of the continent.

Conditions on this passage were not so severe as on my previous visit to this region, though, in all conscience, they were bad enough aboard that half-tide rock of ours. But the winter had passed, and we had not to suffer such terribly long dark nights as those experienced in the *Elginshire*. As is so often the case, the worst weather lay to the westward of the Horn, where we went through the usual trying period of peril and stress.

One bitter cold night of storm and darkness stands out from all the many others.

The ship was flying eastward under foresail and lower topsails, battered and harried and tormented by a tremendous pursuing sea and furious wind . . .

It was midnight. I had just left the helm, where for two hectic hours the maddened ship had been mine. Another apprentice on the lee side of the wheel had manfully lent me his aid to hold the frightened vessel somewhere near her course. It was a heavy responsibility but in that ship—always shorthanded and doubly so now by the loss of several sick or injured hands—we older boys had to play fully the part of men. And there was no comforting wheel-house to guard us from the great roaring crests which leaped hungrily upon us, at times threatening to sweep the poop. That was the reason for the lashings which secured the pair of us to the wheel-box.

Wet, tired, perhaps a little unnerved after that two hours' ordeal, I reached my room in the deck house, having passed safely through the dangers of the swirling main deck . . .

Striking a match, I lit the oil lamp, faintly illuminating the dingy, damp hole. Over the deck washed three or four inches of water, monotonously yet swiftly, for the ship was rolling badly.

Standing there in dripping oilskins and sou'wester, I drew my sheath-knife to cut myself the comfort of a fill of plug. As I did so my thoughts turned to the unlucky man who had relieved me at the wheel. His ordeal was really worse than had been mine, for he had been roused, a few minutes earlier, from his warm bunk to stand in the most exposed place in the ship.

The cook suddenly raised his grey head to gaze at me with haggard eyes. "Christ! What a night!" he said. "I must be getting too old for this game for I can't sleep at all with the racket and the rolling."

"Now, Cookie," I admonished, "she hasn't been running so badly. I know because I have been at the wheel for the last two hours. And I know another thing too. Here's one bold *marinero* who is going to have a darned good sleep, racket or no racket."

The words had scarcely left my lips when I sensed that something was amiss, that something out in the dark, blustering night was about to menace the ship.

It has often been said that a good helmsman could tell, even though blindfolded, by his feet upon the wheel-gratings that the ship was running off her course. That was the sixth sense which was operating in my brain that night.

The ship was swinging wildly to starboard—that I knew, boxed up in that cubby-hole in the midship house; that I knew even before the first great sea strode aboard unhindered, the full length of the starboard rail. It hit the deck-house a titanic blow, completely overwhelming it, and poured in upon me through the warped door. Shortly after, another giant roller swept over the ship so that she seemed dead beneath my feet.

Slushy sat up in his bunk, alarmed. He was sailor enough to know the ship was broaching to. Without a word to him, watching my chance when she rolled to looard, I pushed open the door and scrambled out on deck.

After the lamplight it was intensely dark out there, but I dared not pause one moment. Jumping on to the pin-rail, I was over the sheerpole and half-way up the weather lower rigging before the next monster roared aboard the ship.

When my eyes adjusted themselves to the darkness, they saw a scene of wild disorder. The wind, instead of being aft, was now a little abaft the beam, pinning me against the rigging. The ship had swung so far off her course that she offered her low-lying starboard side to the furious onslaught of the seas, which swept over her full length. Out of that foaming turmoil the three masts jutted gauntly, almost as if without support.

The great half-filled foresail, partly edging the wind now, thundered—to be answered by the topsails. The ship lay like a dead thing, and I knew exactly what she was crying out mutely for us to do to help her. Those fore yards would have to be braced sharp up to throw her back to her course again. On the poop a whistle was shrilling and a hoarse voice shouted in the darkness...

And now we were faced with the direst danger which can beset the crew of any square-rigged vessel. Those fore braces, on their pins in the waist, were situated in the most dangerous spot of all. To man them while we put those yards on the backstays might mean the loss overboard of half our crew. For the main deck was filled with solid water.

Then the old ship decided herself to save us that hazardous adventure. Though the wind blew unabated a lull came, such as is experienced sometimes between the worst Cape Horn seas. With way still on her, the ship began to feel her helm, slowly falling off. The sails, filled again, were quietened now as she gathered speed. Slowly the wind and sea drew aft again, and some of the deadening load of water left the deck.

The ship was off before the wind again, the crisis past. And I stood in the lower rigging watching her getting into her stride once more. And then, seizing the opportunity when the heavy water on deck had rolled to looard, I entered the room again.

The cook lay scared and grumbling in his bunk, sucking comfort from his glowing pipe. "What are they playing at aft there, letting her broach-to like that?" he growled. "Are there no sailors left to steer ships properly?"

"Shut up, you old tyke!" I told him, "you know dam-all about steering ships anyway. And if you had been drowned it's what you richly deserve." Throwing off sou'wester and oilskin jacket, I turned in, sea-boots, wet oilskin pants and all, for the cry of "all hands" might come at any moment. On nights such as this the most dangerous hours were midnight and four a.m. when the wheel was newly relieved. The relieving helmsman, freshly wakened from his bunk, his eyes as yet unused to the darkness, a little bewildered perhaps by the noise and rush of the ship staggering before the gale—how could he be expected to get the "feel" of her immediately?

* * *

We were off the Horn almost to the very day on which Lubbock passed that lonely spot in the *Ross-shire* in 1899. He had been privileged to gaze on that rugged, storm-swept outpost, whereas our ship was far away to the s'uth'ard. Old Jim, aft there, was taking no chances. We sailed far south of Diego Ramirez, and nearly 80 miles from the Horn itself.

It was late afternoon when we crossed the meridian of the dreaded cape. Several of us had been sent aloft to tighten up the gaskets before nightfall. Swinging on the main t'gallant footrope, we paused to look around.

A sombre pall of heavy, gloomy cloud lay over us, unbroken anywhere. The sea, rolling in great undulations from the west, was even greyer. Far away to the s'uth'ard, dwarfed by distance, leaned a little, toylike barque. Outward bound, close-hauled under topsails and foresail, she struggled to make westing against the everlasting adverse wind and current.

And then, away to the north of west, the heavy cloud opened suddenly to permit the setting sun to glare malevolently on us ere it passed below the tumbling horizon. There was something strangely baleful in that yellow eye spying at us through the round hole in that mantle of cloud. The sickly, eerie rays lit up the crests of the ponderous procession of rolling seas; they touched our sails and rigging, gilding them faintly for several minutes. And then that watery orb was gone, and darkness crept over the vast lonely ocean...

* * *

There were eight days in the variables before the south-east trades were reached—eight days during which the ship lay becalmed inertly. As she rose and squatted sluggishly in the long, greasy ocean swell, the canvas pounded the masts incessantly, causing more wear and tear than a month of gale.

The Old Man, growling to himself about this annoying delay, prowled restlessly about the poop; the idle man at the wheel whistled softly for a breeze. And come it did at last, ruffling the water in its path, quietening once more the sails as they settled to their task.

While the ship swept up the South Atlantic the usual process of beautifying her for her homecoming went on apace. Alow and aloft, she was painted throughout, and the old mate was a past master in the art. The white panels of deckhouse, bulkheads and bulwarks were picked out in a pretty shade of green.

It was while she was in the trade-wind belt that life was pleasantest aboard the ship. And the most enjoyable time of all was the second dog watch, that brief period of sociability and interchange of yarns.

The two old men of the crew fell into the habit of visiting me frequently, usually singly, for the only poor seating accommodation the tiny room offered was my sea-chest. The cook would still be in the galley, poring over one of his beloved novelettes, so that we would have the place to ourselves. Sometimes Slushy spent a few minutes in the evening waging deadly warfare against the innumerable cockroaches which infested our ship. Portions of their anatomy were always to be found in our food or tea and coffee. The cook would boil a bucket of sea water and then swirl this potent weapon down the back of the stove. Hundreds of cockroaches were slaughtered thus, but there were thousands more to take their place.

Old Sails, whimsical, care-free sea vagabond, entertained me with many tales of ships he had sailed in long ago. Over sixty, thin and by no means robust looking, he was one of the cheeriest and best sailors aboard. A rolling stone who had gathered no moss, to whom all trails were the same, he told me of his long, hard life in sail. There was nothing to sadden or depress him in the fact that he was alone in the world. Yet he had married and had children in early life. But they had died long ago, all save one, and he and that sole survivor had drifted far apart.

One evening he spoke a little bitterly of his daughter, the last of the family left. "She's a bloody lady now," he told me. "Yes, a bloody lady, for she married a man with money. And now she doesn't want the likes of me. When I called at her house last time home her maid turned me away from the door."

MIKE O'BRIEN, WHO FOUGHT THE SECOND MATE,
AT THE WHEEL OF THE "ARCTIC STREAM"

Poor old Sails, what had he to show for a life of toil and hardship? Nothing; nothing but his unspoilt outlook, the miserable clothes he stood up in, and the handful of tools of his trade. But there was something which was his besides—that art which enabled him to cut a topsail with a roach "like the curve of a woman's cheek," as he often said, unconsciously using the term of a poetic simile.

Though this old fellow was small and thin to the point of emaciation, he was intensely tough and capable of great endurance. In Bahia he had been refused permission to go ashore. Ignoring this decree, he decided to swim the half mile between ship and shore. His preparations amused us greatly. Into a small, black-painted canvas bag he put a battered tin alarm clock (perhaps for barter purposes, for he had no money), his shirt and trousers, and a stale scone which the cook had given him.

While the officers were at dinner he slipped overboard on a rope's end. Nobody prevented him from going, for nobody realised the old fellow was serious. Striking out from the ship, he made for the beach. Through a telescope we watched his progress. He was nearing the shore when a boat picked him up, apparently still quite game, though the canvas bag had become a trifle waterlogged.

Nothing further was seen of him for several days. Then he returned to the ship, to be railed at by mate and master. He was, however, quite unrepentant, having enjoyed himself immensely in the company of two native women, in whose hut he had lived all the time he had been ashore.

* * *

Old Bill was the very antithesis of the sailmaker. There was perhaps some cause for the atmosphere of gloom in which his life was spent. For he was the butt of the rough fo'c'sle humour. His was always the task to fetch and carry for the men, to perform the more menial jobs despised by them.

It may be that he found me more tolerant than the others. Shunning the social life of the fore hatch, he would come instead to my room. There would be a shuffle, a snuffle, the gurgle of a foul pipe—and the shaggy head of Old Bill would appear at the door. Climbing over the high coaming, he would come to rest on the sea-chest. Though he received no hilarious welcome from

Q

me, he must have imagined mine a sympathetic ear. For into it were poured all his woes while he sucked at his gurgling clay pipe.

Before me sat the ruin of a man bordering closely on the sixties, often unwashed, flatulent and rather futile. Yet there were signs that Bill had seen better days; there were relics of a good education received in his dim, distant youth, and he spoke in what might once have been a cultured voice. Throughout the voyage it had been rumoured that he was the possessor of a second mate's certificate. Frequently jocular reference was made to this as we worked about the deck, nobody believing that he could lay claim to such a distinction.

One night he came to me as usual. On that occasion there was a sort of triumphant gleam in his watery eye. Putting his hand inside his grubby shirt, he drew out a discoloured parchment. Opening it out, I saw it was a genuine second mate's ticket, dated many years ago.

"Show it to them all, Bill," I urged him, "that'll convince them."

"To hell with them all!" he replied. "You're the only one that's going to see it." Replacing the parchment, he settled down for his customary chat, becoming a little garrulous as he warmed up.

"I'll be glad when this voyage is over," he rambled. "Those brutes for'ad have had it in for me since we left home. And you saw how the mate tried to kill me at Macabi Island. Every dirty job comes my way, and I never get the slightest consideration. I haven't a friend in the world since my poor, dear wife died several years ago. . . ."

The maudlin old ruffian squeezed a tear from one of his rheumy eyes. It trickled slowly down the grime of his cheek. But he hastily pulled himself together, wiped away that unmanly tear, and tumbled out on deck. He had heard the voice of Mike O'Brien shouting out, "Where's that bloody Old Bill?"

* * *

We made the Chops of the Channel in heavy blustering weather, thick as mud, running before a bitter sou'west wind. Already the long ocean swell had left us, replaced by the shorter, savage sea which is found in bad weather on the plateau from which the

British Isles are thrust. The ship, her exact position undefined as yet, was sailing far too fast. It was decided to shorten sail, for no wise mariner would risk making sudden landfall on a lee shore under such conditions.

At a quarter to midnight I went to call Old Sails, for it was a case of "All hands t' th' fores'l!" He was already fully dressed in oilskins, for he had anticipated the call. His head was resting on his arms, and when I spoke to him a tired and worn old man looked up in the flickering light of the dim oil lamp.

"Sonny," he said, "I was just thinking of Christmas Eve over thirty years ago. I remember it well, for we paid off in Dundee several days before the great gale which destroyed the Tay Bridge. I got home on Christmas Eve before the shops had closed, and on my way I bought a few things for the wife and kiddies. . . . Now they are all gone—all except that daughter I told you of . . . . and she's a bloody lady now and doesn't want the likes of me."

Poor Old Sails, the tragedy of his life laid bare! I went out on to the wind- and sea-swept deck, leaving an old, old man with his face buried in his hands. Ten minutes later he was crying out cheerily at the weather gear of the foresail as we hauled the heavy canvas to the yard.

Some hours later, up against the black background of winter sea and sky, between the driving rain squalls, a little light shone out in the darkness—a double flash.

It was the Bishop's Rock, outlying signpost of Britain's coast which had welcomed home from long and often tiresome voyages so many windblown wanderers of the sea.

Kipling has set it down in poetic, manly measure:

> "Beat up, beat in from southerly,
> O Gipsies of the Horn!
> Swift shuttles of an Empire's loom
> That weave us main to main,
> The Coastwise Lights of England
> Give you welcome back again."

O Gipsies of the Horn! Surely we had earned the right of inclusion in that brave body of ships and men? With the assurance and comfort of that friendly, gleaming light, the foresail was set again, and the main t'gans'l too.

The Lizard was passed, our numbers flying gaily to the signal station ashore. In their dusty office in the heart of Glasgow, the owners would soon know another of their ships had all but won through the perils of the deep. With that great blessing, a fair wind, we romped up Channel. Though the wind was not actually off the land, the sweet fragrance of Old England crept out to us. The earthy smell of ploughed fields, the scent of hedgerow, and of grass and trees.

The wind had freshened, so that we took the main t'gans'l off her. The Turk and I furled the landward side as the ship flew by the chalky cliffs of the Isle of Wight. Our work done, we lingered a little to gaze on the shore. Suddenly, striking an attitude, throwing out an arm towards those bold, white ramparts, I cried out, "Albion's proud shores!"

The Turk, swinging nearby on the footrope, looked curiously at me before shrugging a shoulder and remarking disinterestedly, "What you spik, you bloody fool?" Had it been the shining domes of the mosques of Constantinople he might have understood my mood.

We strode through the narrows of the Straits of Dover on a cold, dark night. Everywhere we looked there flashed buoys and brilliant shore lights. The traffic, too, was thick, and old Jim, on the poop, was feeling the strain of it all. The old-time windjammer master hated such narrow waters, for the big square-rigger was essentially of the open sea.

Shortly after midnight a powerful Dutch tug ranged up alongside, having spied the vast blot of our towering canvas.

"What ship is that?" a voice enquired in the darkness.

"*Arctic Stream,* Peruvian coast for Leith."

"Are you taking steam, Captain?"

"What will you charge?" from our cautious skipper.

"I'll tow you to Leith for £140," came the answer.

The Old Man paced the poop a few times, and then, buoyed up, no doubt, by a courage of similar nationality to that of the tug, called out, "No. I'm sailing my ship to Leith dock gates!"

We all felt bitter disappointment at that. But it was unthinkable that our skipper would agree to pay for towage when there was plenty of God's good wind for nothing. As we were soon to learn, that tug could never have held us in the wild weather which followed.

We had not got far into the North Sea when the wind freshened to a gale, jumping later from sou'west to nor'west and blowing with great severity, putting the ship on the dead lee shore of the whole continental coast.

It was in the early hours of the middle watch that we took the foresail off her. As the canvas was dragged to the yard, fighting against clewgarnet and buntline, and leechline, the crests of the seas rattled ice-cold on us as they blew clean over the ship. Up there in the freezing cold we stood on the swinging footropes as we fisted the cruel canvas, inch by inch, under our straining stomachs. When it was all but muzzled a fierce squall, accompanied by stinging sleet, beat down upon us, tearing the folds from our clawing, bleeding fingers.

A hardened old hand on the footrope next to me, shaking his fist at the lowering sky, defied God with foul curses to come down and face us on that yard. In a lull, at last the heavy sail was gasketed—to be followed by the three upper topsails.

The ship having been snugged down, all hands lay aft to the shout of 'Grog Oh!' Under the mate's supervision the steward dished out the fire water. I have no hesitation in stating that we youngsters swallowed our tot like the men, feeling somewhat cheered and comforted by it, though the bulk of our watch below was gone.

During the following week the ship lived in a world of her own, a narrow world of restricted, indeterminate horizon, bounded by the flying spindrift and driving sleet squalls. Her position was pure conjecture, for no sights were possible. Occasionally a hardy North Sea smack flitted ghostlike by under a rag of sail. Once or twice steamers, our lifelong enemies whose aid we now sought, blundered near us, paying no attention whatever to our miserable paraffin morse lamp as it clattered out, "How does St. Abb's Head bear?"

At last, when all hands had had more than enough of the North Sea's venom, a light was picked up from the mizen-top. Far away it blinked—May Island, at the entrance to the Firth of Forth. When daylight came weather conditions moderated and sail was put on the ship. She could just lay her course, the wind having backed to the south and west. Once inside the Firth the sea moderated, and the ship made good going.

The bastion of Bass Rock was passed, the sea-birds screaming as they wheeled about its rugged cliffs, reminding us, in a small way, of the feathered myriads of Macabi. A fussy tug came down to meet us, her crew criticising our weather-beaten appearance in broad Scots as they leaned over the rail. Our foxy old skipper was not for taking steam yet; the tug ranged close alongside and kept pace with us as we swung up the Firth. It really looked as if the Old Man's remark to the Dutch tug had been no idle boast.

In the afternoon the wind decreed otherwise, hauling slightly to the westward. The tug's rope was passed aboard, and we went aloft to stow the canvas for the last time.

That wintry evening found the ship lying quietly at anchor, her shoreward side lined by meditative sailormen who gazed eagerly at the twinkling lights of Leith as they sucked at their pipes. To-morrow they would cease to exist as a crew, to be scattered to many different sea ports. The more fortunate would return to hardworking wives who, no doubt, were looking forward to a land of comparative plenty after a starvation half pay allowance of many months. The Greekie-man and the Turk were itching to see again their beloved 'Cardiffie.' Many of our deep-sea warriors had no fixed plans except to get ashore to start spending their hard-earned money. There were, no doubt, plenty of sharks of both sexes awaiting them to assist that spending, perhaps even now looking out at the riding lights of the ship and licking their chops in anticipation.

The ship made fast at the quay next morning. The mate glanced aloft and along the decks, and then said quietly, as was the custom, "That'll do, men." Sea chests and bags were rapidly passed ashore. They and their owners were escorted triumphantly away by the greedy sharks who lined the quayside, regarding all sailors as their legitimate prey. Hasty handshakes were exchanged, 'So-longs' were shouted—and the crew disappeared.

Old Sails was one of the last to leave. I walked part of the way to the town with him. At the bend of the dock road he stopped to say good-bye to the old ship, while I stood mute beside him. He was muttering to her as if he had forgotten my presence there:

"Ye tried to drown me that time we took those heavy seas to the west'ard of the Horn. Aye, ye tried to drown me pretty near every time we ran into bad weather. I called ye the dirtiest, wettest, most contrary bitch I ever signed on in. But ye could sail, and now—damme, but I don't want to leave ye!"

I left him there—still talking to the ship, and never since have I clapped eyes on the whimsical old fellow. He must have set his course many years ago for the place where 'There shall be no more sea.' He was of a type which mechanical progress has left far behind, a true sailor grown old in the real service of the sea. No recollection of his name comes to me a-down the years—for to all he was just 'Old Sails.' But I can still hear his voice raised happily in some catchy chorus of his boyhood days; I can still hear his long-drawn, eerie cry as we trimmed the yards to the wind. God rest that old shipmate's bones, wherever they may lie!

*　*　*

No epicure enjoyed his flamingoes' tongues as did we that first shore feed of bacon and eggs and fried potatoes, eaten in a nearby cafe. How we cleaned our plates vulgarly with bread, wiping up every smear of that delicious fat. The pretty Scots waitress came over to make out the bill. Preening her curly hair, she enquired casually, "Is there onything mair ye want?" "Yes, please, miss," we chorused, "just take these plates out and fill them up again." Her eyes goggling with surprise, she did as we bid her. From a corner she and the manageress watched us devouring the second helping. The latter came over to us, an amused smile on her face. We told her what ship we came from.

"Aye," she remarked dryly, "I hear they keep ye pretty hungry in thae ships."

Several days later there remained aboard only the captain, his wife, their daughter who occasionally came to stay with them, an old fellow who filled the dual role of cook and steward, and myself. The work of discharge had commenced. Down the hold a number of men and women shovelled the guano into bags, reversing the process we had carried out so laboriously at Macabi.

There was little for me to do aboard, for mine was the post of sort of glorified watchman, attending to the trivial needs of the ship. So it was I was idly watching a pretty girl of seventeen who was helping the others in the hold. She seemed too fair a bud to be listening to the coarse banter of the rough men and women with whom she worked.

A hail from the quayside reached my ears. Looking up, I saw

a neat, serge-clad figure coming aboard. It was Old Bill. Old Bill transformed, transfigured, purified, spruced up almost beyond belief. He wore a natty new suit, in the buttonhole of which was stuck a bright flower. His huge, splay feet were encased in highly varnished boots, on which were superimposed flamboyant spats. He carried a dainty cane and a pair of ultra-yellow gloves. His beard—always his worst feature—had been cleansed and trimmed to a neat point. The whole ensemble was topped by a brand-new bowler hat.

"Holy smoke, Bill!" I gasped. "Those spats! And the gloves! And the cane! In fact, the whole get up! What's the big scheme, anyway?"

He drew me towards my little room in the deck-house. He sat down on my sea-chest, thrust out the offensive spats towards me, and remarked: "It's a girl . . . . a woman . . . . a judy . . . . a skirt . . . . call her what you like." From his hip pocket he produced a flask of whisky. We drank, in the manner of good shipmates, from two battered tin mugs. As I raised my arm I toasted facetiously: "To the girl . . . . the woman . . . . the skirt . . . . call her what you like!"

"I met her in Cardiff just before we sailed outward bound," Bill went on, gulping as the powerful spirit tickled his tonsils. "She's got a café there, and she's going to marry me right away. No more crawling around aloft at night; no more dirty, biscuit-chewing stiffs to associate with; no more cheek from mates who think every sailor is a dog for them to kick. I wrote to her while we were on the West Coast. There was a letter waiting for me at the shipping office, and everything is fixed up. I'm off to Cardiff to-day, and then—what-ho for the nuptials!"

He got up and executed a grotesque, shuffling step-dance.

"Sit down, you rotten hypocrite," I said. "For months you have been snivelling about your poor dear wife, who was the only friend you ever had, and all the time you have been thinking about this bird in Cardiff. Anyway, I can't imagine what the woman is thinking about, marrying a mouldy ruffian like you."

The maudlin old fellow looked sheepishly at me, smiled slyly, dropped his left eyelid in a broad wink, and for answer pushed the flask towards me again. Finally he hobbled ashore up the gangway. Over his shoulder he shouted, much to the amusement of the onlookers, "You see, there's life in the old dog yet!"

On the quay he tilted his pot-hat at a jaunty angle, spread his shuffling splay feet, and twiddled his cane, aping the antics of Charlie Chaplin.

A playful gust of wind snatched the jaunty bowler from his head and sent it twirling among the dockside puddles. The last I saw of my curious, lovesick shipmate was his shambling pursuit of the flighty pot-hat around a shed, the pristine beauty of his spats marred by the greasy mud of the wharfside. And I could imagine him uttering words which were hardly those of love.

* * *

The powerful stench of the guano was not the only unpleasant feature of the work of those men and women in the hold. For the vermin, with which our cargo had literally crawled in the sunny clime of Peru, were even more vigorous after their four months' sojourn in the ship. Perhaps it was they ran about more rapidly to keep themselves warm under the chilly, leaden sky of Leith.

And those Scots women and lassies, unprotected from such activities by the nature of their attire, roundly cursed the little crawling beasties. The men could afford to laugh at this, for lashings around the bottoms of their trousers rendered them more or less immune from the roving propensities of the vermin.

The two rooms on the port side of the deck-house were allotted to the ladies for the purpose of delousing themselves every evening before they went ashore. While I ate my supper in solitude in my room on the starboard side the coarse conversation and vulgar jokes of the women as they stripped themselves would come clearly through the thin bulkhead.

For a month I lived aboard the ship. She would soon be preparing for another voyage beyond a far horizon. The Old Man told me, on one of his visits, that she was to tow to the Tyne to load for 'Frisco.

Throughout that period many complete strangers showed me much kindness. It seemed my old ship had achieved a fame unshared by the other full-rigged ship, *Wray Castle,* lying across the dock. Over and over again I had to recount the history of our voyage.

One morning as I was hoisting the ensign the captain of a 'Ben' boat called to me, inviting me aboard his steamer. At the time I was clad in ragged jersey and dirty dungarees, my feet and legs encased in an enormous pair of old leaky rubber thigh-boots—the parting gift of the second mate—and altogether I looked a very disreputable individual.

My new friend would hear of no excuse. Soon the two of us were sitting in what appeared to me to be a palatial, steam-heated room, listening to his gramophone. The good man fed me lavishly, and loaded me with magazines before I left him.

The time had come for me to say good-bye to the *Arctic Stream*. It was perhaps as well, for the seventeen-year-old bud mentioned before proved not so innocent and budlike as had seemed at first. Towards the end she had, indeed, taken it into her head to assume unwarranted proprietorial rights over my person. On the arrival of the workers every morning she would come up to me, put her arms around me and proclaim, without so much as by my leave, that I was her 'mon.' The roars of laughter from her colleagues always filled me with embarrassment, for, though a little different from the original manse product, I was still a timid youth.

* * *

There is always a certain sadness in leaving a ship. She may have bruised and battered and half drowned you, but that is all forgotten when the time for parting comes.

At the bend of the dock road, where Old Sails had done the same, I turned to say good-bye to the ship. Almost empty, she rode high in the water, and some of the grace of her pretty hull was consequently lost.

Somehow I knew that this was a last farewell; that this was not a mere *au revoir*. She too may have shared that presentiment of mine, for as I gazed long and a little sadly at her the drooping ensign fluttered into life—as though she were bidding me a last good-bye.

A few days later that beautiful ship lay dead upon the bleak Northumberland coast—a battered, twisted wreck. . . .

It is over a quarter of a century since I last trod that ill-fated ship's deck. And of all those men who manned her but three have crossed my path; the mate, who walked aboard the steamer in which I was third mate to press me to sail as second mate with him in Law's four-masted barque *Kinross-shire;* one of the apprentices whom I met recently, after all these years; and the captain, of whom more anon.

What became of my room-mate Slushy I never knew. He has probably departed long since to the place where there shall be no more women—not, at least, as he liked them. After that long voyage spent in such close companionship with that culinary artist (?) it became my habit to remark facetiously, every time I heard acidy women adversely discussing their cooks: "What's the matter with cooks? They're all right. I slept with one for many months and should surely know something about them."

Pretty feeble, you will say. Yes, pretty feeble, I admit, but it was amusing to watch those dames' faces, those disapproving looks, until I hastened to assure them that my sleeping partner was a male.

CHAPTER XV

SWAN SONG OF SAIL

In 1892 — now more than fifty years ago — the shipbuilding yards of Britain sent down the ways the largest tonnage of sailing vessels ever to take the water in one year. From that time onwards, the building of purely sail tonnage dwindled rapidly until, in 1905, the last big British ocean-going vessel, relying solely on sails for its movement, was launched.

That was the fine four-masted barque, *Archibald Russell,* still afloat and owned by Capt. Gustav Eriksen of Finland.

From the British shipyards, at work on that great fleet of square-riggers in 1892, the clamour of riveting-hammers rang out the length of the year.

Paradoxical though it may seem, the metallic voice of those clattering hammers was, to my mind, the Swan Song of Sail.

In the year mentioned, perhaps even several years before, the design of sailing vessels had undergone a change. Gone for ever were the sleek, slim-thighed composite tea clippers and the early semi-clippers of iron. It is true, many still remained afloat in full commission, but the stocks would know them no more. Some semblance of beauty was given to the new huge four-masted ships by their sweetly curved entrances, gracefully moulded counters and long tip-tilted spike booms, under which, to the last, was snugly enthroned the traditional figurehead. But the midship sections were square, wall-sided, and somewhat pathetically symbolic of the struggle sail was waging to retain the seas.

Dire necessity, in the shape of ever-increasing steam competition, had forced the designers to produce a full-bodied hull, capable of great carrying capacity, not too slow on a passage, yet not too heavily sparred to render the ship unfit to be handled by a comparatively small, economical crew. The resultant effort was the four-masted barque, most of which were turned out from the middle 'eighties onward until British shipowners recognised their defeat by steam.

One hundred years ago practically all long voyages were carried out by vessels relying solely on sail to drive them to their distant

SWAN SONG OF SAIL

destination. It is indeed strange, when one studies the history of steam at sea, to find how tardy was the growth of any serious effort to make full use of it as a propulsive power. Conservatism remained deeply imbedded in the soul of both ship designer and shipowner.

Far into the nineteenth century sail held pride of place, many shipowners looking askance at any new-fangled ideas. Sailors, too, have always been amongst the most conservative of people. For centuries ships had been driven by the winds of heaven, surely a most natural thing seeing they were so closely attuned to that other great element which bore them.

The beginning of the end can rightly be set down to the opening of the Suez Canal in 1869. Cutting off, as it did, thousands of miles on the run to India and the Far East, this event literally sounded the death knell of the fleet tea-clipper and those other swift-sailing vessels trading out east.

Many authorities claim the 'fifties and 'sixties as the Golden Age of Sail. Without posing as an authority, I maintain it came even later—in the seventies and eighties, in spite of the Suez Canal —when iron had taken the place of wood in the construction of larger vessels.

Most old salts held up their hands in horror at the idea of an *iron* ship, making use of the scarcely logical argument that 'wood floats—iron doesn't.' I feel sure that once they had overcome their prejudice, after making no more than one voyage in an iron or steel ship, they would never readily return to a wooden vessel again. For the majority of wooden ships leaked considerably when loaded with anything in the nature of an unkindly cargo. The necessary pumping was probably the most gruelling work, should the leak be serious, that any sailor was forced to perform.

Reference has frequently been made to the fast passages of the wooden and composite tea-clippers, and their performance compared with that of their iron and steel successors—to the detriment of the latter.

Such comparison is scarcely fair for the following reasons. The ships of the so-called Golden Era of Sail were small, handy vessels, manned by what now appear to be enormous crews; they almost invariably carried light cargoes which did not tax the ships, which were thus in favourable trim for fast sailing; they received highly remunerative freights, thus dispensing with the continual nursing of gear and crippling economy which became so prevalent in later years.

The logs of most of the tea-clippers show an almost monotonous repetition of such entries as: 'Such and such a sail blown away—new one sent aloft.' It would seem a few sails were a mere flea-bite in the keenness of the competition.

In the square-rigged ships in which the author served, sails were a valuable part of the ship's equipment, and could not with impunity be permitted to be lost. Freights had sunk so low that it was only by the practice of the strictest economy that a narrow margin of profit could be shown. Reckless driving, with its consequent damage or loss of canvas, had it been indulged in, would soon have brought the master face to face with a curt 'Please explain' from the owners.

And then, again, composite and wooden vessels do not foul rapidly when sheathed with copper as was, and still is, the custom. The underwater hulls of iron and steel ships, on the other hand, despite the periodic and liberal applications of anti-fouling paint, were seldom really clean, often on a long passage being heavily encrusted with barnacles and trailing sea-growths.

Crews, too, had been pared down. The divided fo'c'sle of the *Elginshire* contained twelve bunks on each side. Presumably, then, twenty-four men was the crew deemed fit to man her when she set out on her maiden voyage. Though her sail area had not been altered in any way, this number had dwindled to six men in each fo'c'sle when I was in her—just half her original complement.

This deficiency, it is true, had been made up to some extent by the enlargement of the after deck-house (the half-deck) to accommodate twelve instead of six premium-paying apprentices. That was, of course, an astute business action on the part of the owners, who knew only too well what a number of boys were clamouring to take up a life at sea. It furthermore assured them a plentiful supply of officers whose services could be bought cheaply.

With this crew the big barque was really undermanned, and on occasion in bad weather, when several members were laid up sick or otherwise disabled, literally ran away with us.

These facts are mentioned to point out that the latter-day windjammer was in no position to go in for any reckless racing such as other days had known. In spite of this, some remarkable passages were made by the iron and steel ships of the closing era of sail. Many could be mentioned, but one or two should suffice.

The Anglo-American Oil Co.'s ship, *Glendoon,* sailed from Cape Town to New York in 36 days in 1907. This is, I believe, a record for the passage under sail. The usual distance on this trip is 6,811 nautical miles, but the *Glendoon,* being a sailing vessel, must have covered a far greater mileage than that.   A cargo steamer at that time took from 29 to 32 days to complete the passage.

My old ship, *Arctic Stream,* sailed from San Francisco to East London, South Africa, in 75 days, a splendid passage which was only once beaten.

But even these good runs pale almost into insignificance in comparison with that of the four-masted barque *Lawhill* from Melbourne to Cape Town several years ago.

Deep-loaded with wheat, under the able command of my good friend Captain Soderlund, this 51-year old ship sailed (in 1943, when the art of handling big windjammers is supposed to. have been lost) the 11,500 miles in 55 days, a truly amazing feat when one considers the age of the ship and the fact that each of these 55 days was shortened, sailing east, by often over 20 minutes.

The speed of the big barque worked out at over 9 knots throughout the entire passage, an achievement which surely proves to the admirer of the swift tea-clippers of old that it was not they alone which were *sailed;* that here, in a mechanized age, we have one stout-hearted seaman who knows how to urge to the utmost his aged ship.

Well done, Captain Soderlund! Had yours been the opportunity to command those tiny clippers of old, I feel sure you would have defeated one and all, causing those giants of the sea—Moore, Wallace, Woodget, and all the much vaunted others—to doff their top-hats to you in admiration.

* * *

Right up to the end of last century, and even into the opening years of the present one, many steam vessels still clung tenaciously to their sails, so suspicious were their owners of the alien power embowelled deep within their hulls.

But by then most British shipowners had seen the writing on

the wall. And it was surely there, plain for all but the blind to read. That disfiguring smear of smoke on the wide, blue horizon of the oceans was growing and spreading apace. Year by year the red-edged 'steamer' section of Lloyd's Register was thickening—undeniably, inexorably—no matter how old-time sailors and ship-owners with a touch of romance in their make-up scorned the 'tin kettles.'

And then came the blow which did so much to deplete the remaining fleet of British sail. From the French ship-building yards swarmed a host of big sailing vessels to compete with the already hard-pressed British ships. The full import of this invasion was not realised by the sturdy band of British sailing vessel owners until it became known that these Frenchmen were to sail under a Government bounty—a subsidy so substantial that they could circumnavigate the world in ballast without financial loss to their owners.

It has been said that the advent of these foreign vessels was the last straw which broke the British windjammer's back. The result was soon noticeable. Owners who still managed big fleets of sail capable of carrying on, under conditions of fair competition, for many years, became disheartened and sold out at ridiculous prices.

A few of the older, more conservative lines, whose owners may have been foolish enough, or sentimental enough, to love their ships, clung stubbornly to the industry their fathers, in many cases their grandfathers, had built up. From dusty little offices in London, Liverpool, Glasgow, and the other seaports were ad-ministered the activities of their white-winged ships. The utmost economy in even small details was necessary. Their office windows flaunted no flamboyant house-flags; their staffs were small, prob-ably one or two clerks—the senior one, as likely as not, grown old in their service.

And then, of course, there would be the marine superintendent, or 'ship's husband,' a most important man whose duty it was to meet and inspect each vessel at the end of her voyage. This sup-posedly snug 'shore job' was usually his reward for the many years of faithful service sailing those ships in which he now voyaged no more.

*   *   *

"ARCTIC STREAM" IN THE NORTH-EAST TRADE WIND

Oh, I am the wind that the seamen love —
I am steady and strong and true

Thomas Fleming Day

Photo by the author

The years 1909, 1910 and 1911 were disastrous for the old industry. Besides losses to the Red Ensign from knock-out sales to foreign buyers, the usual hazards of the sea claimed many victims. Amongst a host of them the names which come most readily to mind are *Swanhilda, Crompton, Annersley, Kynance, Marion Frazer, Deanmount, Radiant, Carnarvon Bay*. Lloyd's Register had them all there—a pathetic list of brief obituary notices, one on almost every page or two—telling tritely but sadly of the end of those square-rigged ships which would never be replaced.

Why was it so many were lost about that time? Was it perhaps that the art of sailing those big ships was dying too? Or was it that their officers and crews had become inferior through being affected by the insidious creeping in of a 'steamboat complex'? These may have been factors in the loss of so many seaworthy vessels at the time of which I write, though there were still, of course, numbers of seafarers who, even so recently, had never sailed the seas in anything but square-rigged ships.

* * *

Before me lies a cutting from a Shipping Gazette of 1910. The following extract is quoted from it:

'Very gloomy views are held as to the future of sailing ships so far as British owners are concerned. The steady stream of sales at knockout prices, which set in some months ago, still continues.'

The truth of this statement was soon made manifest in the years which followed while I was in sail. Out on the vastness of some lonely stretch of ocean the welcome cry 'Sail Ho!' would be heard. First the royals and then the t'gans'ls would peep over the rim of the ocean—a little white spot in the distance. If we were approaching, her canvas would grow rapidly—upper topsails, lower topsails, courses, and then her saucy jibboom creeping over the horizon, proving once more the undoubted rotundity of the world's surface.

Our ensign would rise, streaming to the gaff-end. We waited patiently for hers to follow. Some member of the watching crew would call out, "That's the old——. I made two voyages in her."

A little spot of red would climb slowly to her gaff. She would still be too far off for us to read her name, but that flag blowing

R

out in the distance looked uncommonly like our own. Then, as we approached, bowing and curtsying to each other, we would make out that little spot of red. It would all too often be the handsome flag of Norway, that sea-minded country which bought so many of our sailing ships while they were still stout and strong, sometimes paying for themselves in a voyage or two. The Norwegian ensign is very similar to our own in the distance.

The skipper would turn sadly to the mate. "Another of our fine ships gone," he would remark. He had never been in steam and loved the windjammers which he sailed.

In spite of this, when I joined the Shire Line, Thos. Law & Co. still clung stoutly to their ships, owning a fleet of twelve square-riggers—all in commission—and no steamers. At one time the fleet had been almost double that number. In the pantry of the *Elginshire* one could still see some of the original crockery, inscribed in pale green with the house flag and the words 'Shire Line of Queensland Packets'—pathetic relics of its former glory,

There were a number of other companies who still (in 1910) managed considerable fleets of sail—notably John Stewart & Co. of London; G. Milne of Aberdeen, the *Inver* Line; A. Weir's *Bank* Line of Glasgow; C. E. de Woolf's and R. Thomas' ships of Liverpool. Lastly, but by no means least, might be mentioned Aitken, Lilburn's famous *Loch* Line which traded for so many years to Australia. There must be a number of people still living in the Antipodes who remember the first view of the Australian continent as seen from the deck of one of the fine Loch liners. Of all these companies the Loch Line was the first to sell out. Under outlandish Scandinavian names, uninsured and cheaply run, these magnificent four-masters still sailed the seas for many years.

But there was really very little left for sail. Steam was butting in everywhere. Trades which hitherto had been scorned by it were now being flagrantly filched from the ships of 'the sticks and strings.' General cargoes of the better sort were almost unobtainable by sailing vessels. They had to be content with timber-carrying and the poorer class of cargo. There was coal from the Bristol Channel ports, which usually meant the bitter westward passage of the Horn; 'black diamonds' from Newcastle, N.S.W.; nitrate or guano from the West coast of South America, or, most favoured of all, grain home from Australia.

The good-hearted, sporting Australians did much to keep the last of the square-riggers at sea. It was through their love of, and interest in, the sailing vessel which had done so much to open up their wonderful country that many of these were not forced to lie-up indefinitely, rusting at obscure moorings.

Australia was, indeed, the Mecca of the last of the ships of sail. Fortunate were those who were borne by the wind to its hospitable shores. Memories of many happy days in port there come back to me, and I can recall innumerable kindnesses shown to a lonely 'light-the-binnacle boy' far from home.

* * *

The ship of sails has folded her great broad wings in sleep for ever. And there are some—foolish sentimentalists, perhaps—who mourn her passing as are mourned our beloved dead.

It was she who blazed the trail across the vast, unknown oceans; she who performed the rough spade work which rendered safe the path of her snorting successors.

And the language of the sea has died, a language reaching far back into the early days when oars were cast aside and man set about perfecting the art of using the wind to aid him in his lengthier voyagings. No more will ring along the decks of a British ship that well-known cry, "Lee fore brace!"—bugbear of the sailor drowsing in the tropic night.

The song of the chantyman is stilled for ever, that brave, heartening song without which the work of those square-rigged ships could never have been carried out efficiently. This refers to vessels of the orthodox type where everything was done by pully-hauly on ropes. Such things as brace- and halliard-winches were unknown in the ships in which the author served. What was sung, if they sang at all, while they twiddled the handles of those winches I do not know, never having been shipmates with those labour-saving contraptions.

Some sea-minded reader will remark, "But the songs of the sea will never die out. We often hear them on the air. They will be preserved for ever."

They will be preserved for ever! By whom—a bunch of emasculated crooners gathered together round a microphone in an overheated studio?

Those chanties were created for a purpose. That purpose is now dead. For the love of Mike, then, let them die too, instead of casting them to the tender mercies of a pack of dinner-jacketed warblers who never even smelt deep water, or knew the manly song of wind on mast and spar and distended canvas.

There are many of us older ones, those of us who have passed the half century, who can still look back with pride and pleasure on our days in sail. My mind is filled with memories of those brave old voyagings, when we had nought but our stout arms and God's clean wind to take us to our distant destination. The life, of course, was not entirely dog-like though, in all truth, it was hard enough. The one amazing thought for me is how we managed to carry on our work of sail-making and sail-taking at night *without artificial light of any sort*. After one bell no light of any kind, other than the lamp in the binnacle, was permitted aboard. As has been said before, the most of our work aloft was carried on at night, and when the kindly moon and stars denied us their pale illumination we could but feel our way aloft amongst that towering, spidery rigging.

But there was something which the steamboat man missed at the end of a long voyage—a feeling of satisfaction, perhaps even an elation such as must have been known by the Vikings of old when their homing port was made. And when the last mooring-line was made fast and the mate had cast his eyes aloft to note the neat trim of those lofty, broadspread spars with their close-furled sails—those great white wings which had driven us so far—there was something deeper than mere satisfaction for us when he spoke his last few simple words of dismissal—"That'll do, men."

Let us, then, drink a toast to the windjammer which is no more. *Ave atque Vale!* Hail and Farewell, brave old ships which have passed for ever.

But is it for ever? Is it not possible that the day may dawn when man, surfeited and grown weary of the stride of his vaunted progress, will turn again to the simpler things?

Should he do so, he will find God's good wind, which is not merely of to-day or to-morrow, ready for his needs once more. He will find "the Trades" singing their age-old triumphant song—and the great West Wind still sweeping over the illimitable spaces of the Southern Ocean.

*　　*　　*

Before closing this chapter I have a confession to make, a confession which has never been made to any living person before. I, who had so often while in sail heard steamships and their officers so foully maligned, when in charge of the watch in one of those ships nearly committed the unforgivable crime of destroying one of the last of the windjammers . . .

I was at the time navigating officer in one of the Clan Line steamers. It was the middle watch, and the moon sufficiently strong to make the horizon ideal for star sights—a branch of my work in which I was particularly interested.

Before taking my sextant from its box, I swept the sea from ahead to abeam each side with the powerful night-glasses. Nothing was in sight.

Taking five stars—two east, two west for longitude, with an ex-meridian of the Pole Star for latitude—I made perfect contact with the horizon, clear in the stellar telescope. Then, having told the apprentice on duty with me on the bridge to keep a good lookout, I stepped into the chartroom to work out the sights.

They fitted in beautifully, and I was just about to prick off the position on the chart when the apprentice stuck his head in at the door to report. "There's a funny little green light on the port bow, sir," he said, quite casually.

A "funny little green light on the port bow"! That must surely be a sailing vessel crossing our bow. Dashing out on deck, I looked over the weather-cloth. My heart nearly stopped beating! There she was, a great, dark shadow on the sea and the sky—a big square-rigged ship running to the eastward for the Straits of Gibraltar, so close that it seemed no action on the part of either vessel could prevent collision. And that other ship had the right of way, and it was up to me to do something *immediately*.

In the *Nautical Magazine* I had recently read an article in which the writer attributed the sinking of so many sailing vessels by steamers to an under-estimate of the speed of sailing ships. That article was the salvation of that big barque, and of me, too, that night. Had I altered course to starboard that windjammer would undoubtedly have been cut to the water's edge—and I would have lost my certificate.

"Wi-jao chikar!" I roared at the lascar quartermaster, without a moment's hesitation. The ship swung almost immediately—

just in time. As our bow swung to port the barque's stern barely drew clear. I heard the many little sounds I knew so well—the drumming of wind on canvas and the patter of reef-points, the gurgle of the water around the rudder-head.

But, above them all, I heard a louder and far more insistent sound, a hoarse cursing through a megaphone which seemed oddly familiar. It was, of course, though the words were unintelligible, the same foul invective I had heard under similar conditions from the windjammers in which I had served.

That apprentice, duly strafed, assured me he had kept a good lookout with the glasses while I had been in the chartroom. Undoubtedly, some wraithlike patch of mist, thin yet dense enough to obscure that ship, had enveloped her until she was almost upon us.

*   *   *

Some of us who served in sail foolishly imagined the lordly steamship to be more or less immune to the onset of wind and wave. How false was this idea was proved to us most graphically during one of the wildest nights it has been my lot to spend at sea.

The ship, a full-powered, well-found steamer but flying light in ballast, was bound from London to Liverpool. The weather had been ugly and threatening as the turning point of Land's End was rounded. In the afternoon it had become positively filthy. A nor'west gale, increasing in force with amazing rapidity, put the wicked coast of Cornwall dead to leeward of us.

At four o'clock, when the short winter's day was all but done, the second mate came to me. "Come on, young fellah," he said, "the mate's forgotten the *pouri wallah* (lookout man) up in the crow's-nest. He's been up there for hours. None of the lascars will go up, so you and I are going to bring him down."

The ship had been headed right into the gale to attempt to make an offing, for the land was all too close. As she pitched heavily into the already high sea, solid water broke over the fo'c'sle head and, thundering aft when she lifted again, burst madly against the bulkhead of the midship section.

Watching our chance, we swiftly covered the well-deck and scrambled up the steel ladder of the foremast, the second mate leading. A few seconds later the ship thrust her nose into a wall of water which buried the whole fore-deck. High up in the cross-trees though I was, the fringe of that avalanche struck me savagely, tearing the buttons from my oilskin coat.

A rather slack and narrow ratlined ladder led up the long topmast to the wooden-barrel crow's-nest, lashed close below the truck. This we eventually reached. Peering over the edge, we found the *pouri wallah,* his lookout days apparently over for ever, slumped in the bottom of the barrel. His thinly-clad body, half covered with sleet, was frozen stiff and he was quite unconscious.

Now we were faced with the problem—how to get him down. As we clung there the masthead swung dizzily and bucked and jerked. Luckily both of us were well used to clinging to such insecure parts of a ship, far from the safety of the deck.

There was a gantline rove through a block close under the truck. Putting a bowline under the lascar's arms, we signalled to the mate to hoist away. The other end of the gantline had been taken up on to the lower bridge, where the mate and his men were clustered.

There was just sufficient drift to hoist the helpless man from the barrel. Then, as the mate started to lower away, our real difficulty commenced. The further down we went the worse it grew. In the mad pitching and rolling, the inert bundle broke away from our clutching hands repeatedly, blowing far out from us in the screaming wind. As the ship pitched extra heavily, back it came again, battering heavily against us and almost throwing us from the mast.

At last we got him down. Quickly he was carried aft, stripped, rubbed all over with brandy, and rolled in many blankets. He recovered eventually and suffered no ill effect.

Halfway through the night I stood on the bridge with the captain. We spoke little as we clutched the stanchions. The wind had reached an unbelievable fury; the ship had become utterly unmanageable, literally refusing to face the gale. With the engines racing madly in the wild pitching, she sagged away to leeward.

From the north-west came an unending procession of steep, raging seas. They climbed all over the ship, faintly lighting her decks with the weird phosphorescence of their angry crests. They smashed the port lifeboat; they broke up deck fittings piecemeal. Up aloft at the trucks and all along the triatic stay shimmered the ghostly light of St. Elmo's fire.

Every now and then the wireless operator came up to report the signals from Poldhu coming through louder and louder. The chief engineer came too—to tell the master the engines could not stand such terrific punishment for long. "For God's sake keep her going!" was all the skipper said to him.

My mind kept dwelling on the one thing—that cruel, rock-bound coast which lay dead to leeward of us, offering no spot of shelter for which a ship might run.

The captain's thoughts must have been similar to mine. Putting his mouth close to my ear he shouted: "Have you got your certificate in your pocket?" It seemed an odd question at such a time. Then he went on: "I don't believe the ship will live through the night . . . it's easier to identify anybody by a certificate . . ."

Mercifully, a sudden and unexpected shift of wind to the south-west enabled the ship to weather that notorious Cornish coast. Had it been delayed, she could never have kept off that leeward shore.

CHAPTER XVI

WAR TO END WAR

THROUGHOUT my apprenticeship my salary had been £5 per annum, plus twelve shillings a year "washing money." The indentures did not state specifically whether the latter sum was to be utilised for cleansing one's person, one's clothing, or one's soul. It could hardly be expected to do all three.

My father had frequently augmented this measly income at the various ports. He, good man, attempting to put by a little for his retirement, was still industriously scribbling sermons, still trotting wearily around visiting his flock, imbibing with the womenfolk the far-too-many cups of tea which etiquette imposed and which, no doubt, severely aggravated the stomach trouble from which he suffered continuously.

But the Lord had tempered the wind to the shorn lamb. Since my leaving home my father's financial affairs had improved greatly. It is truly an ill wind that blows nobody any good. He was the somebody who drew comfort from the evil blast of scandal which stormed against one of the professors of the college.

The man either resigned or was dismissed; there was none to fill his hurriedly vacated chair. My father, a Gold Medallist in German and French in his closing student days, was approached by the perplexed authorities. Could he fill the vacant chair of modern languages? He could, and would, and did—after the consent of his congregation had been obtained. The dual job was filled by him so creditably that it was eighteen months before a permanent man was imported to take over.

The good man's burden had been heavy throughout those long months. With two sons and a daughter studying the arts in an attempt to acquire degrees of various sorts, the extra salary was a God-send.

But the stoop of his shoulders had increased. Maybe his congregation suffered loss through his immersion in his other duties; maybe the ladies, who did not see so much of him, missed his company over that "nice cup of tea." They did not complain,

however, happy perhaps in the thought that their minister was
so erudite a man.

* * *

Now had come the time for me to relieve him of the burden of
my partial keep; to raise the wind with a few pounds to see me
safely through for my second mate's certificate. Walking aboard
a Blue Funnel ship at Birkenhead, I put the position before the
Chief Officer, a red-faced Welshman who welcomed me with an
unexpected friendliness.

"Come along to the shipping office to-morrow," he said. "I'll
get you signed on as A.B., and will pick you for the wheelhouse
afterwards. An A.B.'s wages are £5, but as quartermaster you'll
get five shillings a month more and live two in a room."

"Thank you, sir," I said, preparing to leave him.

"Just a minute," he remarked, "a word of warning before you
go. In this company the crews are very conservative. Some sail
for years in the same ship. Don't mind if you get a few black
looks, for they don't like strangers."

A number of men stood waiting outside the shipping office
next morning. The white collar of the young man hovering on
their fringe looked a little out of place in that bemuffled gathering. The black looks referred to by the mate were obvious, even
had they not been reinforced by sundry pointed remarks which
did not fail to reach the ears of that youngster standing diffi-
dently on the outskirts.

"Who's that young bastard there with the choker on?" one or
two asked of their pals. Well used to the rough language of the
sea, knowing that no direct slight was cast upon his parents or
himself, that youngster remained silent, unaccepted as yet into
the inner circle of the narrow, class-hampered brotherhood of his
future shipmates.

Nevertheless, the job became mine, and I soon found myself
signed on in my first steamer for a voyage to the Far East.
The ship had not yet left the dock when it became obvious
that there was much to be learned in this strange new life. I
saw for the first time seamen wearing gauntlets to protect their
hands as they hove in the mooring lines. Gloves on the hands of
sailors! Ye Gods, what was the race coming to! And then I
realised that they were not sailors at all, and the truth of the

THE NIGHT WATCHMAN ABOARD THE ILL-FATED BARQUE "GULF STREAM"

"OLD SAILS" AT WORK ON POOP OF "ARCTIC STREAM"

jocular remark I had heard so often became apparent. I had now "given up going to sea and gone in steam."

The Bar Light Vessel had been passed before the mate sent for me to come on the bridge, where he stood with the master.

"Take the wheel!" the captain ordered me curtly. Though his father had commanded one of the best known of the white wings of Britain, he was a man I never grew to like.

The elderly quartermaster stepped aside—and I grasped the helm of a steamship for the first time. Sheltered by the surrounding glass, it seemed almost stuffy in that wheelhouse. Over the bowl, a big, bulging lens magnified the lubber's line and the degrees so much that they looked almost like the points on the compass cards I had been used to. The slight tremble of the card puzzled me at first, until I realised that even high up there the pulsing of those unaccustomed engines could be felt.

The ship was steering easily, though the wind and sea were making. Breaking off his conversation with the mate, the skipper came to watch me. Leaning through the open for'ad window of the wheelhouse, he peered down on the card for a few minutes.

Raising his eyes to mine, he barked out, "You're half a degree, off your course!" In spite of my position that nearly made me smile. Half a degree! And many a time, away down south in the roaring forties we had been happy enough to hold the yawing ship within a point or two on either side, thinking we were doing well.

The captain returned to the mate. "He'll do," he said shortly. The mate stuck his head in at the window to speak to the old quartermaster who had been standing there silent all the time. "Shift your gear aft with the men," he said.

As the old fellow left me he growled, "Yer welcome to the lousy job. Now yer just a bloody officer's toe-rag."

* * *

The sombre greyness of evening was changing to the blackness of a dirty night when Holyhead drew abeam. The lights of the town twinkled brightly against the dark, heavy clouds which lay over the land.

The ship was nosing her way down into the Irish Sea. I stood on the lower bridge, handy for any call which might come from the officer on watch. It was a little strange, standing there listening to the dull, unfamiliar beat of the engines. The ship was plodding along steadily against a rising south-west wind and sea. To windward the sky was dark with the promise of coming bad weather. As I watched I saw a squall gathering and bearing down on the ship.

I had witnessed the coming of many such squalls. They had always menaced the ship, calling for alertness and preparation. So it was, unconsciously perhaps, I stood ready for that call which had so often rung along the deck: "Stand by the royal halliards!"

Surely enough, the call did come—two shrill blasts from the whistle of the officer overhead. Running up the bridge ladder, I made my way to him. He was smoking a cigarette, sheltering comfortably behind glass in the wing of the bridge. "Turn those ventilators a little more back to wind," was all he said to me, casually, as if it was a matter of small import.

This trifling duty accomplished, I returned to the lee of the charthouse. The squall, a severe one, had reached the ship. Heavy rain beat down upon her for a few minutes; the shrill note of the wind in the scanty rigging heightened; she listed almost imperceptibly. That, so far as I could see, was all the notice she took of it.

While the ship drove on unperturbed, the officer on watch sheltered in the wing of the bridge, puffing at a gasper. And I skulked in the lee of the charthouse while the engineers forced the vessel along.

At the time of which I write the *Nautical Magazine* was devoting pages every month to heated discussions on the value, or otherwise, of sail training. Comfort, after all, was not everything, I thought, standing there on that steamer's deck. There were other more important things which went to the training of a sailor. In the sailing ship one found them—watchfulness, resourcefulness, alertness, and that mutual interest which every member of the crew must needs have in the welfare of the ship . . .

The squall had passed, but the wind was freshening strongly. I thought of a man with clear blue eyes and a face flayed by wind and spray. "You've got to nurse a ship," he was saying . . . "nurse her all the time . . ."

Away down below me, embowelled in the hull, the powerful, unfamiliar engines throbbed, thrusting the vessel steadily on her

course. Far out on the lee quarter the lights of Holyhead shone
out through the rain again, twinkling clearly against the dark,
black cloak of cloud behind them.

* * *

For several days a westerly gale had been lashing to fury the
North Atlantic. The wind was abating to some extent, but the
sea still ran dangerously high, and the ship lurched and rolled
as she pushed her way to the s'uth'ard. On the bridge stood the
second officer, monotonously surveying the scene of staggering
ship, storm-tossed sea and leaden sky.

Presently, as his gaze passed around the grey horizon, he stiffened. His hand made for the binocular box. After a long look
with those at that dark object out on the weather bow he returned
the glasses to their box and swung the long telescope into position.
After gazing out to windward for some time he blew down the
voice pipe to the captain's room. Then he shouted down the
pipe, "There's a disabled windjammer three points on the weather
bow, sir!"

The burly figure of the master soon came clattering up the
bridge ladder. The telescope passed from the officer's hands to
his. As I stood at the wheel I clearly heard snatches of their
conversation—"Lost her mizen topmast—hull seems sound but the
boats are gone . . ."

Our course was altered, and we rapidly closed with the poor
victim of the recent gale. As we approached, the engine-room telegraph rang "Half speed." Every detail about the decks of the
derelict, for such she appeared to be, was seen plainly from the
steamer.

She was a vessel of eight or nine hundred tons, lying wallowing
in the trough of the sea under foresail and lower topsails. The
only damage aloft was the loss of the mizen topmast, the fall of
which spar had crushed the bulwarks to matchwood on one side.
As our skipper had noted, the boats were gone and the blocks of
the empty falls clattered against the barque's side as she rolled.
Every now and then, as the ship fell heavily into the hollow of
the seas, the topsails and foresail pounded the masts with a sound
like cannon fire. Occasionally a heavy sea leaped aboard, to wash
about the decks in a welter of white water until it had passed
overboard again through the shattered bulwarks.

Her hull appeared sound. she still rode the high sea pluckily, and there was a note of contempt in the captain's voice as he remarked, "I thought those Norwegians were sailors. I wonder what possessed them to leave their ship like that . . . "

Is there a more forlorn object in the world than a sailing ship abandoned at sea? If so, it would be hard to name. Every spar, every rope seems to shout the fact that she has been deserted. And it needs no glance at the wheel to learn that no helmsman stands on duty there.

Our siren wailed out a long melancholy note as we encircled the derelict. But, though her side lights were still burning, there was no sign of life, no sound except the sad surging of the sea and the echo thrown back from those slatting sails. A thorough search of the surrounding sea revealed no trace of the missing boats and crew.

The day was drawing to a close, the sea still running high—too high to lower a boat without grave risk in the growing dusk. To capture that waif of the sea would mean a valuable loss of time, and time is money afloat as well as ashore in times of keen, cut-throat competition.

Reluctantly the master rang "Full Ahead" again. As the steamer swung on to her course once more he remarked, "We'll report her, that's all we can do. The owners would not thank me for wasting time taking her in tow."

The derelict soon faded into the gloom of the evening, untended, unguided, pathetic and almost human in her loneliness . . .

*　*　*

So we strode on towards the Far East, caring little or nothing for the wayward wind which heretofore had governed so arbitrarily my wanderings. Through the Straits of Gibraltar we passed; through that narrow exit from the Mediterranean which at one time the valiant, ancient seafarer regarded as the End of the World.

That grim sentinel, the Rock, was left far behind and Port Said was reached. There we entered the "ditch in the sand" which, when it was opened in 1869, had thrown out of business for ever the white-winged tea clippers.

Old Williams, in releasing the wheel to me at the commencement of our passage, had called the life of a quartermaster a "lousy job." This had seemed to me an exaggeration until that foreign pilot came aboard to see us through the first half of the Suez Canal.

He was intensely highly strung and did his utmost to impart to all on the bridge his nervousness. As I stood at the wheel, though the long ribbon of the narrow waterway stretched clearly for miles ahead, he had me utterly confused. Jumping about the deck, he yelled frantically as if some crisis were at hand: "Hard a-starboard! Steady! Hard a-port! Steady!" until he had me sweating at the wheel. "Captain," he roared, "is this one of your number one quartermasters?" "Yes, he's all right—if you give him a chance," was the sarcastic reply of the skipper. I was on the point of telling that pilot to go to hell, or to come and steer the ship himself when my watchmate stuck his head into the wheelhouse to say, "Don't take any notice of that bloody frog. Just keep her nicely in the middle."

* * *

The ship spent a few days in Vladivostok. It was before the glorious Revolution which is reputed to have set free the enslaved millions of Russia. My most vivid impression of that port is of swaggering Tsarist military officers—and prostitutes. The sidewalks were literally thronged with both; it would be difficult to say which were the more numerous. And each was as easily recognisable as the other. For the technique of the *fille de joie* is the same the world over, whether she be dumb, or speak Russian —or just plain, homely English.

In that strange place, with its weird, back to front lettering on shops and public buildings, I felt more alone than ever before. And then I entered a Chinese restaurant where, at least, the proprietor spoke to me a form of English. While I sampled those hitherto untasted dishes I was thankful to that Chink for his friendliness and for his understanding of my tongue.

The ship sailed for Nikolaevsk, in Southern Siberia. In the River Amur, on which that port lies, she inconsiderately ran aground, putting us to immense trouble to get her off the mud. In that desolate spot, where young icebergs floated down the river, no assistance was available, for those were the days before cargo vessels carried wireless.

It was necessary to shift part of our cargo of bagged salt from No. 1 hatch to right aft, in order to lift the vessel forward. For

two days we toiled, carrying every bag up a brow which had been
rigged by the carpenter, over the midship section, and then down
a similar brow on to the after deck. It was a task which nearly
killed me, for I was still far too light for such heavy work.

How we cursed those bags of salt! During their stay in the
hold they had assumed all sorts of shapes, many having saw-edges
which rasped our shoulders, flaying the skin even through our
shirts. My back became so raw and chafed and salt-infested that
sleep was impossible. I had decided to tell the mate I could not
carry on—when the ship considerately floated clear.

In Nikolaevsk we loaded a full cargo of beans for Denmark, a
holdful of "musical fruit," as was said by the vulgar wits of the
crew. Calling at Vladivostok once more on our way south, we
took aboard one passenger, a German merchant who was anxious
to reach Singapore without delay.

*   *   *

It was night when we approached Singapore, homeward bound.
Suddenly the darkness was stabbed by a number of searchlights
which speared the horizon. The captain, in conversation with
our German passenger, remarked casually, little dreaming the import of that unusual activity ashore, "What's on to-night? Perhaps
they're holding some sort of celebration at Singapore."

And then, slithering alongside in a silence befitting the Silent
Service, a warship challenged us, her searchlight sweeping us from
stem to stern as she steamed alongside. "What's on to-night?"
our Old Man called across the water.

"WAR HAS BEEN DECLARED ON GERMANY!" was the
startling answer.

The passenger had left the captain and now stood alone in the
wing of the bridge. To me his words came clearly, almost in the
nature of a prayer repeated over and over again, "Lieb' Vaterland! Lieb' Vaterland!"

On the fore deck the crew, lining the shoreward side, were
cheering raggedly. Why do men cheer when war is declared?
Why did they cheer then, particularly then, when the bloodiest
war of all time had commenced; when millions were to give their
lives futilely in the stench and the filth of fetid battlefields? If
that is all men find to cheer about—why cheer at all?

As the searchlights stabbed that night, dimming the brilliant, peaceful stars overhead, a spark was glowing in Europe—a little spark which was soon to set the world ablaze, enveloping in destruction millions of brave men who had no real grudge against one another . . .

So "Der Tag" had come at last! The Kaiser's slavering war hounds were now unleashed, a-thirst for blood. The war to end war had begun.

The war to end war! What ill-conditioned fool invented that poor joke? Had it been called the war to begin war it would have been nearer the mark; to begin war of a new and filthier beastliness than any battlefield had even seen before . . .

* * *

We lay several days off Falmouth awaiting further instructions. While we were there a number of big German sailing vessels were towed in by naval craft, the sails clumsily stowed on the yards by the willing but inexperienced ratings. For after their capture the sullen Hunnish sailors refused to take any part in the working of their ships.

Taking bunkers at Swansea, we sailed for Christiansand, in Norway, to discharge. Our departure from the Welsh port had been delayed by a bit of trouble with the crew, who had been informed by their union delegate that the North Sea was strewn with German mines. Steaming without lights, we safely reached our destination, though even at that early date the U-boats were already a serious menace to shipping.

* * *

Another voyage was made by me under the aegis of the well-known and imposing blue-painted smoke-stack, in one of the finer ships on the Australian run. Sydney still made her strong appeal to me. The number of windjammers there had dwindled since my previous visit four years earlier.

Before leaving Singapore, homeward bound, we took aboard a distressed British seaman who was so ill he had to be carried up the gangway on a stretcher. Two nights later, when my relief had taken over the wheel at four bells, 2 a.m., I went straight down from the bridge to see the poor sick man, who had not spoken for many hours.

The D.B.S. was dying. That was clear even to me, young and unversed in the many mannerisms of death. He was lying on

s

a stretcher-bed in the alleyway, where he might get some relief from the hot, stagnant air. The light was dim there, so that it was necessary for me to strike a match to find out how he fared.

And then I knew the D.B.S. was dying—that his time was near at hand. Making my way at once to the doctor's room, I ran my hand noisily up and down the lattice of the door.

"Doctor," I called out, "the D.B.S. is very bad. Will you come to him?" There was no answer but a grunt from the bunk. My knuckles rasped the slats of the door again as I called out louder.

The light was switched on, and there was the sound of resentful movement from the bunk. Presently the door was opened, and an angry man faced me. "The D.B.S., Doctor . . . " I began.

He was fairly bristling at me. "What do you mean by disturbing me like this in the middle of the night!" he blazed. "I know that man is dying. Nothing can be done for him, young man! You understand—nothing!" Slamming the door in my face, he climbed into his bunk once more.

That doctor was a callous brute. He might at least have seen the man. It seemed to me a cruel, heartless thing to let that poor creature die unwatched—alone. After fetching a hurricane lamp, drawing a box close to the cheerless bedside, I sat there nervously awaiting the end.

It was queer, but I did not even know the poor devil's name. He was just the D.B.S. to all aboard—some worn-out bit of unwanted flotsam who was destined to die far from home. The night was perfectly calm, one of those which are so frequently experienced in the Indian Ocean. The sky was blue-black velvet, and the stars shone so brightly that their reflection on the still water was almost as vivid as themselves. But Death, stalking the world, busy with his grisly ministrations, cares nothing for the beauty of the night or the hour of the day. And he stood so near me then that it seemed the foul odour of his musty raiment and the putrescence of the grave already poisoned my nostrils.

As I sat there beside that poor stricken stranger, the subdued noises of the ship came to me. Two firemen far below in the stokehold argued hotly as they rattled their shovels on the plates. There was the muffled throb of the engines, the hiss of our passage through the water.

Above all was the rasping gasp of the dying man's breathing.

His pulse had almost ceased. I leaned over him, thinking some last moment of consciousness might release a message from his lips. He suddenly struggled up, clawing as though for breath, and then fell back dead. In the flickering light of the upheld lamp his glazing eyes gazed blankly into mine before I closed those lids for ever.

What malady was his no one seemed to know. His face, as I covered it with the rough blanket, looked like clay.

*   *   *

In my native city I obtained my second mate's square-rigged certificate, after three weeks at the excellent school on Eden Quay. The absence of the anticipated exultation over my success reminded me vividly of the subduing words on the old brown flower-vase, which stood on the dining-room table of the Sandymount manse from my earliest childhood:

"Pleasures are like poppies spread;
    You seize the flower—its bloom is shed."

Modestly, with one or two of my cronies, my victory was celebrated over several glasses of Guinness. Nevertheless, my heart was glad, for I was now an officer—and somebody else was the bloody toe-rag.

*   *   *

The windows of the shipping offices of Liverpool were brilliantly adorned with house-flags, putting me at a loss which one to enter. Suddenly the rampant lion of the Clan Line caught my eye. The Clan liners ran a service to South Africa—that was the company for me.

The senior clerk, with a levity not usually associated with such a personage, remarked gleefully, "You're the answer to a ship-owner's prayer! We want a third mate immediately for a ship in Glasgow loading for Cape Town. Sign here on the dotted line!" Obviously, officers were already getting scarce.

At Newport, Mon., a heavy consignment of rails was taken aboard, promising a fairly lengthy stay at the South African port. That suited me fine, for it was five years since I left Cape Town.

The war was already getting into its stride. Women workers were taking the place of the men who were being mowed down in thousands by the insatiable maws of the clamouring guns. Many sonsy lassies worked in the Newport docks. They were a

cheery, high-spirited crowd. Watching them as they approached
the dock gates every morning, I envied them their happy, care-
free outlook on life, which put to shame my miserable, introspective ponderings.

As they neared him, the policeman on duty would call out,
"Show your passes, girls, show your passes."

"Show your passes, girls, show your passes," they would mimic
him, flirting the backs of their short skirts aloft as they skipped
along. The bobby would attempt to look embarrassed, for those
cheery girls entirely omitted to pronounce the initial letter of the
word describing the cards which gave them entrance to the docks.

* * *

And so I came back to South Africa, to the parents I had not
seen for five years, if not in triumph at least in possession of what
I had sworn on the *Elginshire's* deck to obtain before returning.

On my first arrival in that great country the shadow of the
South African War still lay over the land. Now, on my second
coming, a greater shadow than ever lay over the entire world.
The bitterness and enmity of previous hostilities had been confined
to a comparatively few thousands of people. Now they had
broadened and spread until the whole world was aflame.

There are some misguided folk who see in warfare something
ennobling and uplifting. God forgive them, for they know not
what they do or say. Or *do* they know, and is perhaps warfare
not a stimulus to progress, as is said by some, but just part of a
rotten system in which the few are permitted to fatten ghoulishly
on the suffering and the sorrow and the outpouring of the rivers
of blood of the multitude?

When will war cease, one well may ask, seeing little hope in
the future, no security beyond the short, uneasy periods between
ever-recurring wars of a fiercer nature? No lasting peace can
come till the hearts of men are cleansed of their greed and avarice
—greed for money, greed for power.

At this point Tennyson's stirring words, written many years ago,
might well be quoted:

> "Ring out a slowly dying cause
> And ancient forms of party strife;
> Ring in the nobler modes of life
> With sweeter manners, purer laws.

"Ring out false pride in place and blood,
The civic slander and the spite;
Ring in the love of truth and light,
Ring in the common love of good.

"Ring out old shapes of foul disease,
Ring out the narrowing lust of gold,
Ring out the thousand wars of old,
Ring in the thousand years of peace."

Christ was crucified on the Cross nearly two thousand years ago
—for what? Even the spread of Christianity has failed to alleviate
the curse of warfare. Some, indeed, of the bloodiest wars of old
were fought under the inspiration and impetus of religious fer-
vour. The perfidious Kaiser had the effrontery to cry out while
he raped Belgium: "Ich mit Gott, und Gott mit Uns!"

One day recently the master of a ship remarked to me while
his vessel was being docked: "You'll never end war until every
history book is burnt." That's a start anyway. Burn the lot—
yes, even those stirring volumes which describe so graphically the
Glorious Deeds that Won the Empire, on which so many of us
were fed along with our maternal milk.

* * *

Steaming repeatedly through submarine-infested seas, I saw
something of the "ennoblement and uplift" of war in that great
struggle which was vainly fought in the hope that the cancer of
war would be abolished for ever. And there was little to glorify,
ashore or afloat, except perhaps the heroic patience and indomit-
able spirit of the common people, to whom final victory brought
little or no material gain.

Many readers probably witnessed that most tragic of sights—
the departure of a troop train bearing off the soldiers who were
returning from leave to the battlefields of France. If they did
they will never have forgotten that heart-rending scene . . .

A train was about to leave Liverpool for the Channel port where
those brave men would embark for the shambles on the other
side. The unhappy warriors stood about the platform of Lime
Street station, close to their allotted carriages, the paraphernalia

of their calling heavy about their shoulders, their uniforms still soiled by foreign mud.

The womenfolk were there too, of course, for women have ever sped warriors on their quest, however worthy or unworthy the cause might be. Close to me a young girl, obviously *enceinte,* was bidding farewell to her soldier husband. Entirely oblivious of gawking onlookers like myself, she hugged and caressed her man, speaking to him ridiculous, intimate little names of endearment, kissing him again and again. Many other couples were doing the same, but somehow that young girl and her boyish husband claimed my attention. They were so young, so full of life. Theirs should have been the happiness of their home, the peace of their fireside, the joy of their unborn child.

The bloody dice of war were loaded heavily against that poor boy. Over in that shambles the guns were clamouring for blood, and yet more blood, and thousands upon thousands of lives were to be claimed by them ere they were silenced for a few, uneasy, fleeting years.

The train moved away. That girl, who had been sobbing before, broke down completely and cried so broken-heartedly that none of the older women there could comfort her. And I, seeing that poor tortured bit of a girl, her unborn child warped by sorrow within her womb, could have cried, too, had I the courage.

Surely any thinking person can read in such an incident, trivial perhaps in itself, in the agony of that poor girl which was being multiplied a thousandfold throughout the land, a terrible indictment of warfare. Yet we still speak superiorly of "the beasts of the field," knowing full well in our hearts that we can learn many illuminating lessons from them in the art of decency and decorum. Why is it, too, that we use so glibly the terms "barbarians" and "barbarism," knowing that no barbarian ever perpetrated the horrible atrocities of coldly calculated mechanical warfare.

*   *   *

It took a long time for the minds of my Lords of the Admiralty, cramped by a surfeit of officialdom, to realise how serious was the menace of the U-boat. Ships leaving British ports were armed, of course, armed (usually) with a 4.7 gun and, at first, *one* trained gunner to man it. If the ship was bound for the South Atlantic this gun was removed at Gibraltar—to be placed aboard some homeward-bound vessel. If her passage led her through the Mediterranean, the gun would be retained as far as Port Said.

With this poor equipment hundreds of ships set out unescorted to face the prowling, murderous, underwater Hun. It took many months and the loss of hundreds of valuable ships and lives to make my Lords, sitting pretty in Whitehall, understand that something further was needed to protect Britain's lifeline on the sea.

Steaming many thousands of miles east and west through the Mediterranean, that 10-knot ship of mine plodded—unprotected save for that pop-gun with its solitary gunner. Wreckage of all sorts and swollen bodies floated there, and the wireless chattered ceaselessly with the many SOS calls from ships around . . .

One afternoon we steamed north of Crete, no other vessel in sight. The sea was unusually calm, the water greasy in its stillness. Suddenly a periscope showed up on our port beam. Immediately afterwards the torpedo was making for us. The mate, on watch, had seen that U-boat. "Dow chikar!" he shouted to the lascar quartermaster without a moment's delay. Though it was a fairly long shot, we would have been struck but for the mate's prompt action. As the torpedo approached, the periscope appeared again to watch the explosion.

But the ship was swinging fast already; the torpedo rushed harmlessly past at arm's length from the rudder.

One night we steamed up the Irish Sea, alone, blacked-out except for a shrouded glimmer from the compass-card. It was intensely dark; a dreary south-westerly wind blew over the wintry sea, driving before it a heavy cheerless rain.

When I took over the middle watch from the third mate, I found the captain on the bridge too. It was at the height of the unrestricted U-boat activity; so thick were the submarines in the vicinity that we were not even sounding our whistle.

Dangerous and mad, somebody will say. Yes, dangerous and mad in the extreme—but many things are dangerous and mad in the dark days of war.

Stooping down to the dim, unlit, white face of the engine-room telegraph, I saw that the pointer stood at "Half Ahead." I knew by the quick throb of the engines that that was a lie. "We must make that tide at Liverpool," the skipper had said—"besides we don't want to loaf about with submarines all around."

The third mate and the captain went below, the latter to fill his pipe while he had a look at the chart. With the visibility practically nil, I continued peering ahead, my mind filled with anxiety at what I considered the excessive speed we were steaming.

Suddenly I saw something resembling the breaking of the sea at the base of a towering cliff. That black cliff, very fine on the port bow, was the huge bulk of a vessel almost on top of us; that turmoil of white water was her bow wave.

I had to make an instantaneous decision. The obvious action seemed to be to alter course to starboard. No such order left my lips. For I felt convinced that any alteration of course in that direction would throw the after part of the ship across the bow of the other vessel, so close was she. I could picture our crew, all living aft, mangled as they lay in their bunks. To ring "Full Astern" would probably have had an even worse effect.

Therefore I did nothing, except to order the quartermaster to watch his steering carefully. The huge bow sheared past ours. The vast bulk of a big, two-funnelled passenger ship tore abeam of us. The dark water, tossed back from one ship's side to the other, boiled in that narrow strip between us.

I blessed that rattling door of the chartroom and the slight deafness of the skipper. He was an old man. Had he come out just then he would have died of shock!

Like our ship, no pinpoint of light showed throughout that great, long hull. Strangely enough, no hail came from her bridge. Silently, save for the sound of tormented water, she passed on a parallel course—and disappeared immediately into the blackness of the night. As I stood in the wing of the bridge I felt on my face the wind and displacement of her passing! I cursed her for her mad speed. And yet, on second thoughts, it may have been the impetus of that very speed which kept us apart.

The captain rejoined me, puffing at his new-lit pipe. "We'll slow down a bit," he said. "There may be other ships about."

"Yes," I agreed, "there probably *are* other ships about."

To his dying day the old fellow never knew how close destruction had approached him that cold winter night in the Irish Sea.

* * *

Far later than should have been, when shipping losses were

mounting alarmingly, the convoy system of protection was adopted. While this gave a certain measure of safety to the merchantmen it placed upon them many additional cares and worries. The average deep-sea man likes plenty of room; to be bunched in close proximity to twenty or thirty other vessels, each with its individuality and contrariness, gave many a shipmaster nightmare. It was, nevertheless, amazing how efficiently the system worked.

Many incidents in connection with those convoys come to mind as these remarks are penned. It would take a volume to relate them all. One great affliction we always prayed to be spared was to be placed astern of a wallowing Geordie tramp. With such a ship ahead, one had to keep a wary eye on her. One minute she would be correctly in position in line ahead, the next, especially at the time of cleaning fires, she would be almost under one's bows.

One of the most amazing mix-ups I ever experienced was when our northbound convoy got foul of a westbound one from Gibraltar. Some brass hat had blundered, and blundered badly. We met at 2 a.m. on a pitch dark night with a light mist covering the water. We were hopelessly mixed up before any action could be taken. Rushing into the chartroom, I switched on all the lights with the master switch. We just missed cutting a destroyer in two; another ship crossed our bow so closely I could have tossed a biscuit aboard. There were a number of collisions—we could hear the shouting and crashing of steel against steel. Next morning half of the strangers were with us, and half our convoy had gone west with the other ships.

In the grey of a bitterly cold winter's dawn in the Irish Sea we steamed close alongside a big transport packed with soldiers. Suddenly she was torpedoed, the huge column of water leaping several hundred feet into the air. I have often wondered how she fared, or rather, how that horde of khaki-clad men fared. The ship was obviously doomed. Our last glimpse in the uncertain light showed her settling fast, her rapidly listing decks swarming with frightened men.

One afternoon a Harrison boat next to us was struck. As the torpedo shattered her side the frightened Lascar lookout man at the fore-topmasthead climbed on to the edge of the barrel and hurled himself into the sea, twisting and turning like a rag doll as he fell. It is strange how little things are noticed at the time of crisis . . .

Another day we were steaming down Channel alone. A light easterly wind ruffled the water, bringing to us the dull, rumbling growl of the hungry guns over there in France.

The mist had thickened to fog, narrowing our view to several hundred yards around the vessel. Suddenly, from right ahead, came the sound of heavy gunfire, near at hand.

The fog became patchy, then lifted sufficiently to show us one of the latest of the big U-boats shelling a French steamer. Although she had not been hit, there was chaos aboard that ship. With their vessel apparently still moving at full speed the crew were lowering the boats to abandon ship. On our approach the submarine crash-dived. As we steamed close by the Frenchmen, looking a little foolish, assured us they had not been hit.

Once more the fog settled down; nothing more was seen of the Frenchman or the U-boat. But there were other ships about, one of which ran us down while steaming madly at almost full speed in thick fog. Our vessel had been stopped, blowing the prescribed two long blasts. Suddenly the huge bulk of the other ship appeared out of the fog, travelling fast and heading right for our midship section. Our skipper promptly rang "Full Ahead," giving the engine-room the "double ring" of emergency. That action undoubtedly saved the ship. Instead of cutting us down to the waterline amidships that blundering, heavily-laden stranger struck us aft, smashing in the poop. And there she left us, without stopping to see how we fared.

Her name was painted out, as was the custom, but we knew she was British. The usual little detail which always imprints itself on my mind in a crisis was there on that occasion. In the wing of the bridge of that steamer the skipper stood, bulky in sou'wester and oilskins. As he gripped the rail he swayed to one side, in the manner of a cyclist turning a corner, vainly attempting to swing his vessel clear of us.

We put into Falmouth later to lick our wounds before proceeding to Glasgow for repairs. That night, endeavouring to make that same bay in the fog, the Frenchman who had evaded the submarine by our timely appearance ran aground on the rocks of Killygerran Head and became a total loss.

Nearing the end of another voyage, we were steaming up towards the Straits of Dover. As I stood on the bridge in the afternoon watch there was a tremendous explosion on the port bow. The ship almost stopped, and appeared to settle steeply for'ad. From the engine-room came an uncanny noise as if the engines were falling through the ship's bottom, something like the loud rattle of a few coppers in a child's tin money-box. The Lascar crew immediately rushed the outswung boats, praying to Allah for protection and to us to lower the boats.

The captain came running on to the bridge. "What's happened?" he enquired. "I think we've got the dull thud," was my answer. "See if the engines are still in the ship," he ordered me.

At the engine-room door the third engineer's scared white face was looking out. Down below the engines still pounded away. And when the ship was sounded we found she was not leaking, nor had she suffered any harm. That afternoon the Straits were swarming with floating mines, probably both enemy and our own. Like great black peas broken loose from their pods they floated about. The escorting destroyers sped ahead to sink them by gunfire, expending much ammunition in the process.

So that ghastly U-boat warfare went on, and brave merchantmen died by the thousand, and hundreds of valuable ships, shattered by mine and torpedo, went to their watery grave. The climax was reached, as most people know, in May, 1917, when the sinkings had soared to a perilous tonnage, and the position looked grim indeed. Had losses continued at such a pitch Britain might easily have starved.

On a number of occasions I passed along the Channel at that anxious time, seeing everywhere the work of the dastardly Hunnish pirates who had perfected for their foul cause this new type of warfare. Masses of wreckage floated about; in the ears of the wireless officer on watch screamed continually the SOS calls, many close around us, pathetic proof of the supreme effort Germany was making to starve proud Albion into submission.

My Lords of the Admiralty, sitting by now not quite so pretty in Whitehall, were perturbed. They decided to invite some of the humble and hitherto slightly despised merchant service officers to attend instructional courses in gunnery, etc., at the various naval bases. This invitation included even the treacherous Japanese, who were, of course, our allies at the time.

So it came about that I was, for a few days, the guest of His Majesty at Chatham, where I lived aboard the big man-of-war *H.M.S. Hibernia*. The cabin of the Admiral's secretary had been allotted to me.

My first night aboard, shortly after dinner, the man who looked after the room and myself came to me, a pound note outstretched in his hand.

"Excuse me, sir," he said, "but I found this behind a glass above the wash-basin. I cleaned out this room thoroughly when the last officer left, and it wasn't there then. It must be yours."

"Thank you," I said shortly, pocketing the note.

No recollection was mine of having placed that pound there. It was, indeed, extremely unlikely that I had done so. Shutting the door, I drew from my pocket my wad of notes, result of a recent generous pay-day. Futilely I counted them, knowing full well that I had no idea how many should be there. Those were the affluent days of bachelorhood, when a quid was neither here nor there—before the acquisition of a wife and family had put for ever an enumerated rubber stamp on every pound note in my possession.

A few minutes were spent pondering over the problem which had been thrust upon me. Under similar conditions my father would undoubtedly have sought inspiration from the Scriptures. Why, then, should not I? The name of Solomon leaped into my mind. That good man, despite his somewhat promiscuous philanderings with his three hundred concubines, has always been regarded as the transcendence of wisdom. What, after all, are several hundred lights o' love compared with the inestimable attribute of wisdom?

Solomon had threatened, when faced with a situation somewhat akin to mine, to carve in two with a sword a live baby. It would surely, then, be a simple matter for me to rend in twain a mere Bradbury.

Opening the door, I called the man into the room. Handing him a ten shilling note, I took it upon myself to treat him to a short homily on the merits of honesty. He went away delighted with the ten bob. To be perfectly candid, to this day there still exists in my mind considerable doubt about the real ownership of that pound.

* * *

My brother, a lieutenant in the Royal Flying Corps stationed at Biggin Hill, invited me down there for a week-end to see something of the war from his point of view.

The training camp was under canvas, for it was summertime. All day those youngsters zoomed and boomed close above the tent tops in the crazy box kites they were forced to fly in those far-off days. Sometimes they even crashed amongst those tents, rarely surviving such an accident.

One afternoon we stood watching a budding pilot firing on a ground target just outside the camp. He roared down repeatedly, his gun spattering the ground. And then, before our startled eyes, he failed to pull out of his dive and crashed, with engine all-out, into the hard earth.

We started to run towards the wrecked machine, thinking we might help. As an ambulance man rushed past us he shouted to my brother, "I wouldn't go over there if I was you, sir. He's finished. The engine has gone right through his guts!"

* * *

It has been said that the devil looks after his own; that only the good die young. Whatever the reason for my good fortune, I survived the terrors of the U-boat and the deadly mine, though many were not so lucky, for half the Clan Line fleet was sunk.

The end of that war to end war came one day as we proceeded eastwards through the Mediterranean. Early that morning we had sighted one of the latest of the U-boats on the surface outside the Straits of Gibraltar, probably the one which had the distinction of sinking the last large British man-o'-war to be torpedoed. A burst of cheering reached us from the nearest escort vessel. Then came the message: "An armistice has been signed. Hostilities have ended!"

It took a lot of readjustment to revert to the piping times of peace. That night, steaming once more with blazing lights, after four years of black-out, it seemed to us a little too tame and safe at first . . .

So the war to end war was over. But the bickering and the muddling and the wrangling went on long after. And when peace came again to the world, it was but an uneasy cessation of hostilities in which that same cruel foe was permitted to gather strength for revenge. And our million dead were soon forgotten.

Forgotten, too, were many of those who returned alive. They, also, were left to rot, like the million dead—left to rot in the gutter, where they were driven to eke out a precarious living selling piffling toys, or peddling shoddy writing pads from house door to house door.

Many beautiful poems were written about the glorious valour of those men. Oh yes—many beautiful poems were written. "In Flanders fields the poppies blow. . . ." "Lest we forget . . . . lest we forget. . . ." And so on, *ad nauseam*. We forgot damn soon. And all those beautiful words meant exactly nothing but—beautiful words.

And in his lair, wherever that may be, the God of War did not even bother to put aside his weapons. Chuckling as he wiped the reeking blood away, he set about resharpening them, ready for his next campaign. . . .

* * *

At the end of 1918 my father wrote to me rejoicing over the successful termination of the War. He referred to the past year as *Annus Mirabilis*. It had indeed been a wonderful year, for the Hunnish hordes of Germany had been utterly defeated.

Writing on the eve of the New Year, he said: "To have lived to see such a rosy dawn after the darkness of weary years is matter for profound thankfulness. Yet more privileged will be those whose lives are dedicated to ushering in the perfect day, repairing the ruins, and realising social ideals lying yet ahead."

Poor deluded man, poor deluded world! He little thought that the slogan "War to end War" was but a parrot-cry; he little dreamed that in less than twenty-one years the same powerful forces of evil would be unleashed once more.

Poor deluded man. He was tired and ill, though his brave spirit was unquenched. The sands of life were running out for him. He never saw another earthly New Year's dawn, rosy or otherwise.

CHAPTER XVII

HERE, THERE—EVERYWHERE

The Red Ensign is no Magic Carpet from which to view the world at will. Hide-bound in her relentless quest of remunerative freights, the path of the merchant ship is always restricted and ofttimes unromantic.

Nevertheless, far afield I wandered, here, there, everywhere—more or less—visiting and re-visiting many ports, and finding much of interest on my wanderings.

London has always been regarded as the hub of the universe, and probably still is, in spite of the challenge of that gigantic mushroom, New York.

Somehow I never felt at home in London, though my voyagings took me there on many occasions. It may be that one has to be born in that great metropolis to appreciate fully its dingy charm.

My first visit there as a very young man filled me with confusion at the vastness of that immense human bee-hive. For hours I trod wearily the hard pavements, seeing but a tithe of those historic buildings.

Among them all the Tower, playing strangely on the chords of my imagination, appealed most to me. Dawdling through those priceless relics of Britain's chequered past, I spent several hours within those somewhat sinister walls. When I finally emerged into the anaemic sunshine of a London afternoon, my mind, fresh from the atmosphere of a long-dead past, refused at first to re-adjust itself to the roar and bustle of the present. Instead of the leisurely passage of sedan chairs, or the stately, measured tread of palfreys' hooves, gigantic, snorting motor-buses thundered past. . . .

As I strode along, an unknown ant in a seething anthill, thousands of faces, mostly fixed and white with the pallor of the city-bred, flitted past. It was a sea of eyes which surged along like some great river in spate; mostly sad eyes from which little happiness shone out. There were, of course, a few glad eyes; in spite of my youth I knew that they belonged to the girls and women

who, poor souls, walked the heartless streets to find the where-
withal to live, however sordid living had become to them.

I looked in vain for the proverbial cheeriness and cheekiness
and saucy *elan* of the Londoner. Those famous attributes were
missing that afternoon. Perhaps my indecisive footsteps had taken
me to the wrong part of the city; perhaps some temporary gloom
had spread over the people who swarmed around.

*   *   *

Hearty singing reached me from a nearby, well-lit hall. Glad
of a chance to rest, I passed inside. The singing ceased just then.

My entry had been noted by a young woman in the poke-bonnet
of the Salvation Army. She came down the hall towards my seat,
taking the one next to me and turning earnestly towards me.
Under the becoming brim of the bonnet her face was beautiful;
calm and serene with the utter serenity one rarely sees except on
the faces of those who have died peacefully in their sleep.

She leant over me, her great, tranquil eyes looking searchingly
into mine. "Have you ever been saved?" she asked quietly. "No,"
I answered, "not to my knowledge. Does it hurt much?" She
showed no sign whatever of annoyance or distress at my irreverent
and foolish jocularity.

"Come with me, come up to the other sinners," she urged,
gently pulling me by the arm. But I remained glued to my seat.
After further unsuccessful persuasion she left me to return to the
end of the hall.

There were but two sinners in the throes of being saved that
night, a young girl and a hideous, ragged old man who looked
decidedly verminous. No doubt that unpleasant little matter was
of minor importance at the moment, and would be attended to
later should the necessity exist. The officer in charge was praying
loudly and extravagantly over the two kneeling figures. Then the
music blared out triumphantly if a little stridently, and the two
cleansed sinners rose to their feet.

Both were exhorted to tell all those present how they felt. The
young girl was too shy to utter one word, but the poor, broken
old man addressed the audience willingly, beseeching those who
had not been saved to become so at once, and thus be re-born.
Poor old fellow, he looked more like death than the miracle of
re-birth.

"WHITE WINGS THAT NEVER GROW WEARY" *Penso*

. . AND NIGHT CREPT OVER THE DARKENING SEA . . . *Penso*

I rose to go, the beautiful eyes of the young woman who had spoken to me gazing sadly at me out of that calm and lovely face. Turning at the door, I saw she was still gravely watching my departure. . . .

Some years later another person, equally kind but lacking the beauty of that 'Army' lass, endeavoured to bring to me solace and salvation. It was at a time when tragedy had cast me into a slough of despond; when my very soul was weary and sick; when the shadow of life had completely obliterated the sun.

A friend suggested that I should interview an exponent of the doctrines of Mary Eddy, one who had the reputation of having given renewed happiness to many sunk, like myself, in a quagmire of despair.

Like so many of her cult, the Christian Scientist was a woman, a fine, big, handsome woman with clear, fearless eyes and a strong, dominating personality which completely overawed me. Those eyes bored into mine as we sat closeted alone one morning; it seemed to me they were probing far into my skull, right into that confused mass of matter which passed for my brain.

Suddenly she commanded me to get upon my knees while she prayed. Her prayer was so long that my position became, both mentally and physically, decidedly uncomfortable. Earnestly she called on Heaven to turn me into a beautiful flower. I saw her but once again; before any such floral transformation had taken place the sun shone through the shadow once more, and I severed my brief connection with Christian Science. No doubt there are many harassed souls to whom it brings peace and comfort.

* * *

When night had crept into the London streets I came to realise some lodging must be secured before it had grown too late, for it was unnecessary for me to return to the ship until the morning.

My wanderings had taken me far afield. I found myself in one of those intensely depressing little squares which abound in the city. High, gloomy, seedy houses frowned down morosely on the few stunted trees which clung precariously to life within the spiked railings enclosing them. Probably a hundred years or more ago those same houses were the homes of the gentry—the prosperous business folk of the city.

The passing of time had wrought its dissolution on them; now they had fallen into such a state of disrepair that most of them were nothing more than poor lodging houses. Illuminated signs proclaimed this to the weary passer-by seeking, like myself, some haven in which to come to rest for the night. Choosing one door which looked slightly more attractive than its fellows, I pulled the old fashioned bell-handle, causing a faint tinkle in the rear of the house.

Before this tintinnabulous summons was answered, an overwhelming urge came over me to bolt—before that gloomy door opened. But my feet were too tired to respond to this impulse. Already a fat, blowsy woman was regarding me enquiringly. In answer to my request she replied: "Yes, I have several rooms vacant, and one is just what you want."

As we stood in the dim, gas-lit hall, the dingy wallpaper oozed the pungent odour of onions. Why is it that the lower orders invariably swamp their culinary efforts with the fumes of that potent, penetrating root?

Most London landladies are garrulous; this one was particularly so, until, in the end, she saw her fine flow of words was lost on me. Putting a match to a candle, for the stairway reared dismally unlit aloft, she asked me to follow her up to the third floor.

She threw open a door with a gesture such as might have ushered some privileged guest into the regal quarters at Buckingham Palace. Then, touching the candle-flame to the old fashioned fish-tail burner, she was gone.

The little room was dirty and foul-smelling. Throwing open the window to its utmost, I looked out over the vast ocean of drab roofs which stretched as far as the eye could see. Removing only jacket and shoes, I spread out on the damp bed with its unattractive, grey linen. The furnishings were plain; a tiny washstand, underneath which reposed an enormous, battered chamber-pot, one side conspicuously missing; a broken chair; a little dressing table supporting a fly-spotted mirror, and a few rusty hooks behind the door. That was all.

My eyes kept straying up and down the wallpaper. For it was a vague design of rambler roses; clusters of them, ambling without visible support up and down, spaced with geometrical precision on those dirty walls.

How incongruous, rambler roses blooming in such a foul spot!

But they weren't really blooming—how could anything sweet and wholesome bloom there? Perhaps they had bloomed thirty, forty, fifty years ago. Now no scent was theirs, no scent but the sourness of the exhalations of the hundreds who must have tarried here awhile before passing on their way on the morrow.

Where had I last seen rambler roses? Wasn't it around the doorway and clustering the hedges of that pretty little cottage where, strolling the fragrant countryside of Wicklow, I had paused to take tea? That was surely a far cry from this sordid place.

Unwilling to get between the discoloured ramparts of those cold, damp sheets, I lay musing thus, thinking, too, of that pretty girl in the poke-bonnet. It was mean not to have let her save me.

Not only the expectation of the onslaught, at any moment, of the Little Boys in Brown kept sleep from me. . . . Nothing but blank, locked doors faced me in the gloom of the third floor. Stumbling noisily down the creaking stairway, I went in search of the lady of the house. Sounds of gaiety reached me, a chink of light showed from a door at the rear of the ground-floor.

Awkward and embarrassed, I pushed open the door—to disclose a cheery party in full progress. A dozen or so men and girls sat around the table, which was littered with Guinness' bottles and glasses containing the dark, heavy liquid. The blowsy woman sensed my need at once.

"Come in," she gushed, for the potent fumes of the stout had filled her by now with the milk of human kindness towards one in distress. "These are all my friends. Just a little celebration, you know. . . . And just fancy me not telling you! We're a little old fashioned here. Come through to the backyard, young man."

There was little room between the backs of the crowded chairs and the wall. Squeezing past, I had to brave a battery of coarse innuendoes from the men and knowing glances and saucy winks from the girls. . . .

The place was dark, except for what dim light filtered in from the yard. Striking a match, I peered around. Something white lay on the filthy floor. Striking another match, I bent down over that white object.

There lay a mutilated Bible. Its holy pages, outraged as far as Chronicles, cried out silently, helplessly to heaven. . . .

That was in London. In London, the so-called hub of the universe; where the King lives; where the churches are almost as plentiful as the pubs.

* * *

Some of those of us who have wandered the world have slept in strange places. Twice have I lain down to rest in doss-houses, most pitiful lodgings of all. The first occasion was prompted by idle curiosity, the second a case of dire necessity, when I found myself jangling a few coppers—my all at the moment—in the belated streets of an unfriendly city.

To spend the night in those streets, or on a seat in a park, was unthinkable, for the winter was severe, and heavy snow covered the city in a mantle of chilly white.

A seedy old man, to whom I spoke at a corner, accompanied me to a dilapidated building, where he told me he often procured a bed for a few pence. On payment of this humble sum, my new-found friend, whose ghastly cough proclaimed him in the last stage of consumption, and I were taken into a large, whitewashed room containing about twenty beds. These, with the exception of our two, were already occupied.

My companion quickly removed his ragged outer garments, and was soon under the blankets. But I stood hesitant there, gazing with misgiving at that filthy bed. One of its previous occupants —there must have been many since those foul bedclothes had last been washed—had obviously made a very determined and partially successful attempt to commit suicide by cutting his throat. The top end of the upper sheet was soiled hideously with congealed blood.

Taking off nothing more than boots and raincoat, I lay down uneasily, pushing as far from my face as possible that hideous sheet. There was no switch inside the room to put out that glaring light. An attendant looked in occasionally, completely ignoring the oft-repeated suggestion: "Why can't ye dowse that glim?"

Little sleep came to me. It was a relief to watch the slowly growing winter's dawn creeping wanly through the window-grime. Most of the occupants there were old, broken men who had regarded my entry curiously and yet disinterestedly. During the night the place had been filled with their strange animal smells and sounds, and their uneasy mutterings and coughings.

My neighbour had stirred restlessly and continuously, his withered frame tortured by that ghastly, hacking cough. When daylight came the attendant brought in for sale a tray of cocoa and hunks of bread and margarine. My friend insisted on buying me a mug of steaming cocoa and a 'doorstep' for a penny.

We roamers sleep in many places. One of the best, for me, was that lowly bed on mother earth at Jonkershoek, the stars my canopy. It is surprising how comfortably one can sleep on the ground, provided a hollow is scored out for one's hip-bone.

* * *

It was not until some years later that the opportunity came my way to visit that other great city, New York.

The wild, storm-tossed passage of the Western Ocean was accomplished at last. The colossal Statue of Liberty, with upraised arm, welcomed our salt-encrusted ship in from the sea. The gigantic, bizarre buildings, seen by most of us for the first time, reared dizzily skywards close at hand as we came to anchor in the stream.

For several days a savage blizzard raged, blotting out the huge skyscrapers, and piling high the snow upon our decks. And then, so capricious is the climate of New York, a few days later the great city sweltered under a heat-wave.

* * *

One of the officers from a ship astern of us offered to show me round the city. He suggested, as a start, a visit to one of the glittering cabarets of Broadway. He informed me, as we met one afternoon, that besides showing me around New York he was going to introduce me to two very charming young women.

The ladies were awaiting us at one of the gaudiest of the many sparkling places which abound in the city. They glanced with obvious approval at our new uniforms as my friend introduced me to them. Both young women were good-lookers, beautifully dressed, and what would be called in equine circles high steppers.

As we entered, the murmur of many voices swept towards us, the clatter of swiftly-handled crockery, and the sob and wail of saxophones. It was an enormous place, around the central dance floor of which many tables were arranged. Taking our seats at one of these, my friend, the perfect host perfectly at ease, ordered cocktails, and then more cocktails, before proceeding to the more serious business of the tea and enormous cream cakes.

We were close to the band, which consisted of a number of coal-black negroes, immaculately dressed in 'tails'. It was a hot afternoon; those niggers sweated and puffed at their saxophones and drums, swaying their bodies in a wild rhythm as they played.

Presently a scantily-clad girl came bounding on to the floor in front of the band. From where we sat the heavy coating of her make-up and the unnatural glitter of her eyes showed up all too clearly in the searching lights. Though she did not look much to me, beyond the beautiful moulding of her almost naked white body and legs, she must have been a well-known favourite. For the crowd gave her tumultuous applause.

She started to dance, and as she danced she sang, if that word could be applied to the hideous caterwauling which emerged from her lips. The saxophones tripped in, softly at first, gathering force as though to egg her on.

Though the girl looked fairly fit she kept on telling us all: "I've got the Blues! I've got the Blues! I've got the YAKAHULA BLUES!" contorting her body wildly as the music swelled and quickened. It may have been that she was actually suffering from some dire malady as yet unknown to medical science.

My attention was divided between the prancing girl and the huge negro who conducted the band. He had turned from his instrumentalists; his eyes never left the girl; his body swayed to the barbaric music, keeping time with hers. And on that great, ebony face there was a *hungry* look.

The music ceased, the girl tripped away, the band mopped their glistening faces. My friend, enjoying himself immensely, called for more cocktails with which to quench the seemingly unquenchable thirst of the ladies.

And then the dance was on. My partner (we had sort of paired off long ere this) looked at me enquiringly. "I'm sorry I don't dance," I told her, "my education has unfortunately been neglected." She disguised her chagrin well, and then, while the other two trod a measure, if that old term is suited to the steps of modern jazz, she settled down to tell me all about herself.

She was, of course, married—her wedding ring shone newly on the small hand with which she squeezed mine gently as she told me what a nice boy I was. With the cocktails whispering within her, she became uncomfortably, embarrassingly communicative and confidential. It did not take long to lay bare before me the tragedy of her life. Her husband had been crippled a few months before, crippled hopelessly—crippled for life.

And what of her? She, poor, ardent woman, was now a wife in name only—those were her actual words.

* * *

The saxophones still wailed and crooned in that glittering place of spurious happiness. But I wanted to be gone, without, of course, causing offence to my companions. My new-found friend remonstrated with me, attempting to delay me there while she told me of her beautiful home, with its shady grounds in which her husband was forced to spend the long day, lying helplessly in a wheelchair under the trees.

We parted at the door, in the cold disapproval of my fellow officer. How could I go, he asked me, while there was still so much to do and the day was yet so young? There were many other spicy cabaret shows where we could look in before we dined. I said goodbye to the three of them in the street, and have never seen one of them since that day. The lady had already pressed her address on me. Standing there on the thronged pavement, she whispered to me to come to-morrow.

I cannot recollect her name, but I know what it should have been, for she reminded me of a certain character in the Bible. My name was not Joseph; she had not actually caught me by the garment. But the meaning of her words was clear even to an unsuspecting fool like myself. Mrs. Potiphar, that must surely have been her name . . . . Mrs. Potiphar.

The Campbells, individually and collectively as a clan, may be a poor lot. How many times had I suffered at school the cold stares of my classmates when that unfortunate incident, the massacre of Glencoe, cropped up! On such occasions I used to hear them muttering at me the hideous word 'Murderers!' Perhaps we have even been murderers, but there are some things at which we draw the line.

The activities of the many philanthropic bodies in existence cover an enormous field, stretching from the haughty heights of indigent duchesses down to the dismal depths of mangy cats. It would seem, however, that there is scope for further effort, something in the nature of a Society for the Relief of Wives in Name

Only. This suggestion is put forward entirely free, gratis, and for nothing.

In New York I found at first no chord of friendliness, with the exception of a huge policeman who sat in a little office through which we passed on our way to and from the dock area.

"Where were you born?" he asked, the first time I went out.

"In Dublin, if you know where that is," I replied. He positively beamed at me.

"So you come from Dublin! Come in, boy! Sure anyone from Ireland is welcome here. But we don't want any of thim goddam lime-juicers here!"

In the great canyons of those unfamiliar streets I wandered, between those amazing, skyward-rearing buildings, in the express lifts of some of which I shot aloft at a speed unknown before. That rocketlike flight leaves one almost breathless at first. One gazes down at one's toes, expecting to see one's viscera squirting out of the shoe tips. And the descent is just as bad, for one's heart and lungs and brains feel as if they were struggling to emerge from the top of the head.

Everywhere we went in that city it was made plain to us that we were foreigners, aliens amongst those who spoke a language which was our own. Never before, not even in Vladivostok, which was almost exactly on the opposite side of the world, had I felt so strange and lonely.

The whole place was a hive of feverish activity; the Elevated Railway cars roared past with a far more strident sound than the dear old Liverpool 'Overhead.' Stridor was the note which smote one's ear on every side.

After the hectic rush of the homing automobiles, there was a temporary lull before the scrambling night-life began. And then, as darkness drew on, the placid, twinkling stars were paled to nothing by the gaudy, flashing advertisements, moving ingeniously, which blazed aloft from most of the buildings.

* * *

Through the foolish action of a shipmate it was nearly my lot to experience the cold discomfort of a Yankee prison.

Prowling the streets, we occasionally sampled the local beer (it was just before prohibition) as we passed along. The saloon keepers, anxious over the proposed legislation which promised to deprive them of their lucrative trade, exhorted their patrons to stand firm against this iniquitous curtailment of their vaunted liberty as citizens of the great U.S.A.

These places were festooned with placards, some witty but mostly intensely vulgar. One such which I remember enquired baldly and facetiously: "Where, and how, can we make water if there are no saloons?"

We decided, having tasted of the American wassail-bowl, to eat at one of the restaurants, which abound in New York. In the States one does not breakfast, or dine, or supper—one just 'eats.'

My companion, like myself, had never been to America before, most of his voyagings having been on the Indian run. He, as was the case with so many of his kin, had become used to regarding himself as something of a 'Burra Sahib' every time he stepped ashore. It had consequently become his habit to bully all and sundry with whom he came in contact at each Indian port which happened to be favoured by his presence.

That might work very well in India, amongst a crowd of servile and dispirited natives. Here, under the glorious Star-spangled Banner, where all men were theoretically equal, things were entirely different. The stranger within those gates, especially should he be a Britisher, had to walk very warily and watch carefully his behaviour. This my friend was soon to learn.

As we sat awaiting our meal he became impatient, cursing loudly the mighty U.S.A. and all pertaining to it. We were being watched from a corner by a bunch of Italian waiters, who had, no doubt, spotted us for a 'coupla limeys'. Suddenly, before he could be restrained by me, my companion seized a large, full bottle of tomato sauce and crashed it on to the tiled floor.

It went off like a bomb, shedding its crimson contents far and wide; on adjacent tables, on the walls, on us—even on the ceiling.

That bunch of macaroni-eating waiters made a rush for our table, screaming at us, clawing in our faces. Then came in their wake the fat proprietor, an Italian too, who pushed his satellites roughly away and faced us angrily.

There is in my mental make-up some queer kink which invariably causes me to see some amusing point of relief in the direst crisis. So it was on that occasion. Happening to glance round at the next table, I saw a large, fat man fumbling for his handkerchief, cursing loudly the while. A great gout of crimson sauce had struck him right in one eye, and was oozing slowly and bloodily down the side of his face. Several onlookers were calling out repeatedly, "Call in the cops an' get those guys slung out!"

It took all my persuasive powers, and a sum out of all proportion to the damage done, to smooth the matter over. But worse was to follow before the night was done.

It was late. We had decided to return to the ship, a decision which met with my approval, for my shipmate had worked himself into a dangerous, unruly mood. We stood looking into a brightly lit shop window in a fairly quiet street. Suddenly, without any warning, he lifted his heavily-shod foot and smashed it through the glass. There was a loud crash, and we started to run. I was afraid he might have cut his foot or leg badly; fortunately that was not the case.

People called out, and one or two police whistles shrilled in the night. The sounds of hot pursuit were all around us. How we ran! I have never sped so fast in all my life, and my companion, whom I had imagined a little drunk, kept up with me in that swift race.

We dodged down all sorts of side streets, getting hopelessly lost in a maze of alleys. Somehow we evaded the hue and cry, which gradually grew fainter in another direction. Eventually we reached the ship, tired out. Never again, I vowed, would I step ashore with such a dangerous shipmate.

The Americans are reputed to be a religious people. Theirs is a land of many curious cults, the home of the world-wandering, emotional evangelist. I set out, one Sunday evening, to find out wherein the ceremony of their religious ritual differed from, or resembled, that of my own upbringing.

The service at that church on the outskirts of New York appeared to be entirely undenominational. As it drew on the people, warming to the exhortations of their minister, became at times a little too rowdy for the sober decorum which had been fostered by my father's pulpit.

It was an amazing thing for me to sit there listening to the walls of a church echoing the loud clapping of hands, and the stamping of enthusiastic feet upon the floor. This novel experience left me, as I passed out into the night again, with a strange feeling of having been cheated of something which should have been mine. Where was that sickly-sweet flow of melancholy which would surge over us as children while we sang:

> *'I am but a stranger here,*
> *Heaven is my home,'*

and when the solemn atmosphere of the church enveloped us with its oft-repeated theme that man is mortal—that even we children, scarcely on the threshold of life, had got to die?

Why should the church harp everlastingly on the mortality of man? Why not let us poor wights run our allotted three score years and ten as cheerfully and as merrily as possible? To the average normal, healthy human being, however strong his faith in the hereafter, death can never be made attractive, even should the stench of his approach be disguised by myrrh and incense and flowery words.

The average man must surely be puzzled exceedingly when he considers the maze of denominational difference which harasses the modern church. Putting this point to a minister once, I enquired meekly: "Does the Bible itself not state that a house which is divided cannot stand. How, then, on this ruling, can the church continue to exist?"

He paused, looking perhaps a little embarrassed, and then replied slowly: "Put it down to the contrariness of human nature. That's the only answer I can give you."

Another man of God, more resourceful than his colleague, to whom this matter was mentioned, remarked blandly and without hesitation: "Has it not been said in the Good Book: 'In my Father's house are many mansions'?"

With apologies for this digression, let us return to New York, scintillating city of ingenious, glittering night signs and gaudy, risque cabarets.

In spite of all its empty searching after pleasure by night and its unrest and bizarre splendour, it can, or could at the time of the author's visit, teach the cities of Britain one lesson at least in decorum.

For hours we could walk those streets by night without being confronted by that pernicious pest—the wandering woman seeking her prey. How different from the streets of any British city! The street walker is a blot on our national life. She lurks everywhere; her insinuating voice importunes one at almost every corner— brazenly or with some semblance of discretion according to her age and the time she has been 'on the game.'

It would, of course, be too much to conclude from the above remarks that prostitution in New York and other American cities is non-existent. That conclusion would be far too sweeping and entirely erroneous. Vice of all sorts undoubtedly exists, but, as far as we could see, it did not *obtrude* on the casual stroller taking the night air in the streets. My friend the Irish policeman, to whom I mentioned this subject, told me that solicitation was regarded as a serious offence in New York, and was severely dealt with.

* * *

The ship had partly loaded a general cargo at Brooklyn for the Philippines. She now crossed the river to fill up with case oil for Beirut, in Syria.

The utmost precautionary measures were taken against fire during our stay in Bayonne. Judge, then, my dismay when I discovered that my jacket was on fire while I was still inside the barrier guarding the whole area, the result of stuffing the pipe into a pocket, alight after a few furtive puffs.

The stern Irish guard was about to deal very severely with me, when I asked him if he could still remember Sackville Street and the smell of the dear old Liffey. He was overwhelmed immediately by a softening nostalgia, his stern look broadened into a smile as he helped me to extinguish my burning clothing. It is truly marvellous how the brotherhood of Irishmen smoothes out one's difficulties in the States.

It was with no sorrow or regret we waved farewell to the colossal Statue of Liberty, watching soulfully but detachedly our departure. Some day I hope to return, for on that far-off visit no opportunity was mine to meet the right people. Since then it has been my privilege to meet and become friends with scores of American seafarers who have touched at Cape Town, ancient Tavern of the Seas.

It may be that those of us who were brought up in the somewhat narrow environment and outlook of a British atmosphere cannot see eye to eye with the citizens of the U.S.A. on every

point. Nevertheless, they are a warm-hearted, kindly people who
are ready to extend the hand of friendship to any Britisher who
attempts no superior airs and is prepared to forget about his old
school tie.

CHAPTER XVIII

IRISH PENNANTS*

THE Port of Beyrout, at that time, was primitive indeed. It was, moreover, severely handicapped in all its activities by the Anglo-French dual control which existed there. From one pierhead of the little harbour fluttered the Union Jack—from the other the Tricolor. There was no great measure of love lost between the two factions, and 'incidents' occurred occasionally.

The ship lay off shore, anchored about half a mile from the beach, the 8-gallon cases of oil and petrol being discharged into lighters. The lighters were towed by a diminutive tug towards the shore, where they were anchored just outside the breakers. The cases were then cast overboard, and left to find their way ashore through the surf.

It was all intensely slow, so slow that the ship lay there for several weeks. As the cases made their bobbing way through the breakers, they were grabbed by the waiting natives, who piled them high on the beach. Time lay heavily on our hands until the mate made his great discovery.

I found him on the bridge, his eye glued to the ship's long glass. He did not remove it when I asked: "What's up?"

"Look at that!" he said. "That beats Bournemouth and Scarborough and all your fancy seaside resorts at home. What a sight for sore eyes! Have a squint!"

Focusing the telescope on the beach, my eyes beheld a scene the like of which they had never viewed before. Into the eye-piece of the glass leaped the figures of twenty or more young women as the telescope was moved about.

Here, surely, was the secluded, sun-kissed haunt of the Bathing Belles of Beyrout. In the curve of the bay, under the overhanging high cliff, they disported themselves gaily, playing all sorts of prankish tricks upon one another as they skipped about the beach, or ran care-free in and out of the surf.

---

* *Irish Pennants*: Odds and ends fluttering untidily from the spars or rigging of a sailing vessel.

I have seen many daring bathing costumes, but none quite so daring as those of the Beautiful Bathing Belles of Beyrout. For, one and all, they were entirely in the nude.

Those of the female sex who read these words will, no doubt, consider it a mean trick to have studied that engrossing scene through the medium of a powerful telescope. It must be admitted by the author that some such thought did pass through his mind. This feeling, unfortunately, was not shared by his shipmates. But those young women, gambolling happily and playfully on the golden sands, suffered no harm from the rude gaze of the men aboard the ship anchored in the offing, to which they had apparently given no thought.

At first we foolishly imagined we might see those nymphs come swimming out to us, long hair a-streaming, like the horde of charmers who invaded the whaler *Dolly* when Hermann Melville called at Nukuheva, Marquesas Islands, in that ship a hundred years ago. That incident is graphically described in his fine book 'Typee'. But those enticing syrens never ventured beyond the surf, and no woman set foot aboard our ship until one evening a small boat, rowed by a boy in his teens, came alongside to put on our side-ladder a gaudy young woman with bold, flashing eyes. She passed aboard unchallenged, leaving the boy to tend his boat. She walked right forward; she walked right aft—speaking no word, while the lascar crew looked on in wonderment and the officers sniggered behind their hands.

It was obvious that she had nothing to sell—beyond herself. And there were no buyers amongst the whole crew. She passed down the ladder, silent still. But when she reached the boat and shoved off she raised her impudent eyes to us, lining the rail, and scathed us foully in a tongue we did not comprehend. . .

I had intended, before leaving that port, to travel to Damascus, only a short journey from Beyrout. But the whole country was seething with unrest, and murders were commonplace. The captain refused me permission to go by rail to the place which my father had visited so many years ago, when he toured the length and breadth of the Holy Land so arduously on donkeyback in 1881, for, of course, no railway existed there in those early days.

* * *

At Port Said, that sink of iniquity where, in spite of Kipling's words, East does meet West, an adventure came my way which might easily have proved fatal.

The ship was coaling; the dust and noise of the yelling natives had become almost unbearable when a fellow officer suggested a drive in the cool of the evening.

Boarding a two-horse open carriage, we ordered its driver to take us out along the Canal road for an hour. We had not gone far when we realised our instructions were not being carried out. That rascally driver had deliberately taken us to the hinterland of the filthy town. There was something evil and sinister about the whole locality. In the foul side lanes lurked shadowy figures, peering out, watching our approach.

Suddenly the driver pulled up his horses. Climbing from his seat, he pretended something was amiss, fiddling with the harness. Then, raising his head, he called to those lurking shadows in the lanes.

Swiftly they came running towards us. Several grabbed the horses' heads, holding them down. Realising our danger, we jumped to the ground, and made for the open door of a native shop—the only sanctuary in sight. As we neared it our pursuers came upon us, slashing repeatedly at us with cruel, short-handled, long-lashed whips. My companion, a big heavy man, cried out like a wounded bull, and I realised for the first time the work done by the S.P.C.A. There was agony in those searing, slashing blows.

Hurriedly the door of the shop was slammed in our faces, and bolted on the inside. With our backs literally to the wall, we turned to face our murderous assailants, many of whom were armed with long wicked-looking knives. It was obviously the aim of that mob to bring us down with the whips, and then to finish us off with their knives.

Fortunately that fate was not to be ours. A bright light swept the road; a huge army lorry pulled up nearby. Those good-hearted Australians had taken in the situation at a glance. As they jumped from the lorry, the crowd of thugs scattered like chaff in the wind. Back to their foul lairs in the alleys they scuttled, leaving on the ground several of their murderous whips and knives.

Hilariously, full of hops and good cheer, those Aussies took us back to the waterfront.

Next day, as the ship steamed through the Canal, I told the

pilot of our adventure. Regarding me gravely, he remarked: "You were lucky. Not long ago an officer off a ship was murdered. They would kill you here for the clothes you stand up in. His body was found in the street next day—stark naked. The murderers were never caught by the police. They never are!"

* * *

Before leaving Cape Town my father had said to me: "If you ever go to Calcutta be sure to see the site of the Black Hole. On the occasion of that atrocity 146 British prisoners, some of them officers captured by the Nawab of Bengal, were herded into a room 20 feet square. With only one small grating to admit air to that fetid prison, it must have been hell in there that sultry night in July 1756. Next morning only 23 remained alive—and two of those survivors were relations of ours. One was Major Brattan, and the other Captain Gilliner."

At last my ship had reached Calcutta. Stepping ashore, I hailed a *gharry wallah*. My knowledge of Hindustani at that time practically nil, I asked him: "You savvy Black Hole of Calcutta?" "Ha, Sahib," (Yes, Sir), he replied, motioning me into his carriage.

I had been told the site of the Black Hole was not far away, and was a little puzzled over the length of the drive. Finally the driver stopped at a house from which came singing. He cracked his whip loudly. The door opened immediately, disgorging half a dozen young Indian women, who surrounded the *gharry*.

That ill-begotten son of Satan had apparently completely misunderstood me, for he had made a bee-line for this hideous native brothel!

Realising that some mistake had been made, fearing they would lose their prospective prey, those women clawed at me, screeching like a bunch of witches. One went so far as to attempt to grab my hat from my head to take it into the house— an old trick which is probably practised the world over. Seizing the whip, I lashed the horses into a gallop, leaving that yowling mob standing in the street. Later the driver dropped me close to the ship, and what I sought was found without difficulty in a few minutes.

The original building had long since disappeared, but the site was clearly marked in concrete, on which an inscription has been embossed. It told the details briefly, describing how 123 bodies had been removed in the morning and cast into a ditch close by.

Standing there alone in the still, hot Indian night, I tried to

U

picture that scene which had been enacted exactly 160 years ago.
The weaker ones had, of course, been trampled to death on the
floor by the stronger in the frantic struggle to reach that tiny
grating. It was a glaring instance of the survival of the fittest.

But there was no great pride, for me, in the thought that two
of my very distant relatives had been of the fittest; had gone into
that hell-hole—and come out alive. There was, nevertheless, a
touch of satisfaction in the knowledge that our family had
produced two such darned fine tramplers as the bold Major and
the doughty Captain!

*   *   *

A number of years spent on the Indian run, covering the whole
coast from Karachi to Chittagong, gave me the opportunity to
see something of the fringe, at least, of that great, teeming land.
There is an immense fascination in India, and for the student of
sociology an enormous field lies there. It is a land of unbelievable
contrast, the Rajahs and their kind living in a world of fantastic
wealth, while millions of impoverished workers spend their lives
in abject penury.

This must be obvious to even a careless onlooker who steps
ashore at any of the ports. It is little wonder that vice and beggars,
many wilfully mutilated to enhance their value, and child
prostitution are met with on all sides. So teeming is the population,
so poor the unskilled worker in India, that nowhere else can
human life be held so cheaply. As we lay there in the Hooghly,
many bodies floated about in the muddy water, bobbing almost
unnoticed against the ship's sides as they passed down the river.
Even the police did not bother to fish them out, for religious
principle demanded that they be left untouched.

In Bombay we discharged a cargo of coal. The steam winches
remained silent while the ship was invaded by a horde of men,
women, and even little girls. So cheap was labour there that the
coal from our holds was discharged into lighters *entirely by hand.*
A procession of half-naked creatures, varying in age from ten or
twelve to sixty or more, *carried* that cargo out of the ship to
throw it into the lighters alongside.

Some of those half-starved girl-children precociously importuned
the officers repeatedly, willing to offer, at an age when European
girls would still be playing with dolls, their under-nourished bodies

for a few pitiful annas. How, in God's name, can those pampered, pot-bellied rajahs and princelings lie at rest in their great, gold-canopied beds while such foul things go on?

At Chittagong, too, loading the precious tea which has brought untold wealth to the few, while poverty is the lot of the miserable workers who toil and gather and prepare the fragrant crop, we saw the same thing.

About the docks clustered a host of beggars, waving mutilated stumps of arms, or hobbling on crutches while they cried out piteously for an anna or two. Precocious, wizened urchins, mere boys in their early teens, were there, the self-appointed guides who offered the passer-by opportunity of pastime or amusement. The stock-in-trade of those foul little pimps was usually several older sisters, perhaps even a young aunt.

"School teachers, sahib. Very nice, sahib. All the same white like master. You come look-see, sahib! . . ." they would pester us as we made for town, clinging tenaciously to the *gharry* while they loudly called their wares.

Why was school-teaching a special attraction, we often wondered? Never has the oldest profession in the world been so closely allied to the honourable one of that of a school teacher as by those filthy little urchins.

* * *

At the termination of each of my world wanderings I returned to Dublin, like some nostalgic pigeon winging home to its loft. It was obvious, on each recurring visit there, that the political position was growing tenser. The climax was reached, as most people know, in Easter Week of 1916, when the Rebellion (glorious or tragic as your point of view suggests) flared up.

My return from sea—to sit for my mate's certificate—just missed that sorrowful eruption. The ruins of the city had scarcely ceased smoking when those old grey streets welcomed me once more. It was a saddening sight to gaze on the burnt-out shells of buildings, on the tottering empty walls of the great Post Office.

Pathetic as were those visible, unhealed wounds, they were as nothing compared with the long-nursed, bitter hatreds which were unleashed at that unhappy time.

One might well cry out: "How long, O Lord, how long?"

Even in a deeply religious country like Ireland the gentle teachings of Jesus were flouted on all sides.

* * *

I was almost ready to sit for Mate when a visitor called to see me at the Navigation School. It was my old friend the captain of the *Arctic Stream*. Several years had passed since we had parted on the deck of that ship. He looked older and seedier than ever. His shaggy eyebrows obstructed the view of his piercing eyes even more than before.

He told me he was now master of a captured German barque which had been renamed *Tridonia*. She was to sail in a few days for the Mexican Gulf. And then he asked me if I would sail in his ship as second mate. It was obvious that he was most anxious that I should say yes. Square-rigged officers were becoming scarce. A few, of course, still remained, sail-struck youngsters who hated to desert the old love, or disgruntled elderly men who had left their transfer to steam too late.

Seeing my hesitation, the old fellow took on the attitude almost of a suppliant. "Come down and have a look at the ship," he urged. "She's the finest sailing vessel in the world." I would not commit myself, knowing how soon that smoothness of his would disappear once he had me safely signed-on at sea.

* * *

The barque's masts and yards had been visible, towering aloft, throughout my walk along the North Wall. The captain and his wife were seated at the table in the roomy saloon. Several men stood by them, cap respectfully in hand. It was plain some of the crew were being engaged for the coming voyage.

The initiative appeared to be entirely in the hands of the skipper's wife. It was she who first examined their discharge books, commenting in unflattering terms on that of one of the men. "Doan't take him, Jim. He's got several bad discharges here," she advised her husband.

When the men had been disposed of, the pair turned their attention to me. I was a little disconcerted by the intensity of their combined attack. The good woman reminded me of the long voyage in the *Arctic Stream;* how well her husband and I had got on together; how much he had always thought of me. To this last remark of hers I almost added vulgarly, "Sez you!" but, my father having been a perfect gentleman, refrained.

Reinforcements were then called, in the rather pleasant shape of their daughter, a nice little girl whom I had met aboard the old ship in Leith. She renewed the attack, and certainly embarrassed me more than her grizzled father and mother. Under the battery of words and pretty glances of the young lady, I felt myself weakening. Now, if ever, was the time to go. The captain accompanied me to the gangway, and before saying good-bye invited me to attend a variety show with them all that evening.

The girl was put in the seat next to me in the theatre. The old man had opened his Aberdonian heart sufficiently to buy her a fine box of chocolates. Throughout the performance she continually leant over towards me to beg me to sail in her father's ship. Without giving any definite answer, I managed to enjoy immensely her company and the box of chocolates. We all walked back to the ship together, parting at the gangway. The captain had asked me to give him a final answer when he called at the Navigation School in the morning.

* * *

Standing there in the night, in the dark and the gloom of the rain-threatened night, that beautiful big barque so close, I meditated on the proposition which had been put before me. Though I knew it would be a mistake to go, she was calling to me with the hundred and one subtle little voices of the sailing ship.

From away up aloft came the murmured song of the night wind, caressing those great spars and rigging, so that the barque listed slightly as she stretched her broad yards out over the quayside.

Some loose running rigging *slap-slap-slapped* against the hollow steel masts. In the darkness, far away down the river, the sad, haunting cry of a few gulls came to me. These are the sounds which have ever sent my mind awandering to distant, romantic lands.

A strong inclination crept over me to march up that gangway to tell the old skipper that I was willing to sail again with him. And then reason took the place of impulse. Sail was dead. Yes, that was the truth. Sail was dead—dead as mutton. A handful of windborne ships might still drag their way bravely around the world for a few more years. But sail was already dead—killed by the relentless speed-cry of the twentieth century.

It might be several years before I could return, several precious years which would virtually be wasted, at least so far as my career was concerned. It would also mean the loss of time and money spent in preparation for my examination; that I would go away to sea at a wage about one half of that paid in steam.

A drizzling rain had set in, drifting over the dark water of the Liffey. Looking aloft once more at the *Tridonia's* huge masts and yards, where the wind sang on its plaintive little lullaby, I turned reluctantly away to start my lonely walk back to town.

The weather had deteriorated into an intensely dismal night. Cursing roundly the sodden Irish climate, I tramped along the road which fringed the river, my raincoat buttoned tightly about me.

I had gone half-way to the city when a voice called to me from the shadows: "Mister, mister! Wait a little minnit!" A figure ran quickly towards me, and as I halted I saw it was a young girl.

She could not have been more than about eighteen or nineteen. Her face was thin but comely. In the light of the quayside lamp her great, sad eyes looked up hungrily and appealingly into mine as she stood before me. She was barefooted; her flimsy dress clung damply to her. A shawl, covering her head and shoulders, glistened wetly; from it, drops of rain ran over her curly hair and slid unheeded down her face.

She hesitated before speaking again. And I, for my part, stood silent there, not knowing what to say. Then she came out with it, in her soft, Dublin brogue: "Mister, will ye go over with me behind that shed . . . an' . . . an' gimme a few coppers?"

I looked at her in amazement. To what abysmal depths had the Sorrowful Sisterhood been reduced! And yet there was no evil in her childish face. She dropped her eyes shyly for a minute. A few coppers! Hell, what was the world coming to! And while we stood there in the cold rain painted, powdered Jezebels, unworthy to lick the numb, bare feet of this poor girl, guzzled their greedy fill of warm food and drank of the choicest wines in the hotels and restaurants a few hundred yards away.

Pressing some silver in the girl's hand, I left her there. Her babbled blessings followed me a long way on the road. They may have been the hollow, mendacious blessings which are showered by the Dublin beggars on the head of the giver of the smallest alms. Somehow, on this occasion I felt that the words which poured from that girl's lips were uttered less glibly and with more sincerity than was usual.

A few pitiful coppers! I could have laughed had I not seen that youthful face so full of tragedy.

*　　*　　*

Opening my 'Daily Sketch' a week later, I saw on the front page, staring me in the face, the words, "British barque *Tridonia* lost". There were several photographs of the survivors, the usual grim smiles on their haggard-looking countenances. The master and four men had been drowned.

The ship had sailed from Dublin in ballast. She was trapped on the Welsh coast, a dead lee shore, by a westerly gale of unusual violence. The vessel was a total loss. I thought of that ghastly week the *Elginshire* had spent in those same waters, and knew how easily that same fate might have been hers. But my ship had been deeply loaded and not unmanageably light in ballast like the *Tridonia*.

*　　*　　*

Later, on subsequent visits to Ireland, the opportunity was mine of seeing a good deal of those troublous times through which the country passed in the years following Easter Week of 1916.

Was there any sense in all that frenzy of bloodshed and arson which swept the whole land after the events of 'Easter Week'?

Ask an Irish patriot and, probably with blazing eyes, he will say yes; ask the average Englishman, and he will mildly answer no. And that is about as far as you get, as with most questions concerning Ireland.

The Irish 'question' has been a thorn in the flesh of England for many, many years. The prick of that thorn can hardly have been eased when it was decided to send to Dublin that swarm of 'Black and Tans', their mission to clean up the aftermath of the Rebellion.

Those tam-o'-shantered adventurers swaggered for a while about the streets of the city. Before long a number of them swaggered no more, and the rest were reduced to patrolling in wire-netted lorries. . . .

In one of the main streets a great, dark stain on the pavement and road caught my eye. A number of onlookers stood staring down as if mesmerised by that gruesome, still-wet patch. I' had heard, some time before, the sound of an explosion—but then explosions rang out throughout the day and night at that unhappy period.

In answer to my enquiry, a man nearby spat at me: "That's all that's left of one of them dirty Black an' Tans!" Another onlooker explained, less vehemently, that a hand-grenade had been thrown at the unfortunate man whose life blood now discoloured street and pavement.

* * *

This was the inopportune time chosen by me for a visit to my aunts in Tipperary, travelling foolishly by motor-bike when the whole country was seething with unrest and murder and arson.

The day was fine and the roads were in good condition, so that at first the ride was most enjoyable. I was passing through a particularly lonely stretch of country, many miles from Dublin, when I was challenged from the roadside. A slouch-hatted, ugly-faced man in a trench-coat, rifle in hand, reared up suddenly from behind the fringing hedge, and roared something at me.

I did not wait to hear his words, for it was obvious he was not merely pleasantly passing the time of day. Bending low over the handlebars, I urged the old Triumph to its utmost. Several bullets whistled past me, dangerously near. Luckily, a comforting bend in the road soon put me out of view of that suspicious character who, had he been a better shot, would undoubtedly have brought me down.

It was then that I realised how compromising was my clothing. Clad in a pair of old army riding breeches and putties, borrowed from my brother, I was liable to be suspect by friend and foe.

Having spent a few days with my aunts, who, brave women, still clung to their lonely country home in spite of danger, I faced the homeward run—still garbed in riding breeches and putties. All went well until I was nearing Naas, some twenty miles from Dublin. Then, rounding a sharp curve, I almost ran into a heavy rope stretched across the road. British soldiers with fixed bayonets closed in around me. The officer in charge, civil enough but coldly official, demanded from me any papers to prove my identity.

Will you believe it—you probably will not— I had not even a shred of paper or a letter with which to establish myself? No, not even my driving licence! It will seem amazing that anyone would imagine he could go careering about Ireland in the midst of "The Trouble", without any means of identification. Evidently he couldn't—for I soon found myself locked up under guard in a nearby cottage.

For hours I puzzled over my predicament, knowing they suspected me of being a Sinn Fein rider. The whole thing was typical of the careless manner in which my life has been conducted. Then I thought of a police official at Kingstown with whom I had become friendly while living near there.

The officer in charge of my captors, when sent for, promised to phone through to Kingstown. Unfortunately it was a Sunday; the man I knew was off duty. It was late evening and growing dark when I was suddenly set free.

Then another trouble raised its unpleasant head. There was something seriously wrong with the carbide head-lamp. (I had not anticipated any night riding.) Persistently it refused to burn. In the lonely country stretches I rode in the dark, trusting that no straying donkey or sheep would cross my path. In order to avoid any further possible trouble, the bike had to be pushed through the villages, for miles along the streets of Dublin. Anyone who owned an old fixed-engine Triumph of very early vintage will know what that meant. To even push that wretched machine it was necessary to remove the driving belt, or to keep lifted, continuously and tediously, the exhaust lever on the handlebar.

* * *

Probably the most pathetic figures which stand out from all the storm and stress of that unhappy time were those fine men of the Dublin Metropolitan Police. Many were destroyed by an assassin's bullet. Their own countrymen, in the belief that the police had given their life's allegiance to the foreign king across the water, shot them down in cold blood. I have a vivid recollection of those conspicuous bobbies standing in the darkling Dublin streets, looking anxiously from side to side, expecting any moment the murderer's bullet.

The enmity towards the Black and Tans was not confined alone to Ireland.

One night late, coming aboard a ship of which I was mate, many thousands of miles from Dublin, sounds of deadly argument reached me from the saloon.

In one corner, his face chalk-white with fear, stood an officer over whom towered a big Irish fireman. Somehow it had come to the ears of the fireman that the poor craven he now faced with murder in his eyes had served with the Black and Tans. Only for my timely arrival and whatever persuasive powers are mine, murder would have been done that night. The terrified ex-Black and Tan left the ship next day, for what he had kept secret so long—none of us had an inkling before the fireman had 'smelt him out'—was noised about the ship.

* * *

My father had often said to me: "Get the highest qualifications you can. There are far too many odd-jobbers in the world."

With these words impressed on my mind, I set about preparing, at that excellent school on Eden Quay, to pass for square-rigged extra-Master.

And then the bottom fell out of everything for me. A cable from South Africa announced my father's death. That kind, wise counsellor was gone—gone to whatever place is reserved for such good men. The loss was irreparable.

But that was not the sum total of my distress. Suddenly, without any warning, the greatest tragedy of my life came surging over me with shattering, stunning effect. A fatal accident occurred on my motor-cycle. A life-time friend was wiped out.

With the cynicism of fate, she lost her life almost at the front door of her own home; she who had shortly returned from abroad, where the danger and discomfort of war had been bravely faced.

There was an inquest in the house. With muddy boots the coroner and his jury tramped noisily into the room which had been set aside for their deliberations. The coroner, attempting to soften the blow, spoke kindly to me. Nevertheless, his words and the bucolic gaze of his colleagues left me with the unhappy thought that they regarded me almost in the light of a murderer.

At the suggestion of the coroner, that clumsy throng stamped heavily across the flagged hall to the little chamber of death, where lay what he had referred to as 'the remains'. The remains! There was something indecent, something almost obscene to me, in the use of that term. A few short hours before, that friend of mine, however cold she now lay there, had been a living, laughing entity, full of the joy of life. And now she was just . . . . 'the remains' . . . .

My eyes were never closed throughout those three days and nights before the funeral. It was wintertime, and the weather wild. The great house, standing in the lonely countryside, was beset by storm and rain.

During those long dark nights I lay awake, staring hopelessly into the blackness which had engulfed those good friends of mine and myself, robbing us all of one we loved. In the wide chimney of the bedroom the wind moaned and wailed and whimpered. Sometimes, in all that wild lamenting it seemed to me I clearly heard the well-known voice—mildly reproving, mildly reproachful —of her who lay so still and silent downstairs, gently chiding me for what had come to pass. . . .

It was impossible to study further. I felt I must leave Dublin without delay. To the annoyance of the proprietor of the navigation school, a little apprehensive of his proud percentage of "first attempt" passes, I sat for the examination, obtaining without difficulty my Master's square-rigged 'ticket'. Thus was lost for ever the opportunity of acquiring the higher qualification.

CHAPTER XIX

THE PERSIAN GULF

SOME SAILORS, far out on the storm-tossed waste of water, may long at times for the life of a farmer. That is not the case with this bold *marinero*. For of all the occupations to which a man can turn his hand, farming must surely be the most exacting. The farmer is almost as much the victim of the vagaries of the elements as the sailor, in his wind- and sea-swept bark on the briny.

From Liverpool I had come to spend some time with my brother on his recently acquired farm in the western Transvaal. Four dejected donkeys took us, at the usual pace of the donkey, in a little cart the four miles from the station.

There was no smiling or tear-stained girl to welcome me there, such as greeted the arrival of the original farmer's boy in the well-known song. There were only my brother, a few natives, and myself on the whole place.

That agricultural interlude impressed on me more than any other experience the truth of the old adage, "Cobbler, stick to your last!" Those huge, long-horned oxen filled me with fear. I would rather any day muzzle an obstreperous topsail in a winter gale than even attempt to inspan those immense beasts. Yet my brother worked with them with the greatest ease and *sang-froid*.

Occasionally, when he was ploughing and the boys were engaged on other tasks, I would act as *voorlooper*, leading those snorting monsters along the furrows. Spurred on by those great, sharp, tossing horns so near my back, the leading *reim* stretched out to its utmost length, I would stumble down the field at the rate of knots, as if pursued by the devil.

The farm was situated in an outlying district, amongst a people who spoke only Afrikaans. Some of them may have been able to converse in English but they did not choose to do so. For they were still a bit sore about the South African War, and did not welcome us "rooineks" amongst them. Over and over again—it was, indeed, the chief topic of conversation— they spoke bitterly of *"Die skade van die drie jaar oorlog."* (The damage done in the three year war). In their ignorance or innocence, they considered the first World War a childish bout of fisticuffs compared with their own particular campaign.

That farm was just about three hundred miles too far from the sea for me. Sometimes, in moments of forgetfulness, hungry for a sniff of that salty tang, I would scale one of the higher koppies to scan the horizon on all sides, ready to cry out exultingly, "Thalassa! Thalassa!" had I seen that well-known blue in the distance.

My brother had no luck at all. The weather continually misbehaved itself, either too much rain or too little. The locusts paid us a devastating visit, devouring every vestige of green which came in their path. But the greatest disaster of all was the loss of a number of cattle. The ladies of the herd inconsiderately chose any old time of the night for their confinements. And my brother, anxious over his heifers as any young husband over his first-born, tended them all.

One night a fine calf was born to a highly-strung young cow— her first. Though the calf was perfect, the delivery did not run its full, normal course. My brother had not seen all he should have seen; it was obvious something was amiss.

A few days later the cow had wasted to a bag of bones; it was plain that she would die. Then my brother performed what to me was an amazing obstetric operation. While he vaselined his arm to the shoulder I stood by in wonderment. "What are you going to do, Bill?" I asked him. "I'm going to try and save the life of this poor thing," he told me.

"You can't do that," I said aghast. "We've no disinfectants— and that brute *stinks* of rottenness! And you've got cuts all over your hand and forearm!"

Stout fellow, he took no notice of me. His arm had disappeared to the shoulder. With a preoccupied look, he was counting slowly . . . "one . . . two . . . three . . ." In my ignorance I thought this was some sort of incantation. Later, he explained that he was carefully tallying the "suckers" as he dislodged them, so that the fetid *placenta* might be wholly voided.

That cow made a wonderful recovery. A few days later she was eating heartily and rapidly filling out again.

A number of petty thefts about the farm decided my brother

to buy a good watchdog. "The Farmer's Weekly" seemed to offer the very thing we wanted: "Boerhound, large, black; splendid watchdog, £2."

The term 'boerhound' — farm dog — is rather elastic, but Bill decided to take the risk. The money was posted; we waited patiently for the dog's arrival. The owner wrote by return. The animal's name was Wallace, which was immediately shortened to the handier Wally.

We set out to meet and greet the dog at the appointed hour. The train having pulled up, we expected to see one "boerhound, large, black" leap frolicsomely from the van. No such thing occurred. Instead, a big, strong crate, resembling somewhat a lion's cage, was lowered on to the platform. Inside, in a decidedly nasty frame of mind, stood Wally, growling angrily and showing all the other customary signs of canine displeasure. There was no doubt about his identity; the label tacked on the top of the crate was perfectly clear.

"That's some dog," said Bill, a bit apprehensively, "he looks more like a young lion to me."

To be truthful, we were both a bit apprehensive. We had often seen dogs travelling docilely on the end of leads; we had come in contact with hot-dogs, sea-dogs, dogs of many sorts and sizes. Never before had we met crated-dog, caged like some forest-bred animal of the wild.

Wally, cage and all, was lifted on to the back of the little cart. Raising his regal head high, peering disdainfully between the bars, he regarded with strong disapproval the four dejected donkeys which would take him, at the usual pace of the donkey, to his new home. Then, swinging round, he gazed balefully into our faces. Never before have I seen such a baleful look. His eyes had a peculiar, greenish, phosphorescent glint in them. The cage rumbled with his low growling.

At the farm we placed Wally's cage on the ground, carefully avoiding putting our hands inside the bars. Squatting down in front of him, we studied the proportions of the shiny black animal. "That's a hell of a lot of dog for two pounds," said my brother.

Then we thought of the packet of sweets we had bought at the Indian store on our way home. They were mostly those little vari-coloured tablets with love mottoes printed on them. You know the kind of thing—what we used to call Conversation Lozenges in our childhood days.

Pulling a few out of the bag—I LOVE YOU; KISS ME, DARLING; YOU ARE MY SWEETHEART, etc.—Bill threw them into the cage. A crunch or two and they were gone, those words of love having made not the slightest impression on Wally's bad temper.

Tiring of this childish game, Bill said: "I'm going to let the blighter out." Wally stepped from the crate, his body vibrating with his low growling as he stretched himself.

Warily at first, we gradually took more and more little liberties with him. Finally, he was my brother's devoted friend and a splendid safeguard about the farm.

* * *

Early one morning the two of us stood in the *kraal*, mournfully gazing down on another dead cow. Two neighbours, stolid, bearded men who had no English, were with us, airing their views upon this sudden mysterious death. They sniffed the animal and examined it all over with the greatest care. They fondled thoughtfully their abundant growth of whisker. Then they both came out with their ponderous decision: "Ja, die blitz het daardie beest doodgeslaan." (That animal was killed by lightning.)

My brother had other views. No lightning had struck anywhere near the kraal during the night. Cutting off one of the heifer's ears, he sent it post-haste to the laboratory at Pretoria. To be on the safe side, we buried the carcase deeply, covering it with lime. The boys had to be watched carefully, for they rebelled against the waste of so much good meat.

Then came the diagnosis—what my brother had expected—anthrax!

Our neighbours were furious with brother Bill. The beast had been killed by lightning, surely the *verdomde rooinek* could see that when it was so plain! The whole valley was put into quarantine, and everybody ordered to inoculate their cattle.

What a job was that! The nervous heifers had to be thrown before anything could be done with them. They went mad under the sharp sting of the needle. A little apprehensive, we left Blom to the last—Blom the magnificent Friesland bull, ponderous, lordly, immense of girth—how would he take the indignity?

As we approached, Blom made no attempt to escape. My brother spoke soothingly to him as he pinched the skin ready for the injection. When the syringe punctured the heavy hide, Blom twitched slightly, turned round to look at us, his nose wrinkled in a grotesque smile—and then walked stolidly away!

Another of our cattle had been found lying cold and stiff. Turning to Bill, I said to him: "It looks like I'm the Jonah here. I'm off to sea again."

*　　*　　*

The arrival of the train at Simonstown must have coincided with the most somnolent hour in the daily life of that drowsy little place. As I alighted—one of a half dozen passengers— the station-master stood on the platform busily picking his teeth while he gazed detachedly far away across the water at some spot approximately in the vicinity of Seal Island.

I had been engaged in Durban to join a ship as mate. Had I shaken the dust of the farm from my feet a little sooner, the job as master of that ship would have been mine. She was small—the smallest in which I had sailed as yet. Nevertheless, she was a ship, and I approached the station-master to find out the best method of reaching her.

"The *St. Aubin*," he said, in answer to my question. "The *St. Aubin*. Yes, she's here in dock. You'll get a cab outside to take you down. I hear there's a wild crew aboard her. They made a bit of trouble in the town last night. If I were you I'd keep clear of her."

A look of sympathy crept into his eye when I told him that I was joining her as mate.

With some misgiving, half expecting a brick or some similar nautical missile to be hurled at me, I passed up the gangway. All was quiet on the western front, so to speak; no sign of life appeared about the deck.

The captain was finally discovered in the store-room, checking cases and packages with the steward. When I enquired about the crew, he remarked shortly, "They're skulking in their quarters aft."

No purpose would be served by postponing my acquaintance with those gentlemen aft, especially as it would be my duty to run them for some months. Entering their domain, I introduced myself. A certain amount of hostility was shown towards me at first. Before long, however, they proved, though decidedly unruly, not a great deal worse than many other men with whom I had sailed. Undoubtedly, they were up against the skipper, who appeared to expect from them the servility of the lascar crews to which he had become accustomed.

The *St. Aubin* was one of the "Rescue" class of tugs built in the first World War, fine, able, single-screwed vessels of 145 feet in length. She had been chartered to tow river craft from Basra to Bombay, a distance of 1600 miles.

We sailed for the Persian Gulf next day, calling en route for bunkers at Durban, Kilindini, and Karachi.

After the ships which had been my home for years, that tug seemed diminutive indeed. But once we had put to sea, I soon found the heart within that little hull was big and valiant. Leaving Durban, we ran into three days' nor'east gale. Pluckily the *St. Aubin* rode those enormous seas like a duck, plodding at slow speed into the teeth of them.

The movement was amazingly uncomfortable to one used to the more leisurely pitch and tumble of large vessels. My room was situated "right in the eyes of the ship", off the saloon under the high fo'c'sle head. Many a time the wild motion nearly threw me from my bunk.

* * *

As we neared Basra, on each side of the Shatt al Arab river stretched immense groves of date-palms, tossing their heads in the prevailing *shamal,* or nor'west wind. The principal industry of this strange land was plain to all—dates. Basra and dates are almost synonymous.

On arrival, we soon learnt the nature of the work on which we were to be engaged for some months. Along the river, which is a confluence of the mighty Euphrates and the Tigris, lay a veritable host of craft of all sorts—relics of the war. Small tugs, great stern-wheelers, refrigeration-barges, lighters of all sorts—all these were there, rusting uselessly along the river bank. They reminded me of an article I had read in *John Bull* called "The Mess of Mesopotamia", in which Bottomley had written scathingly of the enormous waste in that campaign. The river craft we saw represented an initial cost to the British tax-payer of many hundreds of thousands of pounds.

x

Some obscure body of men known as "The Disposals Board" had hit on the brilliant idea that all these vessels might be sold if they were towed to Bombay. It was a forlorn hope—a hope, however, which accounted for our presence at Basra, and also for that of an ex-navy tug, the *Saucy*, recently arrived on the same quest as ourselves.

We were informed, the captain and myself, that our first essay would consist of nine 130-foot lighters. Nine! Vainly we protested that this was too much to expect as a start. Curtly we were told to carry on.

I went to examine that brood of ugly ducks that we were to lead to Bombay. They had been prepared for the tow, we had been informed. That preparation appeared to me shoddy and unseamanlike. Right round each lighter had been secured, somewhat insecurely, a heavy wire bridle, terminating at bow and stern in a large thimble. The work had been done by lascar labour and looked to me most unsatisfactory.

It was useless to complain. We were told that we must sail immediately, so that as much as possible might be accomplished before the wild sou'west monsoon came sweeping angrily over the Arabian Sea. So it was we set off, more than a little doubtfully, with our numerous flock. Official regulations precluded any towing until the Shatt al Arab bar, 70 miles distant, had been reached. Consequently, our chickens had been clustered closely around the tug, three on each side, three lashed up astern. The *St. Aubin* resembled a decidedly harassed Bantam hen with a brood of half-grown Rhode Island Reds clinging to her.

We anchored in the river, looking more like a huge raft than anything else. Through the night we dragged our anchors for a mile or two, that vast bulk hanging heavily on the chains.

There was a spot of trouble with the crew before we sailed. Those unruly hands demanded—and ultimately received—a towing bonus of £5 before they would put to sea. This was never paid to the officers, who created no trouble, and were thus deprived of the bonus.

It was late afternoon when we reached the bar. Everything was ready for streaming. On the way down I had carefully shackled on the shoddy coir ropes, which had been lying exposed to wind and sun and rain for many months. After all had been streamed astern, I took the boat and examined minutely the whole, immensely-long tow as the tug slowly drew ahead. There was no one on any of the lighters. On the last one a mast had been erected, carrying a large white flag which would be visible in the beam of our searchlight.

In the gathering darkness, we set out for Bombay.

Many people imagine the Persian Gulf to be an almost land-locked lake, mill-pond calm under a blazing sun. While this is sometimes the case, the weather can be bitterly cold and the water extremely rough. The *shamal,* which blows over the entire Persian Gulf, often reaches a ferocity similar to Cape Town's famous south-easter, quickly raising a fiendish sea.

Before midnight, the *shamal* was screaming after us, kicking up so bad a sea that the towing-gear was strained to the utmost.

At 6.30 a.m. I felt the tug leap like an exultant boy released from school. Looking aft, I saw that seven of the lighters had broken adrift, the rope between the second and third having parted. Circling back, we dropped the boat, in it four men and myself.

Repeatedly we attempted to board No. 3 in the hope that the tow might be re-connected. In the wild wind and the now raging sea, continuously swept by spray, we were defied again and again by that monster. Like some enraged colossus, it strove to smash us to pulp every time we neared. Finally, rather than lose the already damaged boat and, possibly, our lives, we returned reluctantly to the ship. Before it could be hoisted, the boat was partially stove-in.

There was nothing left for us but to lie off, while we watched the Battle of the Giants. All the lighters had clustered together by now, each apparently intent on one thing only—the swift destruction of its neighbour. It was an amazing and awesome spectacle. Like enraged bulls those ungainly craft charged repeatedly—trampling, snorting, climbing over one another in mortal combat.

Throughout the day dull, hollow reverberations rang out, occasionally the scream of tortured metal. Wounded and torn, one after the other they gave up the struggle, plunging out of sight.

And then, save for the tug and the two remaining lighters tumbling astern, the *shamal* blew over a wide and empty sea.

Saddened and disheartened, we returned to Basra, to be given immediately five other assorted craft, amongst them several ponderous stern-wheelers. These seven, through storm and stress, we delivered safely at Bombay.

*   *   *

It would be impossible, in the confines of one chapter, to do justice to the whimsies of the Persian Gulf, or to the gallant effort of the plucky *St. Aubin.* That job in her was about the toughest I have ever tackled. Backwards and forwards we toiled between Basra and Bombay, past the northward-pointed, tapered finger of the Oman Peninsula, through the narrows which were guarded by the towering light of Little Quoin Island.

Some of those passages, a heavy tow behind us, were nothing short of .nightmares. One trouble, however, had been removed. The recalcitrant white crew had been replaced by double the number of lascars, who were packed, sardine-like, into the narrow confines of our circumscribed accommodation.

Repeatedly, often two or three times in the 24-hours, the whole tow, or the greater part of it, would break adrift. And then, for reasons which need not here be specified, all the danger and anxiety of the boat-work fell to me. In daylight and dark we set off in that plunging boat to attempt to connect up once more, before all those craft had drifted together, thus causing further damage to their towropes.

How weary I grew, as I lay restlessly in my bunk at night, of the hot-foot arrival at the door of the lascar quartermaster. Breathlessly he would call, "Sahib! Sahib! *Burra russi toot geea hai*!" (Sir! Sir! The tow-rope has parted!) Even before his announcement of this disaster, I knew only too well what had happened. For the tug, released from the deadening load of the tow, had already bounded ahead, the bow-wave under my open port roaring in my ears before the speed could be slackened.

Then came the dangerous boat trip in the dark; the hazardous manoeuvre of boarding the necessary craft. The stern-wheelers were the worst of all, for a bristling "duck walk" projected along each side. Had the boat got under this, she and her crew would have been crushed to pulp. It was necessary, therefore, to board right aft, on one of the transoms of the huge stern paddle-wheel. Once aboard, the heart-breaking toil of connecting up began. For hours we often struggled in the dark with heavy ropes, weighty shackles and thimbles, working at times completely immersed in the surging, shamal-tossed sea as we clung to bow or stern. Over and over again those shoddy coir ropes were spliced and hitched, hitched and spliced.

Sometimes only the last craft would break away—to disappear south-eastwards in the spindrift and the murk. It was occasionally impossible for us, handicapped by the immense length of the tow, to recapture those solitary wanderers, most of which fetched up eventually on the southern shore of the Gulf. A number of times, on our way back from Bombay, we explored this coast for scattered lost members of our flock.

At an obscure village we discovered one, a large lighter with a cheeky tug still perched unharmed atop. The local chief proved truculent, and decidedly antagonistic to any claim of ours, refusing point-blank to permit us to remove the lighter. The captain returned incensed to the ship. A wireless message was sent out without delay to a unit of the Royal Indian Marine, which we knew was cruising less than a hundred miles away. When that rather insignificant war-vessel arrived, several of her barkers roared out. So great is the persuasive power of powder and shot that we were enabled to claim our lighter without further interference.

The whole coast of Oman, at that time, was extremely wild and practically untouched by European civilisation. Piracy was said to still exist extensively.

At one place where the captain and I landed, our arrival happened to coincide with the celebration of the safe return of a number of warriors who had apparently carried out successfully a punitive expedition against some neighbouring enemy. Most of those weirdly-clad martial men carried ancient muzzle-loaders of primitive design.

In a big room we sat cross-legged on the floor, no chairs being evident, with the local chief and the leaders of the conquering heroes. Not one word of English was spoken. Large brass trays were handed round, on them a sticky mess resembling, and tasting not unlike, soft soap. Into this glutinous stuff we gouged our fingers, imitating the others, as we helped ourselves to the strange concoction.

At another even more remote village the captain hailed a passing boat to put ashore the wireless officer and myself, our quest the purchase of fresh meat. No European lived there, and our language was unknown. By means of signs we explained our needs. We were then taken to an open-air market place, where were shown to us a few scraggy pieces of fly-encrusted goat-meat.

All around us pressed the dark-faced throng, following everywhere we went. At first a certain amount of deference was paid to us. That soon vanished, and we found that we were being jostled and impudently pressed upon by the crowd.

We returned, a little anxiously, to the beach, hemmed in by increasing numbers of the inhabitants. The *Shamal* had increased in force to almost a gale, blowing directly on-shore. In vain we cajoled the boat's crew to take us off to the ship, under way miles out to sea to avoid the numerous treacherous reefs.

One and all refused to take us off. Then, it must be admitted, we became really scared. Around us surged the throng. On every man's belt, even on the youngsters', rested a kris-like wicked-looking curved knife.

It was growing dusk. To spend the night ashore would be madness. We knew it might be many hours before the ship sent in her boat, even should she do so amongst those unknown reefs before the morning. At last, in the dying light, we managed to persuade a crew to take us off. That pull in the teeth of the wind was long and hard, but those men were well repaid when finally we made the ship.

* * *

The native *dhobash* (ship chandler) at Basra came to my door one morning to announce: "To-night, Mr. Chief, we go see the dancing girls."

The small British colony, decidedly clannish and cliquish, had no place within it for the common sea-faring man. So it was the captain, the ship chandler and myself set out that night, in search of pastime or amusement, to see the dancing girls.

The *dhobash* guided us through filthy, muddy streets in which ancient passing Fords splashed our clothes with mire. It was necessary to plough ankle-deep along the bog of the lesser roads to reach that place.

Looking around, we saw in the dim-lit building ours were the only pale faces amongst the dusky throng. On the platform which answered for a stage sat the orchestra, a weird collection of musicians who played the strangest instruments. The leader, a huge, black-faced man who we were told was blind, twanged and plucked at an enormous instrument like an overgrown mandolin.

The girls came in, swaying and singing, much lighter of skin than the crowd who sat gaping there. Armenians, our guide informed us. Had we expected something spicy, we were disappointed. The girls were clad demurely. Their singing was intensely harsh and unmusical. Every one of them had fixed, to forefinger and thumb, a tiny pair of cymbals, with which she kept up a fairy tinkling while she sang.

The *dhobash*, enjoying himself to the full, leered over towards us, his white teeth flashing in the semi-darkness: "You like him —this girls? You like to meet him—afterwards?" We did not like to meet 'him,' her, or it, neither then nor afterwards. All we wished to do was to get away from the hideous miaowing of that bunch of beauties.

Presently the lights went on. Two attendants appeared with big pitchers of black coffee and a small brass bowl each. Every man present—there were no women—quaffed his mouthful, the communal bowl passing up and down the lines to be filled and emptied.

When it came to our turn, we hesitated. Our reluctance was noticed by our companion. Leaning towards us he said: "Drink! It is an insult not to drink!" Praying that those encircling brass rims harboured nothing more deadly than the milder germs of disease—we drank.

We had grown weary of the show. The Armenians—were they slave girls?—still pirouetted gravely, their faces set in a sad fixed smile, while the tiny cymbals tink-tink-tinkled on finger and thumb. As we rose to go, the leader of the band stared sightlessly at us, the perspiration coursing down his face as he rasped and twanged vigorously at his Brobdingnagian mandolin.

* * *

He was standing in the stable when we walked over from the ship to have a look at him. Earlier in the day his owner, who had won the horse for a few rupees in a raffle, had extracted from me a promise to ride the animal that afternoon. Foolishly I had consented, without first having seen the horse, to take him for a gallop after many days in the stable.

Though he possessed no wings and had not sprung from the blood of Medusa, Pegasus seemed to me the only fitting name for such a noble white steed. The Arab blood was sticking out a mile —from delicate, quivering nostrils to the tip of his long white tail which almost swept the ground. He was in the pink of condition, well groomed, well cared for, and literally bursting out of his skin with spirits.

Approaching Pegasus— he really answered to some outlandish Persian title—I attempted to rub his nose. But he was having none of that. His ears lay flat and his hind legs lashed out viciously, so that I backed away. Doubts and fears began to fill my mind.

In Stellenbosch, as a boy, I had frequently ridden my father's nags when they had wanted exercise. They had sometimes run away with me, straining futilely with skinny, impotent wrists at the reins until the horse grew tired. The cause of that rapid bolt was usually a stinging fusilade of acorns from the hands of the leaders of the girls' school 'crocodiles' out walking in the afternoon. Far from the short-sighted control of the teacher at the other end of the long line, those impudent hussies would stoop quickly to pick up the ready ammunition, which lay so plentifully about the oak-lined roads in summer.

Here was a different proposition. Pegasus was no ewe-necked mount such as had been some of my father's. But the die was cast; it was now too late to draw back. "Send him along at two o'clock," I said, quaking a little. "Though no cow-boy—I'll ride him."

* * *

Sailor on horseback—horse marine—incongruous figure of ridiculous comedy, mention of whom is supposed to make one smile, at least—that was me, ungrammatically, shortly after 2 p.m.

The horse had arrived, reluctantly, in the care of a native groom, saddled, bridled, all ready for the road—wherever that problematic road might lead the pair of us. While Pegasus pranced and kicked about, I carefully examined girths, reins and stirrup-leathers, noting with some satisfaction that the bridle carried a heavy, powerful bit. It seemed to me it would be needed.

The horse did not like the look of me. That was quite obvious. And, apart from the beauty of his perfect body, I did not like the look of him. For there was a nasty red glow in his eye as he glared disapprovingly at me. Candidly, I had the wind up.

The whole ship's company lined the rail to see me off. I almost said to wish me God-speed, but that would be too euphonious a term to use. For my adventure was merely a little side-show for them to while the weary hour away.

Cries, some encouraging but mostly derisive, reached me from the ship. And in all that crowd I honestly believe there was only one who was really apprehensive for my safety—my faithful old ally, the Indian bos'un. "Look out, Sir. That horse is bad!" he called in Hindustani.

Watching my chance, between the squalls of the horse's bad temper, I sprang aboard. The groom released his head.

Pegasus got busy right away, promptly performing a few hand-springs, just to limber up his fore-end. Then he reversed the process by rearing, more or less perpendicularly, a number of times to do the same for his hindquarters.

Miraculously, I still clung there—unsunk.

The horse turned a few catherine-wheels in both directions—clockwise, anti-clockwise—and then paused to note the effect. Bloody but unbowed, I still sat there.

What will he do next, I wondered? Probably suddenly drop to the ground and roll over me. That's a nasty trick which luckily did not enter his mind. Instead, Pegasus took to flight—winged flight, arrow flight—heading for the main road at what might nautically he termed the rate of knots.

Taking the bit literally in his teeth, my beautiful white steed bolted with me. Unable to make any impression on his mouth, my hands chafed and bleeding, I gave up the struggle at length, leaving the maddened horse to his own devices.

The speed of a bolting Arab is swift. The wind whistled shrilly in my ears; frightened natives rushed out of our impetuous way; squawking fowls fluttered anxiously from our path.

My father was brought up with horses in Ireland. He, wise counsellor, had often said to me: "If a horse bolts with you, *keep your head*! He's bound to get tired some time!"

Hot-foot we sped out into the desert for miles. That horse had grit and stamina, and never flagged until the town was far astern, I began to think we were bound non-stop for Baghdad, or for the dim, distant sources of the mighty Euphrates.

Pegasus came to a stop, blowing hard and covered in sweat,

Gradually I got control of him, forcing him to do my bidding. I wanted to dismount, to look him in the eye, to speak to him friendlylike, as one man to another. But I dared not do so, for he might bolt again, leaving me stranded far from the ship.

So I was forced to address him from the bridge, as it were, using the wheedling, soothing words of Irish blarney which had so often been my father's when he calmed a refractory horse in my youth.

* * *

It was late when we returned to the wharf, almost sedately, for Pegasus was tired. There was no more enmity between us, no more foolish pranks. Rubbing that smooth nose as I said good-night to him, I noted the reddish glow had faded from his eye. And I could swear he smiled at me as he quietly turned away. Caked in sweat and dust, it was difficult to recognise the beautiful milk-white charger which had stepped so arrogantly alongside the ship earlier in the day.

I took him out for a gallop next morning, far beyond the town. When we returned there was a note awaiting me from his owner: "The horse is yours—if you want him."

If you want him! That beautiful, sensitive thing, most wonderful of all creations. Of course I wanted him! But he was never to be mine.

It had suddenly been decided to lay the ship up in Bombay for some months. We were to leave immediately. Already the sou'west monsoon was raging over the Arabian Sea, rendering more dangerous and difficult each successive tow. The British Tanker Company had become a bit perturbed over the untended, unlit craft which occasionally broke away from our care, to drift menacingly about the Persian Gulf.

The whole endeavour had been a wash-out, more of the "Mess of Mesopotamia", as *John Bull* had said. And all our blood and sweat and tears had been for little more than naught. Those unwieldy craft were tied up to the moorings in Bombay harbour, there to rust as they had rusted at Basra. They may be rusting at those buoys to this day for all I know.

Just before we left Basra for the last time, I walked over to the stable where Pegasus was stalled. He was munching contentedly a mangerful of oats. He graciously permitted me, as I said good-bye to him, to playfully pull his ears and smooth his soft pink nose and proud arched neck.

As I closed the door of the stable, I heard—or did I imagine I heard?—above the strident ship's whistle which was recalling me, a little soft whinny of farewell. . . . . .

* * *

The captain and myself were compelled to spend several weeks in Bombay, awaiting passages to London in the P. & O. liner s.s. *China*. Most agreeable arrangements have been made for us in the interim. We were housed in a first-class hotel. It was about the only lotus-eating period of my life, all expenses being paid for us, besides our normal wages.

On arrival at the hotel, a shadow followed me into my room. Turning I found a spotlessly white-clad servant standing inside the door. "Hum Abdool, Sahib" (I am Abdool, Sir) he announced, bowing before me. He then turned his attention to my luggage so vigorously that I became a little suspicious of his exact status.

Seeking official information, I found the pompous, intensely superior Indian head-waiter in the lounge.

"Abdool is your private servant, sahib," he remarked unctuously. "All the burra sahibs (big gentlemen) in this hotel have private servants. The management, of course, is not responsible for his wages."

From his haughty demeanour it was obvious that argument with such a personage was unthinkable. His whole bearing screamed at me: "Dismiss Abdool—and your name is MUD." So it was, somewhat unwillingly, I acquired the services of a sort of masculine lady's maid.

On my return to the room I found Abdool already busy unpacking my meagre wardrobe. His long skinny fingers were probing the innermost recesses of my trunk. I stood by, keenly conscious of the many garments which should be there. I had never cared tuppence about clothes. Now, apparently, I was to regret that sartorial indifference.

Abdool rose to his feet and faced me, his sombre eye full of sadness and reproach. "Dinner jacket ne hai, sahib!" he informed me. "No, Abdool," I replied, "alas, there is no dinner jacket."

He shrugged his shoulders in a gesture which spoke volumes, turned to the trunk and plunged his talons into its bowels once more. Abdool's next shock was not long a-coming. He rose and faced me again. "Dressing gown ne hai, sahib!" he announced. Humbled to the dust I had to show a bold front.

"There is no dressing gown, Abdool," I said. "I have always regarded a dressing gown as a most effeminate garment. No real sailorman would use one."

My words were lost on him. In the end I gave him some money to go out and buy me one.

* * *

Once Abdool had got over the initial shock of the lack of garments which every burra sahib was supposed by tradition to possess, he proved a most able and attentive servant. No mother tended her first-born more assiduously than he ministered to my needs. His attentions were at times, indeed, a little embarrassing; for instance, when he stood beside me as I undressed, insisting on pulling the clothes from my protesting limbs and body.

The diurnal visit to the bath became something of a ritualistic procession with Abdool striding solemnly behind me carrying the usual paraphernalia. He would turn on the hot and cold water, testing the temperature carefully, first with hand and then with elbow, before his master was permitted to get in.

It was as well those pampered days did not last for ever. The time came at length for us to sail for London, in the unusual role of passenger.

Abdool was standing by the *gharry* in which he had placed my luggage. I pressed in his hand the *baksheesh* of which I considered him worthy. My largesse was, I knew, on far too generous a scale. Perhaps that is why the melancholy face of Abdool was lit by a look I had not seen there before.

"Salaam, burra sahib," he said, bowing profoundly, "Ek dum burra sahib, bahut salaam!"

There was something in his sombre eye which led me to believe my rehabilitation was complete.

* * *

So I left Abdool—and the East.

Perhaps some day I shall return. For the imaginative a wonderful fascination is to be found there. To this day I can hear the squealing cry of the bromley-kites in the early mornings, and the mysterious, throbbing beat of hidden tom-toms in the scented Indian night.

Should I return I can imagine Abdool waiting for me there. I can imagine him bending over my trunk, drawing from it a brand new dinner jacket and a flamboyant dressing gown. In fancy I hear him saying approvingly, "Achcha hai, sahib—ek dum burra sahib!"

CHAPTER XX

THE ANCHOR IS SWALLOWED

IT WAS A peaceful mid-summer evening when we joined the ship, the mate and myself. The two of us comprised the full ship's company.

Both ship and mate were small, the length of the little vessel being a shade under twenty-five feet, that of the mate slightly short of five, though, with the customary vanity of woman, she claims a full inch more than that. She was a mate in more senses than one, for we had been married in Liverpool that morning.

No briny water caressed the sides of our little sailing vessel. For, paradoxical though it may seem, our port of embarkation was deeply set within the very heart of the English countryside. Wroxham, which we had reached after a tedious, roundabout journey from Liverpool, is one of the principal gateways of the delightful waterways of Norfolk and Suffolk. From it set out, every week-end, a great fleet of little white-winged ships of which ours was but one.

The *Mallard* lay at Loynes' yacht-staithe. I fell in love with her at once. Alongside her nestled the handy centreboard sailing dinghy which we towed astern throughout our pleasant wanderings. A dream of many years was about to come true for me; we were about to sail for a fortnight's cruise on the tortuous rivers and Broads of Norfolk and Suffolk.

Do I hear some hard-boiled yachtsman exclaim disparagingly, "Ditch crawling! A deep sea sailor ditch crawling!" Yes, my hard-boiled friend—ditch crawling. But what delightful ditches! And what a dream of a ship to sail! It is true, the more ambitious Kyles of Bute, or perhaps the Hebrides, had enticed me. But then, what new-made husband, at the very outset of his married life, would permit callously his bride to suffer the dismal pangs of sea-sickness?

* * *

With our stores aboard, we sailed from Wroxham moorings, to tie up later alongside the bank on a lovely, wooded reach of the

Bure river. Here was peace and solitude and relief from the noisy affairs of men.

Our meal was eaten out in the well, the table set beneath the sunset sky. We spoke but little, for it seemed to us we were listening to the great, solemn voice of nature all around. And when nature speaks it behoves man to be silent.

One of the greatest charms of the Broads is the solitude which is easily found should one desire to seek it. For the jazz-minded there is ample scope at the crowded village moorings, where the raucous strains of gramophones ring out continuously. Here, as we watched the slow, grand death of the day in a splendour of western colour, was no man-made discord to mar the peace.

A little wind stirred the tree-tops gently; there was the *plop* of a leaping mid-stream fish. Presently a kingfisher came winging up the river, crying for his mate. In the last of the red and gold of the sunset, his feathers blazed aflame. . . . .

Later, in the mellow candle-light, the cabin looked snug indeed, with its spotless furnishings and dainty curtains. We would not have changed our comfortable, water-borne home for the regal quarters at Buckingham Palace.

I went on deck to smoke the last pipe of the day. The wind was freshening from the sou'west, promising us some grand sailing on the morrow. In the starlit night the waterside reeds and sedge-grass tossed and rustled; baby waves *lap-lap-lapped* the side of the *Mallard* with a delicious, soothing sound. She stirred lightly at her moorings, as if she wished to take us adventuring without delay.

* * *

It was a day of spanking wind and blue, white-dappled sky when we tried out the boat on Wroxham Broad next morning. Up and down the length of the Broad we flew, foaming right down almost to the shallows where the ruminating cattle stood, belly-deep in the sparkling water.

The *Mallard* was a delight to handle after the clods of ships' lifeboats and other clumsy craft in which the most of my sailing had been done. In the narrower parts of the rivers she worked to windward like a steamboat. Our wanderings covered many miles, and a number of pleasant little villages were visited. These appeared to have been almost untouched by the hurly-burly of the speeding twentieth century.

One windy evening we moored at Acle and sat on deck to watch the passing show. First came a huge cargo-carrying wherry bound down for Yarmouth. Those wherries, until recently so common a sight on the Norfolk rivers, are not now nearly so plentiful. Probably motor road-transport has sounded their death-knell. With an enormous, boomless sail, immense mast, and long fluttering wind-vane, a wherry makes a brave show when under way.

Close astern of the wherry came a string of yachts picking out their moorings for the night. One manned by four noisy youths flew past erratically, and was brought alongside the bank with much force and little skill. Everything was in confusion, and I felt sorry for the absent owners of that yacht. I heard afterwards that the boat had been damaged and was leaking. The wonder was she had not been sunk.

What a contrast, a few minutes later, was the arrival of another boat. Her helmsman rounded skilfully in the stiff breeze, she dropped easily alongside the bank, and a plump member of her crew hopped ashore to secure the rond anchors. The boat's crew consisted only of girls—three of them—neat, round-sterned little figures in workmanlike shorts and jumpers. While they stowed their sails in a seamanlike manner, the hulabaloo was still going on aboard the yacht of the four youths. It made me feel a bit small regarding my own sex.

"Another example of the superiority of woman," I remarked, casually, lest my wife should rub it in.

Later in the evening two of those pimply youths passed along the bank. They stopped abreast of the *Mallard*. After admiring her, one of them spoke to me: "Nice boat you've got. Where's your crew?" "There," said I shortly, waving my hand towards my wife, aft in the well.

"Oh!" said the pimply one, in some surprise. "We've got four chaps in our boat." "Thank God," thought I, "that I'm not one of them." The pair examined the boat and mate with great interest for some time. As they turned to go I remarked: "But I've got a good mate." "Oh, really," they duetted, "where is he?" "There," said I, monosyllabically, waving my hand once more in a proprietorial manner towards my small wife.

* * *

THE MATE (AND CREW) OF "MALLARD" TAKES THE HELM

In the more inland parts of Norfolk the river banks are heavily
tree-clad, and the scenery is very beautiful. Towards the coast the
country becomes flat and marshy. Over these marshes the
unimpeded wind came tearing at the *Mallard* and we had some
very exciting sailing.

St. Benet's Abbey, close to which we moored one evening, was an
object of great interest to us. This old ruin, a forlorn lonely pile
originally founded by King Canute in the eleventh century, stood
a short distance from the river. I was deep in contemplation of
a splendid arch at the main entrance when an alarmed exclamation
from my wife drew my attention to a number of massive oxen,
bearing down on us at full speed.

"Those are bulls," she cried out, "I'm sure they are. They look
so savage." Having been a farmer's boy, I could positively swear
they were not bulls, but in her innocence she would not believe
me, beating a hasty retreat aboard the boat.

Sitting on deck later on, I smoked a meditative pipe before
going to bed. The wind rustled the sedge-grass along the banks,
sighing sadly over the wide marsh around me. The oxen had
disappeared. The only life in sight consisted of two little birds,
clinging to swaying reeds as they called plaintively to each other.

The Abbey ruins lay sullen, gloomy and lonely in the grey
evening twilight. There was an unique atmosphere about the old
place. That and the magnificent solitude which enveloped the
boat affected me strangely.

I could visualise the scene as the ancient abbey was being built
by those quaintly-clad figures of long ago; I could visualise it in
its prime, housing those long-forgotten holy men, many of whom
were buried in their marshy beds close to where our yacht was
moored. In the rustling of the tossing reeds it may be that their
voices spoke to me again. . .

* * *

An outstanding feature of the Norfolk countryside is the great
number of windmills which dot the landscape. Some of these
picturesque old buildings bear dates of nearly two hundred years
ago. Many we saw were idle and in a state of disrepair, but some
still turned merrily, their duty the draining of the low-lying land
behind the rivers.

One which we visited was still grinding corn. It stood on a hill in a field red-carpeted with crimson poppies. One old white-dust covered man tended the simple needs of the primitive machinery. Heavy perpendicular ladders of oak, their rungs half-mooned by the tread of generations of millers, took the two of us aloft.

At last I found myself inside the great, movable cowl which roofed the mill. Here the massive tower trembled slightly to the insistent urge of the wind. Looking out, I saw the dip and rise, dip and rise, of the four huge sails. Above, around, beneath me was the busy droning of the wind. Shutting my eyes, I might have been aloft again in a sailing ship at sea.

It was obvious the old man had a great affection for the windmill. Hopping about as actively as a boy, he explained everything to me; the ingenious device which held the sails four-square to the wind; the lever which turned on edge the long wooden slats of the sails when we wished to set the mill at rest.

Sunset was at hand when I rejoined my wife at the lower door.

There I stopped to thank him. And then I saw he was affected by something he wished to tell me.

"Boy and man," he said "I've been working here for nearly sixty years, long before the grand ladies and gentlemen from London came to sail their boats through Broadland. But if you pass this way before long, you won't see this mill working and you won't see me. . . They're putting in an oil engine, and then there'll be no place for me after all these years . . . ." He stopped to lift his face towards the great swinging arms of the mill.

I could picture it all. A garish red brick building butted on to the ancient, lichen-clad tower; the choking cough of an oil-engine tended by a man in greasy overalls instead of the one who for sixty years had listened to the song of the wind in those broad-spread sails above.

We left him there—alone with his mill. At the foot of the hill we trod carefully through the drowsing scarlet poppies. Something forced me to look back and face the westward.

The sun had set behind the hill; the solemn hush of the dying day lay over the land. From the marches below came the mournful cries of the plovers, calling softly to one another. The sky was aflame with orange and gold. Against this setting the mill was silhouetted—dark, gloomy, brooding, a monument to an unhurried, bygone age.

Underneath the sails stood the little man, his face upturned towards them, his whole attitude expressing his dejection. Though no words came to us, I knew he was speaking to the windmill, as he had told me was his lonely habit. Faintly borne by the dying evening breeze, I heard the choking cough of an oil engine . . .

Night was coming on as we hastened on our way, anxious to reach the yacht before darkness crept over the treacherous marshland which bordered the river.

* * *

We were back once more at Wroxham. There was sadness in our hearts at the thought of leaving our little ship. She had carried us safely through fair weather and foul. In her, an all-too-brief glimpse of Paradise had been ours. Now we must needs return to the thronging streets of a city whilst other hands than ours would steer the *Mallard* as she set out again.

I pottered about, loath to leave her. I flemish-coiled the ends of the gear, tucked away a refractory reef-point; I dived into the cabin repeatedly, pretending something had been forgotten. The mate, reading my thoughts, sharing them too, asked quietly, "What would you do if you suddenly found you were rich?" "Buy the *Mallard* and start out again," I answered truthfully.

For the winding rivers were calling to me; the magnificent solitude of St. Benet's; the pleasant meadowlands of the Thurne; the untamed splendour of Hickling. I could hear again the eternal rustle of the waterside reeds, the plaintive call of the birds at evening, and the sighing of the wind over the great, wide marshes.

We left the *Mallard* there—sadly, reluctantly. Back to the dingy little railway station we went—back to the teeming, smoke-grimed streets of a great city.

* * *

At the time of that visit to the Norfolk Broads, over twenty years ago, practically all the craft there were sailing yachts. But even then that pest, the motor-cruiser, was rearing its ugly head, filling the yachtsmen with indignation.

One such motor-boat, humorously named *Halitosis* by its owner in a vain attempt to placate the sailing men, dashed past us many times as it puffed along the waterways. I dread to think what will eventually happen to those delightful rivers. The shortage of petrol during the War may have brought sail into its own for a few brief years. But, sooner or later, the lovely, winding Bure and Thurne will be as completely motorized as the country roads.

The fine sailing wherry, dating back for centuries, has been driven off the rivers by motor transport; it is but a matter of years before the white-sailed boats, swept aside from the Norfolk Broads by *Halitosis* and its numerous progeny, become almost as extinct as sail on the high seas.

* * *

In Liverpool one morning, over the bacon and eggs, I said to my wife; "What now? Isn't it about time I was getting back to sea?" Regarding me with a particularly determined gaze, she replied: "You're going to look for a shore job now, young man."

It has been said man cannot serve two masters. It would likewise seem man cannot be wedded to both a woman and the sea. One of the two must needs be cast aside. So it was, returning to South Africa, alone for the time being, I joined the Harbour Service of the Union. To all intents and purposes, I had "swallowed the anchor". It was, for me, more or less a case of:

> *"And now farewell to Thee*
> *Thou well beloved Sea."*

* * *

South Africa is a much blessed land. Fortunate indeed are those who are destined to live their lives in its golden clime. Specially privileged are those of us who spend their days beneath that grand pile, Table Mountain, the Old Grey Father who has stood guard for centuries over this city, the ancient Tavern of the Seas.

My present position has been held for thirteen years. The life of a marine pilot (one must be explicit, for aviation has filched the word from the sea) is full of interest. There is strain, and stress too, when the Old Grey Father gets really angry and spews his venom at us; when the south-easter hurls itself, screaming, across the white-capped bay, fastening itself with mighty, broadside thrust upon the ships as they pass through the narrow entrances.

And in winter wild north-west gales come blustering in from the sea, rendering difficult and dangerous the task of those who go out to board the plunging, tumbling vessels in the high ocean swell.

The Old Grey Father has watched, serenely, aloofly, and with tolerant eye, the antics of that restless atom called man. Here first came the little, awkward-looking high-pooped vessels of the explorers and pioneers, probing ever further afield—valiant craft and valiant men. Marine progress swept those primitive ships aside, to be replaced at length by the great modern vessels which scorn the same winds that brought to these shores those early pioneers.

But the Old Grey Father does not change—perhaps I should say does not change appreciably, for geologists tell us the huge pile is slowly weathering and disintegrating.

That may be, but one would have to gaze far into the future to view its final dissolution. It is, indeed, not outside the realms of possibility that the mountain may outlast the human race, ravished as the latter is by recurring wars of a growing ferocity, and internecine troubles which may well accomplish its unhappy end.

And then the Old Grey Father, unhurried, unperturbed, sublime, will gaze out once more over an empty land and sea.

*   *   *

Viewed from the bay on an early, peaceful, summer morning, Table Mountain is a truly magnificent sight. Before the sun has climbed the ramparts of the east its first rays are painting delicately the great perpendicular cliffs, which rise sheer from the lower buttresses. Orange and gold and pink, separating, intermingling, so that the stern mantle of greyness of the Old Grey Father has been erased as though by a fairy wand.

Gradually those colours change, the invisible brush creeping slowly, slowly down the cliffs. Then, suddenly, the sun appears, over the massive range thirty miles to the east—and the whole mountain is ablaze with the brightness of the new-born day.

It was one such morning when I boarded a ship entering the bay. As I made my way up from the lower bridge, a woman close to me suddenly threw herself on her knees, her faced turned towards the mountain, her lips moving. "What's come over her?" I asked the captain. "She's a missionary," he told me. "She called out to me just now that she was so overcome by the beauty of the mountain that she had to get down on her knees to pray."

*   *   *

It has been my lot and privilege to handle literally thousands of vessels ranging in size from Irving Johnson's schooner *Yankee* and Villiers' little full-rigged ship *Joseph Conrad* to giants of the sea such as the ill-fated *Empress of Britain* and the illustrious *Ark Royal*. One morning I stood on the bridge of the mighty *Queen Mary* as she came to anchor in the bay. Later, I sat chatting with the captain in his spacious quarters. What a contrast to the master's dog-hole in a Geordie tramp!

In the middle of the following night it was necessary to remove from the *Queen Mary's* side the tanker which had been fuelling the big ship in the bay. From the bridge of the tanker, pointing the megaphone skywards I shouted: "*Mary ahoy!*" No answer. Once more, a bit louder: "*Mary ahoy!*" Still no answer. Then, realising the flippancy, the indignity, I amended my hail: "*QUEEN Mary* ahoy!" From the bridge, towering overhead like the cliffs of Table Mountain, came an immediate reply: "Hello! What do you want?"

*   *   *

In the daily routine of handling ships one comes in contact with many interesting characters. One of the most outstanding men I have ever met is Admiral E. R. G. R. Evans. While he was in charge of the Africa Station his flagship *Dorsetshire* often docked at Cape Town.

On two occasions Sir Edward graciously invited the pilot staff to cocktail parties. Another time we were entertained to lunch. The Admiral is a most delightful host, full of a genial *bonhomie* which removes all stiffness and puts his guests entirely at their ease.

At table I sat almost opposite this remarkable, handsome man. During the meal he related anecdotes and stories of his career. He touched but lightly on the episode of the *Broke* (after which ship his son is named) as if he considered the subject a little too hackneyed.

Close to me sat the Admiral's Flag-Captain, Makeig-Jones, with whom I had a conversation after lunch. He was an enormous man, with one of the palest faces I have ever seen on a sailor. He it was who went down bravely in the Aircraft-carrier *Courageous* when that ship was destroyed early in the war.

*   *   *

It has been my good fortune to meet two men in the world of

nautical literature, both writers whose work must have been enjoyed by many thousands of lovers of the sea.

The name of the master of an Anchor liner I was about to undock one day seemed quite familiar to me, though I had never met the man before. David W. Bone, wasn't that the author of that fine book, *The Brassbounder,* which was published just before I went to sea, thirty-six years ago? How avidly I devoured that tale, lying enthralled on my Y.M.C.A. bed when work at the bank was over, scarcely laying the story down until the last page had been reached.

While we sat in his room Captain Bone modestly told me something of the making of his book, finishing up his remarks with: "*The Brassbounder* sold well—it is still selling—because I told a plain, unvarnished tale of the sea, sticking strictly to the truth."

One happy day Captain F. C. Hendry ("Shalimar") came to my house to have afternoon tea with us. This man is undoubtedly the finest living writer of sea stories. His wizardry of words takes one on a magic literary carpet right on to the seaswept decks of the ships he describes so vividly.

With a number of unpretentious newspaper and magazine articles to my credit, I hung on his words as he described the opening days of his literary career. It started one day when he was 47, an age at which many men would have considered themselves too old to begin. The story he wrote that afternoon was accepted immediately by *Blackwood's Magazine* which, like Oliver Twist, clamoured for more. So it was this unassuming sailor leaped into the forefront of the writers of the sea.

* * *

Towards the end of 1934 a German cruiser paid South Africa what it pleased the Consul to term a 'friendship' visit. After docking this vessel, I was invited to drink a glass of beer with the captain. Suave and agreeable, immaculately clad in well-fitting uniform and wing-collar, he was typical of the slightly arrogant German naval officer. There was nothing particularly noticeable about the man, nor did he appear to be outstanding in any way.

We spoke of the trivialities as we sipped that far-too-cold beer, politics being carefully avoided. Some of us, even in those early days of Nazism, were a little suspicious of Herr Adolf's machinations. The captain shook hands and bowed gravely as I left him. I met him once again, when his ship undocked.

He was Doenitz, of the *Deutscher Kreuzer Emden*, later to become Grand Admiral of the German Navy, and finally for a brief, uneasy period, self-styled Fuehrer of the Third Reich, writhing in its death agony.

Of a very different type was another German who called at our port a year or so before the outbreak of war. He was without a doubt the most objectionable man whose ship it has been my misfortune to board. He was in command of a large, rather obsolete warship showing the flag, the crooked cross of Nazidom, around the world.

He was that affected type of German who terminates every question with either *nein?* or *nicht?* On reaching the bridge, I put to him the usual inquiry aboard naval vessels: "Do you wish me to handle your ship?"

He drew himself up to his full height, glared contemptuously at me through his shining monocle, and snapped out: "In the German navy the captain always handles his ship!" And a poor job he made of it, in spite of his bombast.

Unfortunately it fell to my turn to undock this vessel. It was a cold, dismal day in winter. Part of the crew had been lined up on the foredeck. The remainder squeezed and cuddled and kissed the local girls behind the scanty shelter of the quayside trucks. Those good-looking German boys were apparently irresistible.

A heavy rain-squall swept over the ship while we waited on the bridge. An obsequious sailor hurriedly helped the captain on with his oilskin coat. Meanwhile, the bluejackets stood stiffly on the foredeck without covering of any sort, the soaking rain pouring down on them. I asked the captain if no oilskins were supplied to his men. He gave me that arrogant, contemptuous look before replying: "Do you think I would worry whether my men get wet or not?" He snapped his fingers to dismiss the trivial matter. The rain beat down on those bedraggled sailors, plastering to their necks the long, erstwhile-jaunty ribbons of their caps.

He was a nasty piece of work, that Hun captain. Without wishing him any real harm—I hope somebody dropped a 'block buster' on top of him during the war.

*　　*　　*

Then came World War No. 2. War again after so brief a period of uneasy peace? Yes, war again! War of a filthier beastliness than ever. The man in the street, the backbone of the nation, the man who pours out his blood on some foreign battlefield and gets damn-all for his sacrifice, must well wonder when all this nonsense of recurring wars is going to cease. And while he wonders—and fights—the pot-bellied profiteer, gloating over his money-bags, gathers in the profits.

And so World War No. 1 was continued, after the futile peace of twenty years which had been granted Germany to rearm and gather strength for revenge. But before hostilities had been resumed the world was treated to the humiliating spectacle of the British premier hurrying hot-foot to make his obeisance to Herr Adolf, conqueror-presumptive of the world. Ye Gods! How are the mighty fallen! And how must those warriors of old, those hardy men who performed the Glorious Deeds that won the Empire, squirm in their bloody graves!

The resumption of hostilities, after twenty-one years, brought to Table Bay a stress and a strain of traffic which well-nigh made it gasp. At the time of the South African War over a hundred ships lay anchored there. While those were mostly comparatively small sailing vessels, the present war sent to our port all the giants of the sea, with, of course, the exception of the *Normandie,* lying rather sick on her side in New York harbour.

When it would seem that Mussolini's proud words *Mare Nostrum* were no idle boast—when the Mediterranean had been all but closed to Allied craft—the swarm of ships clamouring for admittance was out of all proportion to our capacity. One morning seventy-two ships lay anchored in the bay. And every berth within our two docks was filled, often double or treble-banked. Throughout that time the weather, as if favouring the cause of the enemy, was most unkind to us for two years. Fierce nor'westers swept in from the wintry ocean; raging south-easters hampered us when summer had come.

The Union of South Africa may well be proud of the effort of its harbours in handling an undreamt-of tonnage, when the whole outlook was bleak and black, when Hitler might well have achieved his plan for world-wide domination. Great liners, the cream of the world's fleets, unknown and untried by the pilots, were docked and undocked often under the most trying conditions without undue delay. Some day, perhaps, the story will be written by some abler pen than mine.

*   *   *

At times I have been called a dreamer, with a note of disparagement in the term. But there is, for me, nothing disparaging in being so-called. Dreamers surely have their place in this workaday world. Every moving poem, every great engineering feat is the work of a dreamer.

So I admit to having had, for many years, a dream. It has ofttimes been said that dreams never come true. Mine, it is my hope, will be the exception to that popular belief. I have always been deeply interested in the deep-water cruises of small craft. All the books dealing with that fascinating subject have been avidly devoured. A little library of those authors has slowly grown on my bookshelf. Those men are of the salt of the earth and the sea, and their number is all too few.

The works of the lonely single-hander are the most fascinating of all. Many people regard the cruises of such sea-wanderers as something which places them outside the pale of sanity. To such folk I would quote Kipling's words:

> *"Who hath desired the Sea? Her excellent loneliness rather*
> *Than forecourts of kings and her outermost pits than the*
> *streets where men gather."*

Many of the small-boat voyagers have called at Cape Town. Aboard their little ships I have spoken with the most of them. When one thinks of their wind-blown wanderings, under sail alone, the swift passages of mammoth liners pale into nothing more than the inevitable outcome of mechanical progress.

Some years ago my dream nearly came true, in part at least. I was in Liverpool, temporarily ashore, when Nutting arrived at Cowes in his little *Typhoon*. The 35-foot ketch, under sail alone, had run from Cape Race, Newfoundland, to Bishop's Rock, a distance of 2,100 miles in just over fifteen days. (The newspaper cutting is before me now).

Writing immediately to Nutting, I offered to sail with him if he intended taking *Typhoon* back to New York. A very friendly letter reached me by return. Unfortunately there was no vacancy;

should a member of the crew drop out, he would be glad of my help. Some days later came a wire: "Glad to have you if possible." To my everlasting regret, I weakly permitted myself to be dissuaded by a brother in England at the time.

Bill Nutting, who was editor of the New York magazine "Motor Boat", wrote to me several times after that, each of his letters cordially inviting me to call on him when in New York. "Everybody comes to New York," he wrote, going on to enthuse over his new boat *Harpoon* in which he proposed to race across the Atlantic against the Duke of Leinster.

Since receiving those letters the opportunity of meeting Nutting has never come my way. And now it is too late. For he has gone, and with him, amongst others, A.S. Hildebrand, author of that small-boat odyssey *Blue Water*. They had chosen the long stormy sea-way which had swallowed up Sinclair's plucky little 23-foot *Joan*.

After leaving Iceland, bound west, they were never heard of again. The coasts of Greenland and Labrador were diligently searched. No sign of the boat, *Leif Ericcson*, or of the unlucky crew was ever revealed. Nutting and 'Hilly', both keen yachtsmen experienced in deep-sea sailing, had met their end far out on the water they loved so well.

* * *

Often I visualise my little ship, and picture her ready to set out on the great adventure. She must not be too big—about 30 feet in length—for if the ideal companion is not available I shall go alone. She will be yawl-rigged, for that seems to me the most easily handled by a small or one-man crew. Many authorities will tell me the yawl is not the ideal rig. What, then, is? Each and all have their faults.

Will that dream come true? Will the chance be mine to visit the many delightful places denied to me as a professional seafarer by the sordid materialism and commercialism of the shipowner? As I eradicate the daily fungus from my face it is impossible to remain unconscious of the grizzling hair, the crow's feet clustering more deeply around the eyes. And undoubtedly the one-time activity of earlier days has departed somewhat. When the opportunity comes will it be too late?

Reassurance comes with the picture of a lean little man who, many years my senior, is doing just what it is my wish to do. Harry Pidgeon was well over sixty when last he called at Cape Town on a lone cruise. I visited him many times, sitting in the little cabin of *Islander* while he told me of his single-handed wanderings. His spare body appeared to be as tough as the sturdy timbers which he had hewn himself to build his boat.

* * *

Eight bells have struck! This book has more than run its course. Eight bells have struck. The watch is aft. Around me are clustered that host of shipmates of long ago. God rest their bones wherever they may lie! Some are yet living. But the majority are dead, amongst them one who disappeared in that holocaust when H.M.S. *Queen Mary* vanished in a pall of smoke and thunder in the battle of Jutland. Thirteen hundred brave men were wiped out in a few seconds.

Overhead, at the for'ad rail of the poop, the mate is looking down at us in the midnight darkness. "The watch is aft, Sir!" reports the second mate. "Relieve the wheel and lookout!" roars the mate from the poop, that old-time High Place of authority which is no more. . . .

The long watch is over. Soon I can go below, for my task is all but done.

As I write these closing words there comes from seaward the wailing cry of a few belated gulls. Through the open window I hear the endless murmur of the surf as it frets against the restraint of the breakwater. At times a certain restlessness creeps over me, and I feel the chafe of the shackles which now bind me to the land. . . .

Eight bells have struck. The watch is over. Before the echo of those resounding strokes has died away, I lay down my pen, my task complete.

THE END

EPILOGUE

Whatever the reader may think of this book, there has been a good deal of pleasure and amusement in the recounting of these reminiscences. And a little sadness, too; sadness such as was known by Robert Louis Stevenson, best loved of all the many masters of English Literature, whose brave heart faltered temporarily while he wrote these poignant lines:

> "Sing me a song of a lad that is gone,
> Say, could that lad be I?
> Merry of soul he sailed on a day
> Over the sea to Skye.
>
> "Give me again all that was there,
> Give me the sun that shone!
> Give me the eyes, give me the soul,
> Give me the lad that's gone!"

Give me the lad that's gone! As he penned those words R. L. S. felt as have ever felt most of us who are no longer young. The future is for youth—eager, ecstatic youth— while the past is ours, those of us who have arrived at the half-century; those of us who have reached and crossed the uplands of life, and now gaze down, a little apprehensively, on the all-too-swift decline which leads to what? Oblivion? Perhaps. No man has ever returned to tell us what lies Beyond.

Is it any wonder, then, we look back, a little wistfully? There is so much behind us, maybe so little before. The brevity of life has ever been the plaint of man. The allotted three score years and ten —should he be granted them—are all too short.

Sometimes I feel that my dream will never come true; that my little ship will never set out to take me back to the wide, open sea which I have always loved so well.

Yet can I still go back—when the sun has gone and the shadow has spread, so that nothing remains but a poor husk to be cast into the deep.

The Sea. . . . "It is the companion and the receiver of men. It has moods for them to fill the storehouse of the mind, perils for trial, or even for an ending, and calms for the good emblem of death. . . ."

But I would prefer not a calm but a little wind blowing over the water; a little wind flirting its surface into the tiny wavelets of laughter—laughter when some might say tears should be shed—whispering as they toss merrily their sparkling heads towards the blue-domed sky.

And if a few white gulls, sailing in the sunlight, come crying over my lonely, lowly resting place—that, for me, will be requiem enow . . . .